INDIAN RAILWAYS

AS CONNECTED WITH

BRITISH EMPIRE IN THE EAST

INDIAN RAILWAYS

AS CONNECTED WITH

BRITISH EMPIRE IN THE EAST.

BY

SIR WILLIAM P. ANDREW

GYAN

Published by

Gyan Publishing House
5, Ansari Road
Daryaganj, New Delhi-110002
Phone: 011-47034999, 9811692060
E-mail: books@gyanbooks.com

Distribution Network
gyanbooks.com
India, USA, Canada, UK, Australia

ISBN: 978-93-6280-244-6 (HB)
First Published, 1884

2nd Impression 2024

Printed at: Gyan Press, Delhi.

INDIAN RAILWAYS AS CONNECTED WITH BRITISH EMPIRE IN THE EAST

Author: WILLIAM P. ANDREW

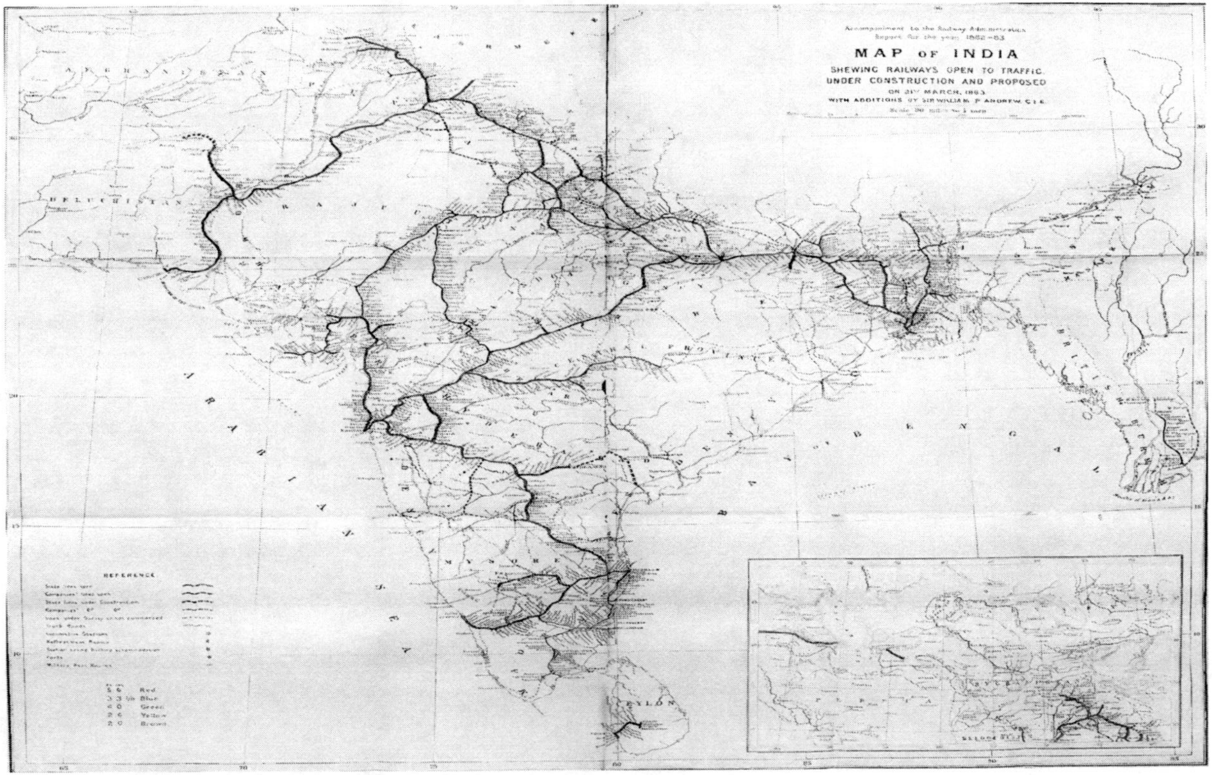
Accompaniment to the Railway Administration
Report for the year 1882–83
MAP OF INDIA
SHEWING RAILWAYS OPEN TO TRAFFIC,
UNDER CONSTRUCTION AND PROPOSED
ON 31ST MARCH, 1883
WITH ADDITIONS BY SIR WILLIAM P. ANDREW, C.I.E.
AFGHANISTAN
BELUCHISTAN
RAJPUTANA
CENTRAL PROVINCES
MYSORE
CEYLON
BRITISH BURMA
ARABIAN SEA
BAY OF BENGAL
REFERENCE
Red
Blue
Green
Yellow
Brown

PUBLICATIONS

BY

SIR WILLIAM P. ANDREW, C.I.E.,

F.R.G.S., Etc.

1846. Indian Railways.

1847. Letter to the Shareholders of the East Indian and Great Western of Bengal Railways.

1848. Is India to have Railways?

1853. Railways in Bengal.

1856. The Scinde Railway

„ Letter to Viscount Palmerston, K.G., on the Political Importance of the Euphrates Valley Railway.

„ Telegraphic Communicaton with India. Letters reprinted from the "Times."

1857. Memoir on the Euphrates Valley Route to India.

„ On the Establishment of a Flotilla of Steam Vessels.

„ London to Lahore; or, the Euphrates, Scinde, and Punjaub Railways.

„ Telegraphic Communication with India. Letters reprinted from the "Times."

„ The Indian Guarantee on Railways compared with the Foreign and Colonial.

„ Tramroads in Northern India.

„ Port of Kurrachee, Depth of Water, and Commerce.

„ The Punjaub Railway.

1858. Colonisation in India and Australia compared.

„ The Indus and its Provinces; their Political and Commercial Importance.

„ Letters reprinted from the "Times" on Telegraphic Communication with India.

1861. The Government Guarantee on Indian Railways.

1869. Letter to the Duke of Argyll on the Completion of the Railway System of the Valley of the Indus.

1870. Letters to Secretaries of State for Foreign Affairs and India on Euphrates Valley Railway.

„ Lecture before Society of Arts on Railways in India by Guaranteed Companies.

1871. Letters to the Grand Vizier of Turkey and the British Ambassador at Constantinople, etc., on the Euphrates Route to India.

„ Letters on the Euphrates Valley Route to India. Reprinted from the "Times."

1872. Paper read before British Association at Brighton on Euphrates Valley Route to India.

1873. Lecture delivered at the Royal United Service Institution on the Euphrates Route to India in connection with the Central Asian Question.

„ The Break of Gauge in Indian Railways.

1874. The Strategic and Commercial Evils of a Break of Gauge in India.

1878. India and her Neighbours.

1879. Asia Minor and Euphrates Valley Railway.

1880. The Bolan and Khyber Railways.

„ Paper read before the Society of Arts on the Euphrates Route to India.

„ Our Scientific Frontier.*

* "In these border-lands (Beloochistan and Afghanistan) to have a rival in prestige and power would be dangerous—to have a superior impossible."—*India and her Neighbours*, p. 319.

INDIAN RAILWAYS

AS CONNECTED WITH

BRITISH EMPIRE IN THE EAST.

BY

SIR WILLIAM P. ANDREW, C.I.E.,

ETC., ETC.

CHAIRMAN OF THE SCINDE, PUNJAUB, AND DELHI RAILWAY COMPANY.

Author of "India and Her Neighbours," "Our Scientific Frontier," "Memoir on the Euphrates," "The Indus and its Provinces," &c. &c. &c.

"Justum et tenacem propositi virum
Non civium ardor prava jubentium
Non vultus instantis tyranni
Mente quatet solida, . . ."

—HORACE.

FOURTH EDITION.

With Map and Appendix.

LONDON:
W. H. ALLEN & CO., 13 WATERLOO PLACE.
PUBLISHERS TO THE INDIA OFFICE.

1884.

To

The Right Honourable

The Viscount Halifax, G.C.B.

THE FOLLOWING PAGES ARE

DEDICATED

IN GRATEFUL REMEMBRANCE OF

POWERFUL SUPPORT AND ENCOURAGEMENT

IN EFFORTS

TO ESTABLISH IMPROVED MEANS OF

COMMUNICATION IN AND WITH INDIA.

THE AUTHOR.

29, Bryanston Square,
July 1884.

CONTENTS.

APPENDIX TO THE SECOND EDITION.

APPENDIX TO THE THIRD EDITION.

APPENDIX TO THE FOURTH EDITION.

INDIAN RAILWAYS.

PREFACE TO THE FOURTH EDITION.

So many years have elapsed since the last edition of this work was published, under the *nom de plume* of "An Old Indian Postmaster," that it appears both necessary and desirable that a succinct account should be given of the more recent progress of railway enterprise in India. With this view, and to make it more clear to the general reader, we will cast a hasty glance at what was accomplished in the early days when the old magnates of Leadenhall Street began to realise the fact that sleepers could be laid and that water would boil in their great eastern dependency, and that nothing was better calculated to arouse, than the whistle of the locomotive, the apathetic

Hindoo to the knowledge of the value of time, and to assume among the nations an aspect of renovated power.

Roadless condition of India before the introduction of railways.

When England became the dominant Power in India, probably there never was a country with a people so rich and intelligent, in which roads were so few and travel so difficult. For the rich the camel, the elephant, the horse and the palanquin, for the poor the pony and the pack-bullock, were the only means of conveyance by land. Springless wheeled carriages called ekkas, drawn by horses and ponies, and bullock-carts, could generally only be used on a few of the main roads, that might be enumerated on the fingers of one hand, or in the neighbourhood of populous towns. In the south-west of India, from November to June, small bullock-carts could travel in certain districts on what have been called the "natural tramways of the country," otherwise in ruts, formed in black cotton-soil, which after two days' rain become a morass impassable for horses, difficult for bullocks and buffaloes, and such was frequently the distress of these animals that they sank under their burdens, and their bones whitening the route acted as land-marks to travellers. Over thousands of square miles wheeled carriages were unknown, and had never been seen by the oldest inhabitant. Merchandise could for the most part only be carried on buffaloes, camels, and pack-bullocks, at a cost of from 6d. to 1s. a ton per mile. Grain merchants were then men of enormous wealth, with agents in large towns, and droves upon droves of buffaloes and bullocks.

The cultivator could find no market for his grain, and other evils caused by the want of roads.

In Central India many a septuagenarian corn-factor laments the good old times, when he bought at what price he liked, and the humble hard-working cultivator could send his grain nowhere, but must arrange for its sale with the grasping money-lender and corn-merchant at his door, or leave it in underground pits, or in fragile storehouses of wattle and mud, or in earthen jars, exposed to fermentation and the ravages of the weevil. In times of scarcity these receptacles of store grain are sometimes opened, and often when the damp has penetrated and the grain fermented the stench is quite unbearable. The poor, driven by famine to eat this rotten grain, die by scores. The mortality is set down to cholera.

Prices varied from village to village, the weights and measures of one hamlet differed from those of its neighbour. Even now in one large grain-producing province there are some seven different tables of capacity by which grain or sugar or salt is sold, and within the last twenty years villagers of the Balaghat district refused to take copper money for any humble purchases that might be made, but demanded cowries.* In one part of the country, grain was almost valueless; in another place, not a hundred miles off there might be scarcity; whilst still further beyond, but yet not very remote, famine raged.

Wandering gipsy-like tribes, called Brinjaras, followed armies with stores, or carried salt, coarse sugar and grain on buffaloes and pack-bullocks during the open season. In the rains, or from the middle of June to the middle of October, that is for five months in the year, there was no traffic, there were no travellers. Pilgrims to religious shrines, surprised by the approach of the rainy season stopped during the rains in the villages where they happened to be, and for the sake of daily food served as clerks or school-masters, astrologers, or village priests, until after some five months' detention travel again became possible. As the country was destitute of roads, so the rivers were but imperfectly utilised for the transport of goods. There were rude country craft, which, if the wind were fair, sailed slowly up or down the stream, and were rowed and poled wearisomely

* Small shells of the *Cypræa moneta*, a native of the Pacific and Eastern seas. Many tons weight of this little shell were annually imported into England, and again exported for barter; in 1848, sixty tons of the money cowry were imported into Liverpool.

against the stream if the wind failed. There was no regular service. A passenger might hope to reach his destination some time or other. Every man's hand was against the merchant, every petty landholder who could collect a score of ruffians exacted transit duties. In the long decay of the Mogul Empire the few roads, and even the canals and irrigation works that once existed, had been suffered to fall into disrepair. It is ever darkest before the dawn. When the English became the paramount power in India, road-making was a vital necessity. But it was not till 1836 that a road was commenced from Calcutta to Delhi, which was afterwards prolonged to Peshawar, a distance of 1,420 miles, at a cost of £1,500,000; it was finished when middle-aged men who saw it commenced, had grown old. In 1842 a road between Bombay and Calcutta, 1,170 miles, was begun, and completed at a cost of £600,000; and a third road uniting Bombay and Agra, 734 miles, at a cost of £250,000, was made. The total cost of all the roads constructed between 1839 and 1849 was £3,460,000. In 1838 over an area of 30,000 square miles in four of the collectorates adjacent to Bombay there were little more than four hundred miles of roads, of which only one half were passable in the rains. All the towns of the interior were during that season so many isolated points; and however important it might

The English Government commence to make roads.

be, it would then have been impossible to pass heavy carriages along even the made roads, which had been constructed without care or cost as to their foundations, were generally unbridged, and had but few ferry-boats.*

The creation of the Public Works Department by Lord Dalhousie, and the commencement of railways in India when there were no roads to feed them.

Though the roadless state of India attracted the attention of successive Governor-Generals, yet it was not until the time of Lord Dalhousie that systematic efforts were made to give India the roads she required. With a view to create them, and to repair and extend irrigation works, he formed the Public Works Department. His rule commenced in 1848. Railways had then made some progress in England. In the first quarter of a century after their commencement in 1825, there had been constructed in the United Kingdom 6,621 miles of railroad, being an average rate of 265 miles per annum. England, indeed, by her admirable system of roads, her organized mail-coach and van traffic, was prepared for the introduction of railroads; but in India, before railroads, there were neither roads nor road-makers. The larger rivers were unbridged, and the Hindoos, at least, thought it would be impious to bridge the holy Ganges, or the sacred Narbada. Both roads and rail-roads

---

* *Report on a Proposed Railway in India.* By Mr. Vignoles, F.R.S., Past President Inst. C.E., dated 22nd September 1842.

had to be made at the same time; there were neither skilled artizans, nor sturdy navvies, nor surveyors, nor engineers. Works had to be carried on sometimes through pathless jungles, over scarcely trodden hills, through tracts of country rendered uninhabitable by wild beasts and miasma.

A great proportion of the Engineers who commenced the railway works did not live to see them completed; they succumbed to hard work in a climate then often deadly. If the first railways thus constructed cost much, is it surprising? Even now whole tracts of country are roadless. In some districts there may perhaps be one made road, the means of communication between two far distant towns. But off that road neither wheeled carriages nor carts can be used; * and there is no system of local traffic that can be utilised to feed a railroad.

"Take," says Colonel Medley, R.E., "the case of the best section of the Scinde, Punjab, and

* In 1881, in the cold season, an officer travelling about seventy miles from the nearest railway and ten miles from the chief civil station of a district, had to collect labourers to make a track between two villages passable for two bullock-carts. It took him eight hours to travel some fourteen miles. On another occasion, in another locality, he found it simply impossible to take a cart anywhere off the solitary unbridged road running through the district. He kept to the plains; he attempted no hills; carts were simply not used and unusable.

Delhi Railway, that from Lahore to Ghasiabad, a length of 335 miles. This is fed by metalled roads only at the stations of Amritsar, Jullundur, Ludhiána, Rájpura, Umballa, Saháranpur, Muzaffarnagar, and Meerut, *i.e.* at intervals of 32, 49, 35, 53, 13, 55, 36, 35, and 27 miles; while the other stations, thirty-six in number, are practicably unapproachable by cart traffic for three months in the year, and during the remaining nine months only at a heavy cost in carts and bullocks, which have to make their way over the village tracks which do duty for roads. To anyone who sees the actual state of the case, the wonder is that a large portion of the traffic ever gets to the line at all. I have shown, indeed, in more than one of my Inspection Reports, from cases that have actually come under my notice, that the cost of cartage to the line, even in fair weather, is from ten to forty times the cost of carriage over the same length on the railway; though even this is a mild statement of the case, for such is the state of the cross-country roads that, in the rainy season, they are practicably impassable by carts, and traffic is more or less suspended all over the country.

"Let it be borne in mind that the above line passes through a richly cultivated and populous country for the whole of its length, and is very much better provided with roads than other lines in the north. The Punjab Northern, the Indus Valley, and the Mooltan and Scinde sections of the Scinde, Punjab, and Delhi Railway may be said to have no metalled feeders whatever; and on the Indus Valley line traffic is practicably suspended during the flood season, *i.e.* from June to October. It is not very wonderful, therefore, that these lines do not pay." *

This being a fair statement of the case in the comparatively dry North-West, the much more deplorable state of things may be imagined in Bengal, where the rainfall is more than double that of the Punjab.

Still, in some of the grain and cotton-producing districts of India may be seen droves of pack-bullocks and buffaloes, the chief transporting media between villages and towns. These means of transport fail in the rains. Unbridged rivers become raging torrents, and country roads alive with traffic in the dry season are mere deserted tracts of mud. Even when made roads exist, they are sometimes so cut up that the best advice to travellers is "keep off the roads"; and you may see bullock-carts slowly dragged at the sides of the road, or, even worse, the whole traffic

---

* *Paper on Feeder Roads for Railways.* By Colonel Medley, R.E., Consulting Engineer to Government for the Punjab and Scinde Railways, dated 27th February 1884.

stopped whilst repairs are in progress, or the road consolidating.

Lord Dalhousie, with his accustomed energy, took up the question of railroads. As Vice-President of the Board of Trade during the administration of Sir Robert Peel, and during the railway-mania of 1845–1846, Lord Dalhousie had acquired considerable experience, experience which enabled him to shape a safe course in India. He held, that whilst it was no part of the business of the Government to conduct an enterprise undertaken mainly for commercial purposes, in which private persons were willing to engage, yet that such enterprise should be directly, but not vexatiously, controlled by the Government of India acting in the interests of the country. In 1842 Mr. C. B. Vignoles, F.R.S., had submitted a report to the Honourable East India Company on the establishment of railways in India. Before this, as mentioned by me in the earlier editions of this work under the signature of "An old Indian Postmaster," the construction of a railroad between Madras and Bangalore attracted attention so long ago as the year 1832, and in 1836 a line in this direction was surveyed by an eminent officer in the Madras Engineers. When the first edition of this work appeared, in 1846, and the Government of India, in spite of many prophesies of failure, were about to commence to construct railways, I ventured to mention that railways would more than double the effective strength of the army of occupation. I said that in the annual relief, infantry regiments were moved from one end of India to the other at the rate of ten and a half miles a day, with six days' halt in a month. It took six weeks to travel at this rate from Calcutta to Benares. In 1845, when the first Sikh war broke out, all officers whose regiments were in the field, were ordered to join the army. About one hundred engineer, cavalry, and infantry officers were required to go from Calcutta to the north-west frontier of India. They were sent at the public expense, and with the greatest despatch! The Postmaster-General could only send three daily! As the journey took sixteen days, travelling day and night, few of these officers rejoined their regiments before the war was over! On the 18th June 1830, Sir Henry Durand, then a young officer in the Engineers, was ordered to proceed from Calcutta to Cawnpore. He started three days later, but did not reach his destination until the 7th September.

But we hasten with our narrative. In 1845 the East Indian and the Great Indian Peninsula Companies had been formed. They found it impossible to raise the necessary funds for their proposed schemes. It was therefore determined

Establishment of guaranteed railway companies, and terms of the guarantee.

by the Indian Government to guarantee to the railway companies for a term of ninety-nine years interest at 5 per cent. upon the capital subscribed; the companies to repay from railway profits the advance on account of interest. The net receipts are paid into the Government treasury. If they amount to less than the sum due for interest, the deficiency is made good to them from the revenues of India; if they amount to more, half the excess is added to the dividend of the shareholders, and the other moiety is applied to the repayment of the sums previously paid by the Government on account of the guaranteed interest. If the receipts are not equal to the amount paid for working and maintaining the railway, the deficiency is chargeable against the guaranteed interest, and the dividend payable to the shareholders is thus reduced. When the whole of the sum given by Government for interest, with simple interest thereon, has been repaid, then the companies are entitled to the whole of the profits. The railway companies have the power of surrendering their works at any time after any portion of the line has been opened for three months, upon giving six months notice to Government, who repay the whole of the amount expended with their sanction on the undertaking.

Government has the power within six months after the expiry of twenty-five or fifty years respectively from the date of the contracts, to purchase the railway at the mean market value in London of the shares during the previous three years. It is also entitled in the event of the railway companies failing to complete the railways, or to work them satisfactorily, to take possession of them, repaying within six months the sums properly expended. The land required by the railway is given by the Government, but at the end of ninety-nine years it reverts to the Government; and if the railway companies have not availed themselves of the power of surrendering, the works also lapse to the Government, which purchases the rolling stock, &c. at a valuation. In any case in which under these provisions the Government becomes bound to repay the capital, or to purchase the railway, it can instead of giving the gross sum pay an annuity.

Land required for railways.

The reasons for the employment of private enterprise in the making of railways are obvious enough.

Reasons for the construction of railways by private enterprise.

1st. Lord Dalhousie, in his famous minute of 1853, regretted the absence of private enterprise in India. He wrote: "One of the greatest drawbacks to the advance of this country in material prosperity has been the total dependence upon the Government in which the community has placed itself, and its apparent utter helplessness to do anything for itself." Hence he maintained that it was the duty of the State to encourage the investment of English capital and English energy in India, by intrusting the work of supplying her with railways to associations formed for the purpose. He foresaw that if such associations could be formed a large non-official class of Europeans would be introduced into the country, who would be at all times both a strength to the Government and a check upon any despotic action, and that if English capital were profitably invested in railways, additional capital would also seek for investment in other industrial undertakings. He welcomed the influx of private English gentlemen and of English capital, of those same men, who, when in 1869 it was determined on the plea of economy to reverse the policy of Lord Dalhousie by the creation of State railways and the discouragement of guaranteed companies, were styled by an advocate in the *Westminster Review*, "adventurers" and the "servants of adventurers," the directors and their shareholders being some of the most eminent servants of the Crown connected with India! By the construction of railways by the State, the flow of British capital to India is checked, and private enterprise discouraged.

2nd. The comparative cheapness of private agency as compared with the proverbial costliness of State industrial departments. We shall show further on, that though some portions of the railways constructed by guaranteed companies have been costly, yet that extravagant expenditure is not necessarily inherent either in the guaranteed system, or in the gauge finally adopted.

3rd. The great facility of obtaining money for expenditure on railways by the establishment of guaranteed companies—as remarked by Mr. S. Laing when Finance Minister of India, "one of their greatest advantages is, that when money is raised in shares with a proper deposit paid at first, you are safe of getting your money when you want it, by making calls. But for this, Indian railways must have been stopped on many occasions from the sheer inability of the Government to find funds." Had Lord Dalhousie determined to make railways by the State instead of by guaranteed companies, no candid man can deny that, owing to the great straits the Government of India has been put to for money by the Mutiny, by famine, and by war, the railways would not merely have, as complained in 1869, cost much, but would not have existed on anything like the present scale: instead of there being 10,000 miles of railway open, there would not have been 5,000. Because the guaranteed companies were such successful pioneers of railway enterprise, the construction of railways by State agency became possible.

Supervision.

Lord Dalhousie, then, having determined to construct railways by guaranteed companies, it became necessary to supervise the expenditure and proceedings of the companies. The Government also selected or approved the line to be pursued by the railway. This supervision is exercised both in England and in India.

In England an official Director is appointed, who attends each Board of the Railway Companies in London, and possesses under the deed of contract a power of veto on all proceedings of the Directors. This power of veto, Mr. Juland Danvers, Government Director of Guaranteed Indian Railway Companies, and Secretary to the Public Works Department in the India Office, has used with rare courtesy and discretion. In India the following rules have been promulgated:—

1st. All questions of general importance shall be referred to the Government for decision.

2nd. Under the above will be included the general direction of all lines of railway, the position of stations, the general arrangements of the more important stations and works; but after the general sanction of the Government has been given to any project, all questions of detail may be disposed of within the limits of the original sanction by their Consulting Engineer.

3rd. All matters of routine, or acts in accordance with rule, precedent, or special agreement duly sanctioned, or undisputed contingent expenditure, may be dealt with by the Consulting Engineer without reference to the Government.

4th. All designs, estimates, and indents, whether for works or for establishments, for carrying into effect objects already generally sanctioned by Government, may also be disposed of finally by the Consulting Engineer.

5th. The Consulting Engineer may, without reference to the Government, reduce the amount of indents, or direct designs or proposed operations to be modified, if he thinks it necessary; but the Agent of the Company in such cases, if dissatisfied with the decision of the Consulting Engineer, may always request that the matter may be referred to the final orders of the Government.

6th. In all cases in which the Consulting Engineer has any doubt as to the decision to which he should come, the question should be referred to the Government for orders.

7th. When the sanction of the Consulting Engineer is given to any proposals of the Agent, in which both of these officers concur, excepting in those matters of great importance specially excepted above, the sanction so given shall, so far as the Government is concerned, be final.

8th. The Consulting Engineer shall submit to the Secretary of the Government a weekly schedule of his proceedings in the usual form, in which shall be explained concisely the nature of all sanctions or directions given under the authority now granted to him.

The Indian Government are fully responsible for all expenditure on guaranteed lines, as much so as if they were State lines.

These powers have been given to every chief Government railway officer in each of the local administrations. We have quoted at length the provisions for the dual government of the lines of guaranteed companies, so that it may at once be apparent that if in any case any of the guaranteed lines have been unduly costly, for such expenditure the Government is as responsible as the companies. For, the controlling powers of the Government have not always been exercised on the side of economy; on the contrary, there are many instances, which will occur to every engineer officer employed by the guaranteed companies, in which the cost of a line has been enhanced by the direct order of the Government. Thus Mr. Bruce, formerly Engineer in Chief of the Madras Railway, proposed to build his stations with low platforms. He argued that what was good enough for England was sufficient for India; but the Government would have high platforms, and so the expense of the stations increased in every way.

Instances in which the cost of a line has been increased by the action of the Government.

Mr. Bidder, Consulting Engineer on the Scinde, Punjab, and Delhi Railway, had framed a contract with Messrs. T. Brassey & Co. for the construction of the Delhi Railway. It was to some extent an experimental work, as no reliable data could be obtained regarding the large rivers it had to cross. To lessen the risk to the company, it was his desire to secure the skill and attention of the contractors in aid of the work by making them liable for the maintenance of all the work, including the bridges, for a period of three years. The contract was sent out to India for the approval of the authorities, and was returned with the remark: "The charge for the maintenance, both as regards time and amount, is too great. Three years is unusual, and in such a climate even two years is excessive." The time of maintenance was, therefore, shortened, and a loss of £200,000 by injury to the works was incurred, which would have been prevented by the payment, as proposed, of £90,000 for maintenance.

On two occasions, as mentioned by me in my capacity as Chairman of the Scinde, Punjab and Delhi Railway Company, in the discussion in 1873 on Guaranteed and State Railways, and on gauges, before the Institute of Civil Engineers, Government engineering officers altered the sites of bridges in the Punjab, to the great loss of the Railway Company.

To give one example. The Sutlej bridge was

built in the most exposed part of the stream, because the Government would have it so, the object being that it might be under the guns of the fort at Phillour. Before the first girder of the bridge was in its place, this arrangement was changed, and all the guns, magazine, and European troops, had been moved eighty miles away to Ferozepore. The truth is, that when railways were first made in India, economy formed no part of the Government scheme. The Government did not narrow the broad view of Lord Dalhousie to the simple consideration whether the construction of a certain line would pay an immediate and direct return of 5 per cent. on a sum equal to the guarantee.

Fares and rates on guaranteed lines.

All fares and rates are fixed with the approval of the Government, and alterations can only be made with the concurrence of the same authority.

Mails conveyed free of charge, and carriage of soldiers, army stores, guns, &c., at the lowest rates.

Railway Companies are also bound to convey the mails and Post Office servants free of charge, to take military officers in first-class carriages at second-class fares, and soldiers, when on duty, in second-class carriages at the lowest fares; also horses, guns, wagons, and military stores at the lowest rate for the time being chargeable for the carriage of such goods, animals, &c.

Lord Dalhousie left nothing to chance. Directly

Determination of Lord Dalhousie to have only one gauge in India.

he had determined on the construction of railways through guaranteed companies, he settled the question of gauge. In his minute of the 4th July, 1850, he writes: "The British Legislature fell unconsciously, and perhaps unavoidably, into the grievous error of permitting the introduction of two gauges into the United Kingdom. The numerous and grievous evils which arose from that permission are well known, and will long be felt throughout all England. The Government of India has it in its power, and no doubt will carefully provide that, however widely the railway system may be extended in this Empire in the time to come, these great evils shall be averted, and that uniformity of gauge shall be rigidly enforced from the first. But I conceive that the Government of India should do more than this, and that now, at the very outset of railway works, it should not only determine that one uniform gauge shall be established in India, but that such uniform gauge shall be the one that science and experience may unite in selecting as the best."

Gauge selected; comfort of Indian railways constructed by the guaranteed companies.

Finally, the 5 ft. 6 in. gauge was selected; and anyone who has travelled on Indian railways can testify to the comfort, speed, and steadiness with which long railway journeys are performed in India. The ordinary railway carriages in England are not to be compared for comfort in long journeys with those in use in India.

Mr. J. Maclean, in his paper on the State monopoly of railways in India remarks: "Lord Dalhousie was determined that India should not be annoyed with that battle of the gauges which had caused so many heart-burnings and wasted so much money in England. . . . It was his ambition to build these new roads on a grand scale, and as solidly as the Romans built; and travellers in India must always feel grateful to him for the comfort which this decision has secured to them. There is no better travelling to be had anywhere in the world than that which is afforded by the guaranteed lines in India! The rolling stock is excellent in quality, although, as is said of the British infantry, there is sometimes not enough of it. The track is thoroughly well laid, and the width of the gauge allows, when necessary, of a high rate of speed and gives every facility for additional power to the locomotive."

Great difficulties to be overcome when railways first commenced in India.

On this system, then, railways under guaranteed companies and with broad gauge commenced to be constructed in India. The difficulties at first were enormous. There was no body of skilled artizans accustomed to the work, or of hardy labourers habituated to the use of the pickaxe; the commonest implement of labour, the wheelbarrow, was unknown and had never yet been introduced. When earthworks have to be constructed the earth is carried in small baskets mostly on the heads of women and children. I have already depicted the want of roads; then the rivers had no boats sufficient to transport railway material. The East India Railway Company, it is said, lost more than 15,000 tons of material* in endeavouring to convey them in native boats. The mutiny of the sepoy army delayed the progress of the railway, and cost the guaranteed railway companies, it has been calculated, some three millions of money; yet the railways steadily progressed in spite of war and disease, and their officers gave the most brilliant examples of courage† and patient endurance. Mr. Juland Danvers, Government Director of Railways, after a visit to India and personal inspection of the railways, wrote: "The civil engineer in India had to contend against the forces of nature to a far greater extent than is the case in this island. He had to overcome the difficulties which the gigantic features of the country placed in his way; he had often only poor materials and inferior labour at his command, and

---

* See *Daily News* of 31st July 1869.

† The gallant conduct of Mr. Boyle, the engineer of the celebrated Arrah defence, is well known.

he had to meet the danger of exposure to a burning sun by day and malarious vapours by night. To his skill and professional knowledge he had accordingly to bring more than ordinary courage and endurance. Many have broken down in the attempt, but their places have been immediately filled by others, and the result is exhibited by the thousands of miles of railway which thread their way over mountain passes, cut through thick jungle, and span huge and uncertain rivers."

The business of a most important contract carried on by a lady on the death of her husband.

In our retrospect of the construction of Indian railways we cannot omit to record that when in 1859 Mr. S. Tredwell, the contractor for the stupendous works on the Bhore Ghat incline, died at Khandála, Mrs. Tredwell, in order to prevent serious delay and embarrassment to the works, conducted with unflinching resolution and high spirit the business of the contract.

Work done up to 1869 when there was a break of gauge.

Up to 1869 the policy of Government determined upon in the first instance by Lord Dalhousie had been consistent: railways were to be made by guaranteed companies under supervision and subject to definite regulations. The main lines had not then, nor have they yet been completed, but the Great Indian Peninsula and East Indian Railways had joined at Jubbulpore, the whole breadth of the Peninsula had been spanned, Calcutta and Bombay, Bombay, Delhi, and Lahore, had been brought into communication with each other. The question of cheap lines had not then arisen. It is as well to pause in our narrative here and to show what had been affected under the system of guaranteed companies in the face of the most stupendous difficulties.

Guaranteed Companies.	Miles Open.	Total Cost.	Net Receipts.	Excess Payment on Account of Interest.
		£	£	£
East Indian . . .	*1,353	29,997,342	7,198,642	5,568,960
Eastern Bengal .	112	2,752,143	417,102	369,053
Great Indian Peninsula	*1,258¼	20,945,620	3,221,365	3,559,248
Madras	781½	9,475,904	1,712,461	2,196,715
Bombay, Baroda, and Central India	312½	7,368,579	869,204	1,513,269
Scinde, Delhi, and Punjab. . . .	666¾	9,308,016	301,809	2,132,854
Great Southern of India	185¾	1,464,533	184,101	210,601
Oude and Rohilcund	42	1,363,298	9,730	130,375
Total . . .	4,711¾	82,675,435	13,914,414	15,681,075

* By the close of 1869, 203 miles of the East Indian Railway had been laid with a double line, as also had 256 miles of the G.I.P. Line. This length is not added to the statement of the miles open, though, of course, it is included both in the cost and interest and receipt statement.

We have not included in this statement eighteen miles of the Indian tramway, afterwards the Carnatic Company, now amalgamated with the Great Southern of India, nor of the cost of the Indus steam flotilla, or the thirty-six miles of State line then open. Our statement includes only guaranteed lines. It appears that in twenty years £15,681,075, or including the Indus flotilla £15,864,344, had, during the construction of Indian railways, been drawn from the Treasury. The average sum drawn was thus £793,000 a year. The above statement shows that the railways had cost in construction £17,545 a mile.

What the country and the Government received in return for the excess outlay on account of the payment of interest to guaranteed railway companies.

For this annual expenditure of £793,000 the mails had been carried free of charge, troops, both horse and foot, had been swiftly and safely conveyed at the lowest fares, and ammunition, camp equipage and equipments, at the lowest rates chargeable to goods of that kind. As remarked by Mr. Juland Danvers, "The saving effected must be considerable, and nearly, if not quite, equivalent" to the average annual charge. The difficulties of Civil Administration had been much lessened, supervision became possible, the Governments of India, Bombay, Madras, found it practicable to migrate annually to Simla, Mahableshwar, and the Nilgherries. Above all, the railways enabled the Government to locate soldiers in healthy stations, and so to diminish the death-rate and improve the physique of European troops. Arsenals have been largely reduced in number, and it has been possible to reduce the European garrison. In 1858 Sir Henry Durand estimated that the Government of India might reduce their military expenditure by one-fourth when the system of rail communication was complete. The hot palatial barracks, sometimes badly built at enormous cost, have become less necessary. The lives of many valuable European officers have been saved. Dotted over the plains of India are to be seen, often in unconsecrated ground, the graves of Europeans, who, ordered to a cooler country, succumbed to the hardships of a long and tedious journey to the sea-coast. Many residents in India still remember the grief caused by the untimely death of Lady Canning. Had the railway to Darjiling existed during the first period of Indian railways that we have described, her life might have been saved, and probably the ripe experience of Lord Canning might have been preserved to Her Majesty's Government in England for many years. The direct advantage of railways by increased land revenue, improved traffic, the development of the cotton and grain trades, will all be shown below. They partly indeed belong to the period from 1856 to 1869, but we prefer to consider the enormous commercial advantages bestowed on India down to the latest date—and once for all.

As recently it has been the fashion, not indeed

of capitalists, but of some officers possessed of great weight in India, to take a very narrow view of the advantage to India of her railway system, to dwell upon the immediate outlay for interest on the guaranteed lines as if all will not eventually return handsome dividends, we think it advisable to state at greater length the less obvious advantages reaped by India from railways. They are the great civilising power in India. Where they have penetrated jungle has disappeared, and the cultivated plains "begin to laugh and sing." Famine in their neighbourhood has been rendered impossible. They have diminished the contemptuous isolation of caste, and have caused knowledge to be sought after. The railways do more for mass-education than all the efforts of the Educational Department. Their influence even on the language of the people, and upon their religious ideas, has been great. The simple peasant, who once attempted by offerings of fruit and flowers and by sacrifice to propitiate the rivers that he could not bridge, has now learnt that the forces of nature may be controlled by man and rendered his untiring servants. On this subject and on the conduct of the independent Englishmen—the engineers and artizans employed by the guaranteed companies in India—we cannot do better than quote from the speech of Sir Bartle Frere, the late distinguished

The indirect benefits conferred on India by railways.

Governor of Bombay, at the opening of the Bhore Ghat incline. He says:—

"Among the many difficulties which beset or were supposed to beset the introduction of railways into this country, was usually placed foremost the difficulty of controlling a large number of independent Englishmen—not like our soldiers bound by the ties of military discipline—not in any way prepared to submit their own will to the mere dictates of authority. We have now ample experience to enable us to judge what foundation there was for such apprehension, and what has been the result. I do not pretend to say that there have not been exceptions among the many hundreds of Englishmen employed in other works, it would be strange if there were not some who possessed the mere animal instincts of courage and strength, and capacity for physical exertion, in a higher degree than that inclination to take the weaker side, the love of truth and of fair play in which as a nation we pride ourselves; but looking at the general results and considering the effects which this invasion of a small army of Englishmen has produced in the country, I think there cannot be a doubt, not only that the fears which some people entertained were entirely chimerical, but that the lower ranks of this railway army, as well as the higher, have left a deep and beneficial impression on the population among which they have been employed, and that the result is one for which our countrymen of all ranks in your service, the artizans and mechanics as well as the gentlemen on the engineering staff, richly deserve the gratitude of the Government and of their country. So far from its being the case that the bonds of official discipline are necessary to prevent the growth of ill-feeling between the Saxon stranger and the natives of India, I find the employment afforded by the unofficial contractor almost invariably more popular than that of Government. . . . I know of no sight more impressive or more full of suggestive topics, to anyone who reflects on the future of India, than such a visit as I lately paid to the contractor's works before they were finished. It was then easy to see how railway works taught the native labourer habits of method and punctuality, habits of truth and honesty in his work, and, above all, habits of independence. It is in this last respect more than in any other that I believe these railway works will have an immense influence on the future of India. We all know that vast sums, chiefly in English capital, have of late years been spent in this country. Let us consider for one moment what has been the effect of all this money being spent in giving a fair day's wages for a fair day's labour. I can safely say that as a rule, this was not known before the commencement of what I may call the railway period; not only were the wages in most parts of the country fixed by usage and authority, rather than by the natural laws of supply and demand, but the privilege of labour was in general restricted to particular spots, and nothing like the power of taking his labour to the best market practically existed. This was partly due to custom, partly to the absence of any but agricultural employment, partly to long ages of despotic and unsettled government; but the result was that the condition of the mere labourer was wretched in the extreme, and the best efforts of Government could do but little to raise him above the status of a serf of the soil. All this has now, I am happy to say, changed, mainly as a direct consequence of these vast railway works; and for the first time in history the Indian cooly finds that he has in his power of labour a valuable possession which, if he uses it aright, will give to him and to his family something better than a mere subsistence, and that there are means open to him of rising in the world other than by the career of the fortunate soldier, or of the chance favouritism of princes.

And what has been the result of this discovery to him? Has it made him more indolent, less inclined to labour, more content to be satisfied with the mere existence that he can now procure with less labour than formerly? I believe there is no one who has any experience in the matter who will not bear me out in saying that this is not the case; the labourer is of course more independent, he is in a better position to make his own terms with his employer, and that, perhaps, is sometimes shown in a manner which his employer does not quite like; but as a general rule I believe the labourer works far harder, and acquires new and more civilized wants, in proportion to the high wages he receives. Follow him to his own home in some remote Deccan or Concan village, and you will find the railway labourer has carried to his own village not only new modes of working, new wants, and a new feeling of self-respect and independence, but new ideas of what Government and the laws intend to secure to him; and he is, I believe, a better and more loyal subject, as he is certainly a more useful labourer. Let us add to this effect on the labouring population the inevitable and irresistible tendency of railways to break the bonds of caste and to destroy the isolation in which the various classes and races of natives have hitherto lived, and you have an aggregate of moral results such as may well be the subject of grave thought to those who are interested in the future of India, and more particularly to us, who have seen in our own time and in our own Continent the vast effects for good or for evil which must follow any great change in the habits of life and of feeling of large masses of the people."

I make no apology for quoting these eloquent words of Sir Bartle Frere at a time when the farther extension of railways in India is under consideration, and when it is about to be determined whether such extension shall be rapidly and economically effected by guaranteed companies, with perhaps an influx into India of those Saxon and Celtic artizans whose good work and example has been so well described, or by the Government of India with the instruments it already possesses. But there is an ample field for all agencies, and all that their combined efforts can effect must for many years fall far short of the requirements of so vast a country.

Sir Evelyn Baring, when Financial Member of Council, acknowledged that the provisions made under different heads for the execution of public works in India were quite inadequate. The policy of Government for the extension of railways in India has not been uniform. It was first determined to employ guaranteed companies, then to make railways by the State, then to enlist private enterprise without guarantee. The most successful agency hitherto employed is that first selected by Lord Dalhousie, namely, guaranteed companies.

Change of policy in railway construction.

In 1869 Lord Lawrence, when Governor-General of India, considered that railways would be more cheaply constructed by the State than by guaranteed companies. Before 1869 no efforts—if we omit the Nalhati line, of which some $27\frac{1}{4}$ miles were open—had been made to construct cheap railways; they were above all things to be solid, sufficient even for emergent traffic, for the conveyance of grain in famine, and of troops, guns, and stores in war; they were to carry their passengers with comfort and celerity. These objects had been secured. But in future railways were not to cost more than £12,000* a mile. So the Governor-General, without consulting independent railway engineers as to the possibility of greater economy in construction, without even attempting to introduce such rules as would secure economy, recorded a minute that the future lines should, "so far as is consistent

* Many portions of Indian railways had been constructed at less cost. Mr. Lee Smith stated, at the Institute of Civil Engineers, that he had constructed $81\frac{1}{2}$ miles of railway at a cost of £6,160 a mile: $37\frac{1}{4}$ miles were constructed during the Mutiny; 44 miles had only cost £5,370 per mile, for earthworks, bridges, culverts, level crossings, permanent way, telegraph, stations, everything complete, except land and rolling-stock. The rails were either 78 or 82 lbs. per yard.

with actual and implied engagements with existent companies, be carried out by the Government itself." It is curious to note how the Indian Government seem unable to look at two sides of a question. No doubt economy in the construction of railways is of great importance, but it may be secured without entailing on the country the evils of a State railway monopoly. Mr. Herbert Spencer opportunely enough, in the April number of the *Contemporary Review*, shows both the evil of State railways, and how that, in the endeavour to avoid one evil, others more potent are often evoked. He remarks that "the law-makers who provided for the ultimate lapsing of French railways to the State never conceived the possibility that inferior travelling facilities would result,—did not foresee that reluctance to depreciate the value of property eventually coming to the State would negative the authorisation of competing lines, and that in the absence of competing lines locomotion would become costly, slow, infrequent. For, as Sir Thomas Farrar has shown, the traveller in England has great advantages over the traveller in France in the economy, swiftness, and frequency with which his journeys can be made." A State railway department will add to that bureaucracy from which India already suffers, and which drives away English capital from Indian investments.

We do not use the term bureaucracy in any offensive sense, but merely deprecate any great increase to that organization of officials which, once passing beyond a certain growth, becomes less and less resistible, and at last works for its own advantage rather than for the common welfare of all. This recommendation for the construction of railways by the State, Lord Lawrence based on the belief:—

1st. That expenditure will be kept more under control than when incurred through the agency of companies.

2nd. That India, owing to the works of the guaranteed companies, now possesses all the knowledge requisite for the administration and control of railways.

3rd. That when a railway passes through native States it is much better that it should be in the hands of Government than in those of a company.

4th. That the Government is better able to command the money requisite to carry on these important public works.

The truth of each of these allegations is doubtful. The first is only true if it is meant that expenditure may be so controlled by the Government as not to be spent at all upon railways when State exigencies are great, or when the Government bring into prominence the urgent need of irrigation works, or the importance of roads to feed railways and desire to divert capital from railways to other objects. If the Government know exactly what they want, what is to be the traffic, what the character and position of the bridges, what the engineering difficulties to be overcome, then expenditure can be as effectually controlled on lines constructed by guaranteed companies as on lines made by the State. If, however, the Government policy is suddenly altered—if, after providing that a guaranteed company shall do one thing, they wish them to do another—if, after directing the construction of a first-class road, they desire suddenly to have less stability and to provide for less traffic at reduced speed, and will not say what they want, but desire to construct a slow-speed railway, and yet to take the credit of a first-class line,—then, of course, it is not so easy to work through guaranteed companies, the reputation of whose officers, taking a loving pride in their labour, is at stake, as through officials to whom it is a merit to obey orders.

Surmounting difficulties and political and military importance of line to be considered in rewarding officers, and not commercial results.

"When it is considered that all the Indian Railway Companies have been engaged for many years in the common object of carrying out and working portions of one Imperial system of Railways; that all these parts of a great whole have been located with the sanction of Government, the construction supervised, and the expenditure controlled, both in India and England, by Officers appointed by Government, and subject generally, as regards appointments, salaries, &c., to a common system of Rules and Regulations, it appears that to introduce as a condition for granting Government aid to the Provident Funds for the benefit of persons employed on the Guaranteed Railways in India, the commercial success of the particular Railway, irrespective of the merits of the Officers or Servants concerned, is not only invidious and unwise, but unjust.

"In many cases the want of commercial success has had nothing to do with the amount of ability, experience, or energy shown by the executive, but has resulted from the physical and other difficulties which have been encountered in the construction of lines, which, on account of their political importance, were promoted and encouraged by Government mainly on military and strategic grounds, but which from their geographical position afforded but little promise of either a speedy or adequate commercial return.

"From this it appears that it is not fair to treat the Employés on such lines, who have had to contend with the difficulties of want of transport, labour, and of almost every appliance for economical construction, in addition to inadequate traffic resources, in order to carry out the objects of the Government, in a less liberal spirit than those who have experienced none of these obstacles in carrying out similar enterprises in a populous and fertile country, which must of necessity yield a certain and large return upon the invested Capital, without any particular merit in those who have constructed or managed the Railway.

"The obvious tendency of such an arrangement will be to discourage many of the old and tried Servants of the Scinde, Punjab, and Delhi Railway Company, some of whom have received the cordial approval of the Government for their public services, and, by attracting the most skilled and experienced men to the lines which have least need of them, will, unless an equivalent in the shape of higher salaries, is sanctioned by Government, compel the Directors of the less fortunate lines to appoint Officers of an inferior grade, and thereby retard the period when surplus profits may be looked for.

"Examples are not wanting in this and other countries of a policy quite the reverse of this, namely, in which the remuneration was made commensurate with the difficulties to be surmounted.

"The Scinde, Punjab, and Delhi Railway Company, in which I am interested, it is fair to state, has had more difficulties to encounter than any other Company in India. When we began the Scinde line, so little was Kurrachee known as a port, that much difficulty was experienced in obtaining freight, and there were no facilities or mechanical appliances there for landing the railway materials. We had to send out boats and cranes, and when the rails and rolling-stock were landed they had to be dragged by camels over miles of sand.

"There was no population available for labour, and we had to import it from China, Persia, Afghanistan, and various parts of India. The soil was obdurate, difficult to work, and little cultivated, and commerce at the lowest ebb. On the other hand, besides the stimulus it would give to a dormant commerce, the Scinde Railway was regarded as the first section of a line of communication of imperial importance, politically, and strategically, which would connect Central Asia, the Punjab, and North-West Provinces with the sea at Kurrachee, which is marked out by its geographical position to be the European port of India.*

"They had to construct and to maintain several

---

* Justice cannot be done to Kurrachee until Scinde is annexed to the Punjaub and the two together constitute one Presidency.

bridges of large dimensions (in the Punjab), spanning perhaps the most capricious and difficult rivers in the world, entailing great hardship and exposure, which have caused the permanent loss of health of several valuable officers employed in their construction, and subsequent maintenance.

"The system confided to the Scinde, Punjab, and Delhi Railway Company has been of the utmost importance to Government, not only in affording efficient help in carrying grain in the emergencies of famine, but in the conveyance of troops and warlike stores during the Afghan campaigns, and, with its branches to the Khyber and the Bolan Passes, is the grand political line in India, and constitutes the readiest and most powerful means of offence or defence on our north-western border.

"Are the men who have planned, constructed, and maintained these lines of inestimable value in a political and strategical point of view in the time of war without or of trouble within our border, however barren the commercial results may be—are they to be less considered and rewarded than those who had little difficulty to encounter in the construction and management of profitable Railways?

"Would the Government of India, or indeed

any Government, apply this commercial test of a paying result to works of magnitude necessary for defence or other State purposes? Do they pay their Engineer Officers, who are constructing the Railway along the Cutchee desert, because it is almost destitute of traffic, less than those employed in the construction of other Railways?

"The Servants of the Railway Companies who have successfully surmounted difficulties, should be equally considered in every way with those whose lines have fallen in pleasant places, without any engineering problem to solve, in a densely peopled country with a large existing traffic, where the profitable working of the Railway would be the inevitable result of such a state of things without the display of any conspicuous ability on the part of those entrusted with the construction and management.

"All the Railway Companies are under one Imperial system, and I desire to see the S. P. & D. Company placed in a position, not superior to others, but on an equality with any other Company which has had entrusted to it the construction of Railways in India.

"I venture to hope that the Government will reconsider this question, and would suggest the formation of a Fund out of Revenue by each Guaranteed Railway, irrespective of their paying more than 5 per cent., to which the Employés should subscribe ; this would be an equitable arrangement, and in accordance with the view that the Railway system is to be regarded as an important part of the machinery of the Empire, and that the encouragement given to the Employés is not to be restricted by considerations of localities, nor measured by financial results."*

But to resume. Whilst the agreement with guaranteed companies allows the Government full control over expenditure on a defined project, it does not allow, without remonstrance, of sudden change in the original proposals on which expenditure has already been incurred, nor does it permit the withdrawal of funds for expenditure on other objects. Can anyone doubt that guaranteed lines could have been conducted with economy if rules such as those issued to officers constructing State railways had been proposed by the Government? We mention a few of the rules :—

1st. In every particular except for road and machinery, the bare necessities of the traffic should be provided for without

---

* Letter by the Writer to the Most Honourable the Marquis of Hartington, Secretary of State for India, dated 21st June 1880.

indulging in luxuries or comforts * which may be postponed till demanded by traffic.

2nd. The lines should be designed for traffic *not exceeding fifteen miles an hour.*

3rd. Fencing should be estimated for; but it is probable *that a change in the law* may allow of its being limited to the vicinity of stations, and other places when absolutely necessary.

4th. The width of bridges and culverts should be reduced to a minimum, say ten or twelve feet, consistently with true economy when in bank.

5th. Large bridges may simply be wide enough to carry the rails, with foot-ways on either side.

---

* Experience shows that this rule is observed on State railways. An officer travelling with his wife and son, after paying first-class fare, were accommodated with arm-chairs in a goods' wagon. This was the only first-class. It is true that the line was only just open for that part of its length on which the officer travelled; and it is true that even if no chairs had been given, the officer would have found it convenient to travel by the train. But the point is not that the first-class rolling-stock was insufficient, but that, in the interests of economy, guaranteed lines should, on similar occasions, have for a time similar privileges granted. Both guaranteed lines and State lines should work in accordance with equally lenient or equally stringent rules.

6th. Economy of first outlay is to be studied in all the adjuncts ; and to this end, station buildings should be of an inexpensive character, the accommodation being restricted to the expected present wants of the traffic. Raised platforms should be dispensed with.*

A guaranteed company can comply with such instructions as well as any State engineer. The hint that the law may be altered, not for the increased safety of the public, but for the more economical construction of a State railway, is a little startling.

The third reason for State railways seems plausible enough to men not acquainted with India, and who may be inclined to regard the Government as the protectors of the people against the greed of guaranteed companies. But as remarked by Sir Bartle Frere, in the speech we have already quoted, not only do the natives of India prefer to serve in workshops and on lines under construction by guaranteed companies to service under the Government ; but native States, not always, but frequently, prefer to have lines running through them constructed by guaranteed

* Compare with the treatment of Mr. Bruce already mentioned, *vide* p. xxv.

companies. The Portuguese Government has employed a company to construct a railway through its territory in India; so has the Government of the Nizam and that of other native States, the most recent being the construction of the Patiala State line by the Scinde, Punjab, and Delhi Company.

The people themselves much prefer to conduct all commercial transactions with a company rather than with the State. Rightly or wrongly, they doubt the impartiality of the State. This is especially the case in Western India. In the event of any damage by delay, or of any disputed rate of charge, if the railway concerned is a State railway, the officers of the Government are themselves the defendants in any actions that may be brought and the judges also. If the railway is managed by a company, then, though Government officers are the judges, they are not the defendants. There is also in a railway managed by a company less of that routine always the subject of complaints, but often very necessary, that is called "red tape." This is a widely spread belief, not only amongst native merchants, but amongst the members of English firms. Some years ago an officer of Government who had to manage a *quasi* trading business found the system of accounts kept very cumbrous, so cumbrous, indeed, that the accounts were generally in arrears and thus useless for all purposes of check. He consulted a Bombay firm as to the best method of keeping such accounts. The head of the firm replied, detailing a simple method which was adopted by the officer consulting the firm, but added in his letter on the subject: "We suppose this system will not be sufficiently cumbrous for a Government office." We may say, generally, not only do the work-people prefer to serve a company to serving the State, but also that the trading classes prefer to have dealings with a company rather than with the State.

The fourth reason for the construction of railways by the State is opposed to all experience. It is notorious that the Government of India are crippled in all their so-called productive public works' expenditure by their want of funds. As remarked by Mr. S. Laing when Financial Member of Council in 1861: "A Government cannot be perpetually raising small loans; and if it can create through the agency of companies a share capital of ten or twenty millions, with five millions paid up, and a certainty of getting the other fifteen millions by calls just as you want it, whether the state of the money market is good or bad, it is an important advantage, and worth paying for." The sum of £2,500,000 is indeed available out of the annual income for the construction of new railways; but the Indian Government, instead of setting aside this sum for the payment of interest at 4 per cent. on a capital of £60,000,000, which it might borrow at once, has, as urged by Mr. J. Maclean, "the pedantry to insist on spending its two-and-a-half millions a year as principal, and thus renders itself incapable of making progress except by driblets."

What a splendid opportunity is now afforded to a wise and energetic Viceroy, to men of the stamp of Lord Dalhousie and Sir Bartle Frere, to provide for the needs of British commerce, to re-open closed foundries and looms, to arrest the fall in exchange, and to enrich by one and the same policy both England and India.

"I projected and advocated the Indus Valley line with its branches to the Bolan and the Khyber passes more than twenty years ago.* In 1863, after two peremptory refusals from the Secretary of State for India in Council, I received permission for the Company to send to India a Chief Engineer with a staff of fourteen Engineers and Surveyors

---

* What is now requisite is an extension from Quetta to Candahar, which place should be strongly fortified and garrisoned: thus we should bar the advance of any force to the Bolan, and be able to attack in flank and rear an army proceeding against the Khyber.

to survey the line from Kotree to Mooltan, who examined the country exhaustively on both sides of the river, and furnished the basis, supplemented by subsequent investigation, upon which the choice of the present line was made.

"This Survey was undertaken and supervised by me, with the hope and expectation that the construction of the line would be entrusted to my Company, and that material benefit would accrue to the public at large, and to the Shareholders, whose interest I have always had so much at heart. The line from Hyderabad to Mooltan on the left bank of the river had been selected, also comparative estimates and every preparation made for its speedy construction, when, from a change of view at the India Office, I was obliged to order further proceedings to be suspended, and to dismiss the staff.

"This was hard upon the Company who had planned and for so many years advocated the construction of this line, which they regarded as an integral portion of their undertaking, "the Missing Link" in their system.

"The delay which followed amounted to the abandonment for several years of a work urged on the attention of Government by Sir John Lawrence, Sir Bartle Frere, Sir Henry Durand, Sir Richard Temple, and many other eminent

Indian Statesmen, as a most important portion of that system which I had devised for the development of the resources of the Punjab and North-West of India, and the border countries, as well as for political and strategical purposes.

"This system, even in its present state, with the Indus unbridged (at the most important crossing, at Sukkur), and the branches to the passes incomplete, has already justified its construction by its augmenting commercial advantages, while its importance in the late campaigns in Afghanistan has been acknowledged repeatedly by the highest military authorities in India, and very recently by Sir Frederick Roberts, who authorised a message to be sent to me conveying his acknowledgments and thanks for the services rendered to him and his troops.*

---

* Movement of troops, munitions of war, &c. during the Afghan Campaigns 1879–81 :—

No. of Specials.	Troops and Followers.	Horses, Mules, and Ponies.	Bullocks.	Camels.	Guns, Artillery, and Engrs.' Carriages.	Military Baggage, Commissariat, and Ordnance Stores.	Frontier Railway Material for Kandahar.	Frontier Railway Material for Peshawar.
						Tons.	Tons.	Tons.
785	538,364	114,156	15,477	8,646	479	145,625	29,892	63,202

"In 1870, Lord Salisbury appointed Sir Louis Mallet and Sir Frederick Halliday to meet me to draw up a joint report with the view of securing unity of design and management in the construction and working of the Indus Valley Railway in connection with the Scinde and Punjaub Lines, so as to avoid, if possible, foreign agency being thrust, as it were, into the heart of our system."*

But instead of carrying out these views, a suicidal and most disastrous policy was introduced, a policy of ostensibly cheap railways of the metre gauge (3 ft. 3⅜ in.), a policy which, by its indiscreet application, has in fact dislocated the railway system of India, a policy which has led to the squandering of large sums of money on the Indus Valley Railway (500 miles from Kotree to Mooltan) the Government having made preparations for the narrow gauge which had subsequently to be abandoned, and to the useless expenditure of still larger sums in the metre gauge railway from Lahore to Peshawar (270 miles).

If the metre-gauge policy had been carried out on these lines, the frontier railways in the event

---

* Letter by the Writer to Juland Danvers, Esq., Government Director of Guaranteed Railways, dated 15th December 1880.

of any disturbance on the North-West border would have been virtually isolated and cut off from the vast amount of rolling stock of the railways in their rear; but after a severe struggle better councils prevailed, and India was saved from a great and ignominious failure.

Break of gauge.

The Government of India having determined to construct railways themselves, immediately proceeded to alter the gauge, and thus to introduce all the evils from which Lord Dalhousie had determined India should be free. A committee consisting of Lieutenant-General Strachey, R.E., C.S.I., Lieutenant-General C. Dickens, C.S.I., Mr. John Fowler, C.E., and Mr. A. M. Rendel, Consulting Engineer to the Government of India, was appointed to consider, not whether having some 5,000 miles of railway, constructed on the 5 ft. 6 in. gauge, it was advisable to introduce a narrow gauge, and thus to dislocate Indian railways, but "to consider the precise gauge and general character for an average narrow-gauge line of railway in India." * The question of break of gauge in India was never before its introduction fairly and fully argued. Could there

---

* *Report on Railways in India for the Year 1870–71.* By Mr. Juland Danvers.

be any greater condemnation of State industrial departments, one of which, the State railway department, introduced so great a change before considering all the consequences. The guaranteed railways and uniformity of gauge were to fall together. To use the words of Lieutenant-General Strachey, the Government of India, in order to extend railways more economically, determined that "all lines should in future be carried out without the intervention of companies, and that the outlay on construction should be reduced to a minimum by the adoption of the narrowest gauge and the lightest rails and rolling-stock compatible with the requirements of Indian traffic."

Had any serious attempt been made to ascertain what were the requirements of Indian traffic, much harm might not have been done. But the opinion of General Strachey, that the Indian railway system had failed financially, and that such failure was due to the construction of railways by guaranteed companies on the 5 ft. 6 in. gauge, was accepted, and it was considered that no railway in India need provide for more traffic than for 840 tons of goods and 1,064 passengers carried over every mile in twenty-four hours.* This, it was

---

* Paper of General Strachey read before the Institute of Civil Engineers.

supposed, was the heaviest traffic ever likely to occur, because it was then the traffic on the East Indian Railway. But the traffic on the East Indian Railway has falsified these figures, 1,417 passengers and 1,825 tons of goods were carried in twenty-four hours, over every mile, in 1882, and the net earnings on capital outlay on some of the lines, part of a system declared to be a financial failure, realised for the East Indian line 8·56 per cent., for the Great Indian Peninsula line 7·11 per cent., for the Eastern Bengal line 10·23 per cent., these being about the most expensive lines in the country. In fact, if only the Government of India will attend to the roads that are to feed railways, and if some reforms, including a reduction for the carriage of grain are introduced, it is hardly possible even to estimate the profits likely to accrue to railways. Who can estimate the loss to railways and to consigners of grain that has arisen from the inability of railways to carry even the existing traffic? Such loss has always sprung from preventible causes. Even famine-prevention railways I should prefer to be light railways on the ordinary gauge, or even tramways, in the absence of roads, which may be economically constructed and worked in sparsely-populated rural districts. But the Government of India, directly they determined on State railways, adopted the narrow gauge system, and rode their hobby to death. It was even decided* to construct the Punjab Northern and Indus Valley lines, those of Rajputana and Indore, and the Chhattisgarh line, on the metre gauge. Fortunately for India, this decision was not approved by engineers in England. They knew too well the evils of break of gauge. A paper read by the late Mr. W. T. Thornton, C.B., when Secretary Public Works Department, India Office, before the Institute of Civil Engineers in 1873, provided an opportunity to discuss the whole question, not of "broad gauge" *versus* "narrow gauge," but of break of gauge. It resulted from this discussion, which I had the honour of leading, and from what took place in the House of Commons and elsewhere, that the 5 ft. 6 in. gauge was adopted for the Punjab Northern and Indus Valley lines. The distinguished engineers and others who took part in the discussion are mentioned below:—

Condemnation of break of gauge in India by the Institute of Civil Engineers.

Against the change of gauge:

Mr. T. Hawksley, President of the Institution.

Mr. G. P. Bidder, Consulting Engineer to the Scinde, Punjaub, and Delhi Railways.

---

* See Report of Mr. Juland Danvers for 1870-71 on Railways in India.

Sir John Hawkshaw, F.R.S., Consulting Engineer to the Madras and Eastern Bengal Railways.

Mr. C. B. Vignoles, F.R.S.

Members of Council of the Institution—

Mr. George Berkley, Consulting Engineer to the Great Indian Peninsula Railway.

Mr. G. B. Bruce, Consulting Engineer to the Great Southern of India Railway, and formerly Engineer-in-Chief of the Madras Railway.

Mr. J. Brunlees.

Mr. T. E. Harrison.*

Mr. Edward Woods.

Colonel J. P. Kennedy, Consulting Engineer to the Bombay, Baroda, and Central India Railway.

Mr. George Turnbull, formerly Engineer-in-Chief of the East Indian Railway.

Mr. Lee Smith, late Chief Engineer Punjaub Northern (State) Railway.

Mr. W. Pole, F.R.S., Engineer to the Imperial Railways of Japan.

---

* Mr. Harrison is now President of the Institution of Civil Engineers.

Mr. W. B. Lewis, one of the Consulting Engineers to the Victorian Government.

Mr. J. T. Wood, Eastern Bengal Railway.

Former Government Inspectors of Railways—

Captain Douglas Galton, C.B., R.E., F.R.S.

General Sir L. Simmons, R.E.

Colonel Sir Frederick Smith, R.E.

Present Government Inspectors of Railways—

Captain H. W. Tyler, R.E.

Colonel Yolland, R.E.

Civil Engineers—

Mr. W. Dennis.

Mr. C. Douglas Fox.

Mr. G. G. Heppel.

Mr. J. Mitchell.

Mr. A. S. Ormsby.

Mr. C. P. Sandberg.

Mr. Price Williams.

Sir G. B. Airy, Pres. R.S., Astronomer Royal.

Mr. W. P. Andrew, Chairman of the Scinde, Punjaub, and Delhi Railways.

Mr. J. J. Allport, Manager of the Midland Railway.

Mr. J. Grierson, Manager of the Great Western Railway.

In addition to these authorities may be mentioned

others who, though not taking part in the discussion, have expressed strong opinions against the change of gauge; as:—

Mr. C. H. Gregory, Past President of the Institution, who has reported officially against narrow-gauge lines in the Colonies.

Mr. G. L. Molesworth, now Chief Resident-Engineer of the State Railways in India, who has also reported against narrow-gauge railways in Ceylon; and

Mr. John Fowler, Past President of the Institution, who reported to the Indian Government strongly against the proposed change in the Punjaub lines.

In support of the change of gauge—

Mr. W. T. Thornton, C.B., India Office, Author of the paper under discussion.

Lord Lawrence.

Mr. Juland Danvers (Government Director of the Indian Railway Companies).

General Strachey, R.E., Inspecting Officer of Machinery and Stores for the Indian State Railway.

Mr. A. M. Rendel, Consulting Engineer to the East Indian Railway, and Executive Engineer in England for the Indian State Railways.

Mr. G. C. Spooner, Engineer to the Festiniog Railway.

Mr. Carl Pihl, Engineer of narrow-gauge lines in Norway.

Mr. E. W. Young,
Mr. G. Allan,
Mr. J. W. Grover, } Civil Engineers.

The enormous evils that would have been inflicted on India, had the Government persisted in constructing the frontier railways on the metre gauge, were happily averted. With Russia at Merv, who can estimate the danger that might arise had there been a break of gauge between Hydrabad (Scinde) and Mooltan, and between Lahore and Peshawar?* But though the maximum evil was thus happily averted, yet enough

* Sir Henry Durand, in a letter addressed to Sir Bartle Frere on the 4th September 1870, says: "I still entertain a faint hope that we shall not commit the blunder of a break of gauge in our Indus Valley and Punjab lines. I was always opposed to it, and only gave way because Lord Mayo would have thrown up the whole thing on a plea of economy. Rather than that, I would tolerate anything, even a break of gauge. But when one recollects that all the inconveniences of a break of gauge from 5 ft. 6 in. to 3 ft. 6 in. (*sic*) only gives a saving in construction of one-tenth, and how dire and costly these inconveniences will be in time of peace, and how ruinous they may prove in time of war, I confess that I think the one-tenth of present saving but short-sighted economy."

mischief has been done by the construction on the metre gauge of the Rajputana-Malwa, and Chhattisgarh lines. Mr. J. Maclean, in a paper read before the Society of Arts on the 15th of last February, mentions that recently in Rajputana "three different trains on three successive days were required to move a squadron of cavalry a distance of 240 miles." Government moves but slowly; but we suppose that already the order has been issued to relay the Chhattisgarh line, the line that will eventually be the direct route from Bombay to Calcutta, passing through one of the greatest granaries of India, which has at present no outlet, and will, with the increase of roads and the reduction of grain rates on the Great Indian Peninsula line, go far to render England independent of America for her corn. The economy of broad-gauge lines with light rails and worked at a low rate of speed seems never to have come practically before the Government of India.

There are no less than five different gauges on railway lines in India:— There are five different gauges in use on Indian railways.

	Miles. Sanctioned.	Opened.
1. The 5 ft. 6 in., or standard gauge - - - - -	7,485½	7,054¼
2. The 3 ft. 3⅜ in., or metre gauge - - - - -	4,951¼	3,091

	Miles. Sanctioned.	Opened.
3. The 4 ft. gauge - - -	$27\frac{1}{4}$	$27\frac{1}{4}$
4. The 2 ft. 6 in. gauge - -	$134\frac{3}{4}$	$94\frac{3}{4}$
5. The 2 ft. gauge - - -	$56\frac{1}{2}$	50
	$12,655\frac{1}{4}$	$10,317\frac{1}{4}$

I do not advocate broad-gauge lines for hilly districts, with stiff gradients and sharp curves, but I desire a uniform gauge for the plains, as what is now a branch to an outlying district may speedily become part of a trunk-line. At first there may well be economies of light rails, slow speed, and cheap stations with low platforms, and generally speaking all those economies now enforced on State lines.

Narrow-gauge railways not necessarily superior to those of broad gauge.

Economy is not necessarily an attribute of the metre gauge; there is no magic in the name. Because it was found convenient to replace the broad gauge of the Great Western by the English standard gauge, it has been supposed that a narrow gauge is necessarily superior to a broader gauge. But if the evidence of Mr. J. Grierson, Manager of the Great Western Railway, be read, it will be seen that a broad-gauge line is not more expensive to work than a narrow-gauge line, and that the change of gauge on certain portions of the Great Western line "did not arise from any objections to the broad gauge, other than a desire to prevent a break of gauge." In some cases in India, arising from the nature and amount of the traffic, or the character of the country, it may be advisable, where isolation is likely to be permanent, to adopt a narrower gauge than the 5 ft. 6 in. gauge now in use; but usually, for jute, cotton, hides, and all bulky stores, crowds of passengers to religious shrines, and the miscellaneous traffic of an Indian railway, and more especially for the conveyance of troops and heavy artillery, the standard gauge is incontestably superior to the metre gauge, and may be as economically worked and constructed with light rails and for a low rate of speed. Or if it be allowed that the first cost is greater, it is abundantly compensated for by the advantage of an interchange of rolling stock, and the possibility, when necessary, of rendering the line capable at small cost of carrying a maximum traffic in emergencies, or as the commercial capabilities of the districts through which it passes are developed.

The carrying capacity of carriages on the 5 ft. 6 in. gauge is, as compared with those of the metre gauge, more than proportional to their increase of weight, as calculated by Mr. Bruce, Consulting Engineer to the Great Southern of India Railway.

Comfort and speed are all on the side of the broad gauge. If it be proposed so to increase the rolling-stock on a narrow-gauge line as to give equal carrying capacity with a line on the standard gauge, then the extra expense would soon counterbalance any saving originally effected. An analysis of the working of some of the principal railways in India during the year 1882, distinguishing between standing and direct charges, may be usefully given.

EXPENSES PER 1,000 FREIGHT TON MILES PER MILE OF ROAD.

	East Indian.	Madras.	Great Indian Peninsula.	Bombay, Baroda, and Central India.	Eastern Bengal.	Sind, Punjab, and Delhi.	Indus Valley and Candahar.	South Indian.	Rajputana and Malwa (metre gauge).	Northern Bengal (metre gauge).
	Rs.	Rs.	Rs.	Rs.	Rs.	Rs.	Rs.	Rs.	Rs.	Rs.
Standing .	3·341	13·138	6·160	8·123	8·039	9·988	9·462	16·404	9·549	14·388
Direct . .	8·942	16·125	15·100	14·148	14·236	14·391	7·585	15·221	12·498	12·213
Fuel . .	0·345	3·469	3·090	2·702	1·908	4·403	3·495	4·305	5·713	3·494
Interest . .	15·682	44·258	18·797	22·468	21·367	29·434	21·258	33·246	18·089	26·843
Earnings, Coaching, per mile . .	8,754	3,376	5,086	7,238	8,748	5,327	1,695	3,229	3,370	2,470
Ditto, goods .	21,744	4,472	19,165	14,527	22,440	8,547	5,302	2,434	6,294	5,365

The excessive cost of fuel on the Rajputana-Malwa line will be noticed. It arises from the break of gauge, which cuts off that line from the Warrora and Mohpani coal on the Great Indian Peninsula line, from the Bengal coal-field, and from the coal measures of Umaria and Johilla. The average cost of coal on the line was no less than Rs. 21·23 per ton; 16,100 tons of English coal were used, costing in wagons at Bombay,

Rs. 15·31 per ton. Had the Rajputana-Malwa line been constructed without break of gauge, it is certain that the saving in fuel alone would in a few years meet any additional cost. When the Umaria and Johilla coal is worked, the necessity for the use of English coal will not exist, as Umaria coal can be delivered at Jubbulpore at Rs. 8·7 per ton. On no line, except that of the Punjab Northern Railway, was coal so dear. The average price may be thus compared for a few lines:—

	East Indian.	Great Indian Peninsula.	Sind, Punjab, and Delhi.	Bombay-Baroda.	Oudh and Rohilkhand.	Rajputana-Malwa.	
Average price of coal per ton in terms of Rs.	2·19	13·10	20·84	15·29	11·77	21·23*	* Had there been no break of gauge, the average cost per ton ought not to have exceeded Rs. 15, and had Warrora coal been taken it would have been less.

Frequently during this brief review of Indian railways we have noticed the evils arising from break of gauge. They may be enumerated once for all.

Summary of evils attendant on break of gauge in India.

1. Rolling-stock cannot be interchanged, so the efficiency of the railway system is

crippled precisely when the lines are most wanted, namely, in exigencies of commerce, war, and famine.

2. The transfer of goods between lines of different gauge is attended in India—
   1st. By great expense.
   2nd. By serious damage, especially to grain, if rain fall.
   3rd. By loss from pilfering.
   4th. By the demoralisation of railway servants by bribery.
   5th. By delay.
   6th. By loss of traffic.

We are sure that no man who has travelled much on Indian railways during the last ten years has not been both grieved and indignant at the immense loss of grain caused to merchants by its detention at railway stations and exposure without covering to heavy rain. Generally speaking, merchants only grumble at their loss, and determine not to send grain far by railway unless the profits are very tempting; sometimes they recover damages. The East Indian Railway Company in 1877 suffered a loss of £28,049 by an unexpected downpour of rain in January. It is a large sum to lose in one year, but it is not a tithe of what is lost in any year from grain lying at small stations in bags exposed to theweather. Such loss diminishes traffic, even if the railway companies have not to pay damages. On the East Indian line the loss in traffic was 123,897 tons of grain and pulse, on the Great Indian Peninsula it was 75,388 tons, and on the Rajputana-Malwa metre-gauge it was 43,859 tons. It thus amounted to 16, 11, and 27 per cent. of the amounts carried on the above lines in 1881. On the other hand, there was an increase of 113,226 tons carried on the Scinde, Punjab, and Delhi Railway, of 55,504 tons on the Indus Valley and Khandahar line, and of 38,434 tons on the Nagpur Chhattisgarh line, of which a part had been newly opened. Other lines show less increase. Thus there was a loss in traffic of 36,497 tons of grain and pulse on all the Indian railways during 1882. The increase on the Scinde, Punjab, and Delhi Railway was considerable, and amounted to 50 per cent. of the grain and pulse carried in the previous year. It is of course alleged that the movements of trade occasioned the decreased traffic in grain and pulse. But all the decrease did not arise from that cause. So great indeed are the necessities of Indian traffic, that although the Directors of the Great Indian Peninsula Railway Company, in their Report for the half-year ending June 1883, announce a partial recovery of their wheat traffic, the fact remains that, as stated by the Bombay Chamber of Commerce, merchants were "obliged to stop purchases against orders, so as not to have unduly large stocks lying exposed at the railway stations, whence they could not be transported by the railway company owing to the deficiency of the company's engine stock." This deficiency had been notorious for years—for three years. Had not these forced stoppages occurred, the purchases of wheat would have been larger. Eventually when money had been lost all round—by the Indian cultivator, by the merchant, by the freight-owner, by England—then the Secretary of State sanctioned an addition of 100 engines to the rolling-stock of the company.

So also the Oudh and Rohilkhand Railway Company had, in 1883, to refuse large quantities of produce "owing to the block at the Howrah terminus of the East Indian Railway." The loss for the half-year ending last December is estimated at £25,000 to the Company alone; to native merchants it must have been very considerable—their wheat was depreciated in value, and in some instances spoilt. Increased accommodation at Howrah has at last been sanctioned. The Scinde Railway had a large quantity of wheat damaged from want of protection at Kurrachee, and had to pay considerable damages to native merchants; consequently increased accommodation at that station has been sanctioned.

It may seem absurd, to those not acquainted with the working of Indian railways, to estimate the loss from pilfering as an evil attached to break of gauge. But whenever goods accumulate at a station, whenever traffic is worked with insufficient rolling-stock, there is always in India loss from theft. In 1877 the Great Indian Peninsula Railway Company paid £32,762 to make good losses from theft. It was discovered that grain going to the famine districts was systematically stolen by organized bands of thieves, aided and abetted sometimes by the servants of the company. Break of gauge causes detention and aggravates losses from rain and theft. The Bombay Chamber of Commerce remarks, in a memorial addressed to Lord Ripon, that the delay at Nagpore "owing to break of gauge, is fully twenty-four hours from arrival to departure of goods, when the traffic going on at the terminus is not on a large scale; but during the busy season, this delay is prolonged to two or three days." The same thing occurs at the Sabarmati break of gauge on the line between Ahmedabad and Ajmere. There is, the Bombay Chamber of Commerce continues, "a very material loss to the trade by the damage and loss in weight caused in transhipping. The goods are roughly handled by the work-people, a portion of the bags are in consequence burst," and weight is lost by exposure to the sun for two or three days. In the monsoon there is a great deal of damage done by the rain. The loss from these causes is estimated at 1 per cent. or about £20,000 a year. This loss occurs at only one break-point; but if the narrow-gauge system were extended the loss to the country would be very considerable. The Chamber of Commerce also says that the mischief done by break of line is very inadequately represented by the loss in money. It is well known that the competition between Indian and American wheat is now so close, that even a smaller margin than 1 per cent. would turn the scales against India and cause much less business to be done by agriculturists, railways, merchants, and freight-owners.*

* The Province of Punjab now produces, says the *Indian Daily News*, about 100,000,000 bushels of wheat annually, of which 25,000,000 bushels are available for export. Indian cheap labour reduces the cost of growing wheat to a low figure, which compensates for the larger cost of freight-charges as compared with the cheaper ocean-freight from the United States. In the Punjab district the Government is constructing irrigating canals, where nearly a million and a half of acres of land were taken up in 1881 for wheat culture, in advance of the completion and opening of the irrigating canals. The American Consul-General at Calcutta, in his last annual report to the State Department, furnishes interesting statistics in regard to wheat culture in British India, which is looming up as a possible competitor with the United States in the markets of Western Europe. According to this report, about twenty million acres are now

3. Confusion caused in the conveyance of troops on lines subjected to a break of gauge.
4. Aggravation of the sufferings of the sick and wounded from break of gauge.
5. The metre gauge is not so suitable for the conveyance of artillery and horses, cotton, jute, and the miscellaneous bulky staples of traffic of an Indian railway, as the standard gauge.
6. In time of war and rebellion the destruction of rolling stock on a metre-gauge line caused by the conveyance of heavy artillery and military stores would be very great, and might be disastrous.
7. The metre gauge will be, so soon as feeder-roads are properly developed and certain minor reforms introduced in the rules and management of railways, insufficient for the traffic on any of the main lines of India.
8. The break of gauge on the Rajputana line has separated the iron ore and lime on the

---

devoted to wheat in India, and the average yield is about twelve bushels to the acre, although high cultivation and a resort to irrigation and manure has, in some cases, brought the yield up to twenty-five and even thirty bushels. The statistics of the English wheat imports of 1882 show that out of an aggregate of 19,044,819 qrs., 8,180,578 came from the United States; 3,233,238 from Russia; 1,978,078 from India; 719,581 from Germany; and 626,460 from Canada.

State line from the coal of Warrora and Mohpani on the Great Indian Peninsula, and of Bengal and Umaria on the East Indian line.

Assisted railway companies

We have already mentioned the attempt of the Government of India to encourage the raising of capital for railway construction through private agency on the exclusive security of the success of the undertaking. The attempt was not successful, but it led to a modified system of guarantee. There are now eleven assisted companies. The length of line sanctioned is 1,327¾ miles, but only 96¾ miles were, on the 31st March 1883, open for traffic. The most important of the assisted companies are the Southern Mahratta, 435 miles; the Bengal and North-Western, 455 miles; and the Bengal Central, 125½ miles. Only two of these lines are on the standard gauge of 5 ft. 6 in.

Contract between the Government and the Bengal Central Railway Company.

The Bengal Central was the first of the assisted companies. The line is of the standard gauge, and twenty miles were open in March 1883. The principal terms of the contract with the Company are as follows:—

Land given without cost.

The Government supply to the Company, without cost, the land required for the line and works, granting a lease, free of rent, for ninety-nine years.

The Company undertake to raise the capital, as it may be required, and to pay instalments as funds may be wanted. Capital.

The Secretary of State for India pays to the Company in London half-yearly interest at the rate of 4 per cent. per annum on the capital of the Company deposited with him until the opening of the undertaking for traffic throughout, or until the 30th June 1886. If any of the sections of the railway are open before then, the net earnings go in diminution of the guarantee. Interest.

All sums advanced to the Company for the payment of interest by the Secretary of State are to be repaid in London with simple interest, at the rate of 4 per cent. per annum, by the appropriation of half the net earnings of the Company in excess of 5 per cent. on the paid-up capital. Repayment of sum advanced for interest.

The Secretary of State has power to purchase the line and its equipment at the end of thirty years or fifty years from the 1st January 1882, and the Company will then be repaid the capital expended, and a bonus of 25 per cent., subject to a maximum payment. Purchase of the line.

The rates and fares are to be within maxima to be fixed by the Government. Rates and fares.

Carriage of mails.

The arrangements for the carriage of the mails, troops, &c., are the same as those on the lines of guaranteed companies.

Southern Mahratta Company.

The contract made with the Southern Mahratta Company was thus summarised in a despatch by the Government of India dated the 22nd June 1882:—

1st. The Company shall raise in such instalments as may be determined upon, and pay to the Secretary of State, the sum of three millions sterling, on which they shall receive interest at the rate of $3\frac{1}{2}$ per cent., paid by an equivalent of rupees in India.

2nd. They shall construct and work the line as agents for the Government, the Government supplying the funds for the construction to the extent of 360 lacs of rupees, the railways being the property of the State.

3rd. The Company shall receive one fourth part of the net receipts of the railway, the Government taking the remaining three-fourths.

4th. For five years from the date of the contract the Company shall be paid, in addition to the $3\frac{1}{2}$ per cent. interest, such an amount as will, together with their share of the profits, make a further ½ per cent. on three millions.

5th. That if a larger sum than 360 lacs is required for construction, the Company may make corresponding payments to the Secretary of State in addition to the three millions, the terms to be settled as the occasion arises, with the proviso that if the Government advance money in excess of three millions sterling, interest shall be paid on the excess at the rate of 4½ per cent. from the revenue before the net receipts are declared.

6th. The contract to be for fifty years, but the Government to have the power of terminating it after the twenty-fifth year; and at subsequent intervals of ten years, or for breach of contract or mismanagement; and the Company to have the right to withdraw at any time on giving one year's notice at end of the fifth year.

7th. On the termination of the contract the Secretary of State shall repay to the Company the sum of three millions sterling, together with any sums subsequently paid to him by them.

The ultimate position of the Company, the despatch quoted says, will be analogous to that of the East Indian Railway. The railways will be the exclusive property of the State, the Company receiving a certain share of the net profits, and holding besides a State security. The usual arrangements are made regarding the carriage of the mails, troops, stores, bullion, &c.

Rates and fares for the carriage of goods and passengers are fixed by the Company with the approval of the Secretary of State; provided that the Secretary of State may require the charges for the conveyance of salt, coal, and food grains to be reduced to any rate not below one fifth of a pie per maund per mile for full wagon-loads, and may require passengers to be conveyed at any rate not below 2 pies per mile, in closed carriages provided with seats.

Special measures should be taken to secure sufficiently low rates for the carriage of the staples of traffic.

It is absolutely necessary that the Government of India should not regard railways simply as so many revenue-producing machines. Lord Salisbury urged, in 1868, that the Government ought not solely to regard the question as one of profits, as they were more than compensated for any outlay they had incurred. Sir Stafford Northcote, when Secretary of State for India, also observed that the political and military advantages to the Government of present commercial railways would be cheaply purchased, even were the railway system more costly to the Government than it was shown to be. As remarked by Mr. Maclean, in the case of the transport of wheat, whatever is charged on the carriage of grain, coal, cotton, sugar, the staples of the country, in excess of a fair profit, is virtually a toll or transit duty levied by the Government on the export trade. The rate sanctioned for the carriage of grain on the Southern Mahratta line is too high. It is one-fifth of a pie per maund per mile. The author of a pamphlet forwarded by the Bengal Chamber of Commerce to Lord Ripon, calculates this rate to be, for wheat, "1·05 shillings per quarter per 100 miles, or double the American rate." So, also, the Eastern Bengal Railway in their contract are allowed to charge "three times the American rate." The lowest rate sanctioned for the carriage of grain is on the Scinde, Punjab, and Delhi railways, one-seventh of a pie per maund per mile, and these railways have but one rate irrespective of the amount tendered. The ordinary rates for small consignments injuriously affect the small trader. It is mentioned in the pamphlet we have quoted, that in America "any discrimination in freight rates between two points dependent only on the quantity of freight shipped, has been held by the Courts to be a violation of the impartial duty due to the public from the railway corporation." In India this distinction of rate diminishes local traffic and injures the small trader.

Merchants, both European and Native, should be considered.

Whatever be the feeling of Government with regard to the construction of railways, successful working will depend on the feelings and interests of the trading community, both European and Native, being conciliated and consulted. The subject of the rates for the carriage of grain is mentioned by Colonel Stanton, R.E., Director-General of Railways in India, in his last report. From the 7th of May last the through rate from Delhi to Bombay *viâ* Rajputana has been reduced 18½ per cent. Lower rates have been adopted by the East Indian Railway. But the Great Indian Peninsula Railway, secure in their monopoly, have not thought fit to make similar reductions, though a lower cost of carriage would, as remarked by Colonel Stanton, "doubtless by stimulating the export of wheat from the Central Provinces, prove most remunerative to the railway, as well as beneficial to the districts concerned." To fully develop the wheat trade of the Central Provinces additional roads are necessary. Colonel Hancock's last report acknowledges this fact. He says that traffic during the latter half of the calendar year will, in the grain-producing districts of the Central Provinces, be gene-

To fully develop the wheat trade of the Central Provinces additional roads are necessary.

rally "trifling in extent, and the monetary result unsatisfactory." There are not sufficient feeder communications. Many of the existing roads are merely fair-weather tracks, and are impassable for carts in the rainy season. It is essential that the main feeders to the line should be bridged and metalled roads, passable at all times of the year. These roads will never be constructed within any reasonable time unless the Government of India assist provincial funds. If the Government of India would attend to the roads, bridges, and irrigation works of the country, and give every facility for the construction of railroads under proper supervision, and be content with attending to these works of paramount importance and pressing necessity, and to promoting the education of the people committed to their charge, and give up all startling political changes, India would make sure progress, and advance rapidly in the career of prosperity and general enlightenment.

Cost of Indian railways as compared with those of other countries.

When the Government of India, by "an act of most extraordinary imprudence introduced a break of gauge in India," * the advocates of this extraordinary measure dwelt upon the excessive cost of Indian railways. It is as well, then, to contrast the

---

* Remarks of Sir G. B. Airey, P.R.S., Astronomer Royal, before the Institute of Civil Engineers.

cost of Indian railways with that of railways constructed in other countries. Of the 10,317 miles of Indian railway, 7,707¾ are constructed on the broad or standard gauge of 5 ft. 6 in. Of this mileage, 862½ miles have a double line of rails. None of the metre or narrow-gauge railways are laid with a double line.

Country.	Miles open.	Cost.	Cost per Mile.	Cost per inhabitant.
		£	£	£
Queensland	867	6,621,189	7,636	26
United States	114,412	1,262,939,957	11,038	25
United Kingdom	18,457	767,899,570	41,550	21
Victoria	1,354	19,746,915	14,584	21
New South Wales	1,313	16,776,642	12,777	19
Canada	8,069	83,122,362	10,301	19
*France	13,150	430,000,000	32,800	12
*Germany	18,080	370,000,000	20,500	9
*Low Countries	3,270	68,000,000	20,900	8
*Austria	12,100	255,000,000	21,100	7
*Spain and Portugal	5,100	84,000,000	16,400	4
*South America	4,880	72,000,000	14,800	3
†India	10,317	142,423,903	13,804	½

* From the last edition (1880) of the *Progress of the World*, by M. Mulhall, F.S.S.

† To 31st March 1884.

I do not place much stress on this comparison. But as Lord Ripon recently compared the Melbourne and Calcutta Exhibitions, I at least err in good company if I compare the cost of Indian railways with those of other countries. All things considered, the advantage is on the side of India.

Influence of railways on commerce, &c.

A reference to the annual administration reports published by the different local governments, will show the influence of railways on the internal commerce of the country. The details are scattered through so many reports and belong to so many provinces that they cannot be given here. But the social effects of the railways may to a certain extent be gauged by the Post Office work. In the year 1869–70, mails were carried over* 50,281 miles, of which 40,586 were travelled by boats, and letter-carriers or "runners," 5,460 by mail-carts and on horseback, and 4,235 by railways. In 1881–82 the mails travelled over 59,667 miles, 46,629 being done by boats and runners, 3,303 by carts and on horseback, and 9,745 miles by railways. These figures show that whilst railroads have taken the place of roads, roads that should feed the railways have not been so sufficiently constructed that mail-carts may take the place of "runners." In the year ending the 31st March 1872, there passed through the Post Offices of British India 93,157,314 letters and newspapers, and the total Post Office revenue was £677,047. In the financial year 1881–82, the number of letters, post-cards, and newspapers that passed through the British Indian Post Office was 171,804,992, and the revenue had increased to £931,174, or by 37 per cent.

---

* *The Statesman's Year Book for 1884.*

The following statistics give the increase of the external commerce of India since the opening of railways.

Year.	Length of line open at the end of each year.	Imports. £	Exports. £	Total. £
1830	0	5,679,000	4,087,000	9,766,000
1848	0	10,571,008	14,738,435	25,309,443
1858	428½	31,093,065	28,278,474	59,371,539
1860	839¼	34,170,793	34,090,154	68,260,947
1874	6,227¾	37,421,031	56,839,857	94,260,888
1878	8,212¼	56,681,462	67,340,849	124,022,311
1883	10,317¼	63,456,197	84,381,723	147,837,920

The exports from India to Great Britain and Ireland have increased since 1870 from £29,890,802 to £39,921,127, and the imports of British home produce into India have increased during the same time from £21,354,205 to £29,059,327. The principal articles of export in 1882 from India to the United Kingdom were: cotton, 3,613,766 cwt., of the value of £9,063,082; wheat, 8,461,004 cwt., of the value of £4,352,270; jute, 5,931,047 cwt., of the value of £4,311,102; seeds, chiefly linseed, 1,511,543 quarters, of the value of £3,614,695; rice, 784,509 cwt., of the value of £3,024,538; tea, 53,576,690 lbs., valued at £3,498,188; dye stuffs of the value of £2,712,374, and the value of the leather, untanned hides, and coffee imported from India amounted, in each case to more than a million of pounds sterling. Before the commencement of railways the export trade in wheat did not exist. In 1881, 9,379,236 cwt. of wheat were consigned to the United Kingdom, which amounted to about one-thirteenth of the entire imports of grain and flour. In 1882–83 the total exports of wheat from India amounted to 14,151,765 cwt. Next to the United Kingdom, France takes the largest share of the Indian wheat exports. So considerable is the anticipated and actual traffic in grain between Nagpore and Bombay since the opening of the Chhattisgarh Railway, even on the narrow gauge, that the Great Indian Peninsula Railway proposes to lay a double line from Bhosawal to Nagpore. In one year the export of grain from the Central Provinces more than doubled in quantity and in value. The area under wheat increased from 3,391,441 acres in 1880–81 to 4,179,982 acres in 1881–2, or by a little more than 23 per cent. As the railways increase in length, uncultivated land is brought under the plough, not only in the Central Provinces but in Assam and Burmah. In the Central Provinces the total cultivated area of 1881–82 exceeded that of the previous year by 6 per cent. In two years, 1880–82, wheat cultivation increased by one million acres. Indeed, in those provinces through which portions of six new lines are reported to be under survey and projected, no less than 42,278 square miles of waste but culturable land await the plough. That is, an area larger that the whole of

England is, though fit for cultivation, still uncultivated. Or, if we consider only the surveyed and assessed area in acres, then, after setting aside 1,879,489 acres for grazing land, there are 11,810,999 culturable acres still waste. The mineral resources of the Central Provinces, too, only want roads and capital for their development. In these fertile provinces limestone, fire-clay, slate, marble, coal, iron, the finest building stones, abound. There are deposits of sulphate of lead and copper, and gold is found in the sands of some of the rivers. The forests contain timber suitable for railway sleepers. The iron resources of the Chanda district were, in 1881–82, inquired into by Mr. Ritter von Schwarz, experienced in iron mining in Austria. It is estimated that Chanda might turn out 260,000 tons of iron or steel annually, and might now open an export trade to England in "ferro manganese" and Brescian steel. The iron and coal of Umaria and Katni are mentioned by Colonel Hancock, Officiating Director-General of Railways, in his Report for 1882–83. Mr. Molesworth, the Consulting Engineer to the Government of India, writes that "the Jubbulpore district contains an inexhaustible supply of hematite, containing about 68 per cent. of iron suitable for the manufacture of charcoal-iron. The iron is on the surface, and may be obtained cheaply without the cost of expensive mining. . . . There is, moreover, in the neighbourhood of the north-west of Jubbulpore manganese ore containing 54 per cent. of manganese."

Government of India.

We have mentioned that six of the twenty-three new lines under survey or projection by the Government of India pass through the Central Provinces. It is, however, too frequently the peculiarity of that Government to survey and project, but to do nothing more. What is required is the energetic prosecution of all the projected lines by Government and all other agencies.

The extension of railways has increased the revenue.

Railways in India have not only created the export traffic of many articles of consumption in England, but have added to the Indian revenue, and have rendered possible the great fiscal reforms recently introduced. The earliest year in which the returns are available on the present system of making up the accounts is 1865–66. In that year, we quote the figures given by Mr. Juland Danvers, the revenue was £53,107,359; in 1831-82 it was £73,695,806.* As fresh land has been brought under cultivation, so the land revenue, in spite of enormous loss from drought, resulting in famine,

---

* *The Statesman's Year Book for 1884.*

has increased. In 1873 the land revenue was £21,375,076, in 1882 it was £21,948,022; and the greatest reform, the one most affecting the happiness of the people, that has been introduced since the time probably of Lord William Bentinck, is now to take place. The cultivator will reap to the full any advantages that may be derived from his expenditure of capital and labour. As Sir Auckland Colvin puts it, the reform to be introduced will give "to the temporary settlement of the land revenue a degree of permanency in the more populous and advanced parts of the country which they have hitherto lacked." The habits of centuries will not at once be overcome, but it is at least probable that the silver and gold hitherto hoarded will be laid out on land improvement. The land will produce more, and railways will transport the increased produce.

Lines existing and projected lines.

We append to this account a statement of the existing Indian railways, and of the five gauges already adopted. There are twenty-three projected lines. An account of these lines is given in the Preliminary Report by Colonel Stanton, R.E., of eighty-one folio pages, and in the Report by Colonel Hancock, R.E., of 414 pages, including the appendices; but it is nevertheless with some difficulty that we learn what it is actually proposed to do in India.

Bhopal, Jhansi-Gwalior, and Jhansi-Cawnpore lines.

In May last, Colonel Stanton, the Director-General of Railways, wrote that he "believed" negotiations had been entered into with a Company to extend the Bhopal line to Gwalior with a branch from Jhansi to Cawnpore. This important line will be 380 miles in length, and will provide communication on the broad gauge between Cawnpore and Bombay by a line 115 miles shorter than the existing one. Since Colonel Stanton wrote, the Secretary of State for India has postponed the consideration of the construction of this line until "the subject of provision for the extension of railways in India" has been referred "to a Select Committee of the House of Commons."

Jhansi-Manikpur.

From Jhansi to Manikpur is a line 180 miles in length, and passing through the important town of Banda. It joins two stations on broad-gauge lines—Jhansi on the proposed line just mentioned, and Manikpur on the East Indian Railway. The line, if constructed on the broad gauge, will only cost Rs. 94,444 a mile, or say, with exchange at 1s. 8d., about £7,870 a mile without rolling stock. Yet the question of gauge is still unsettled!

Etawah-Katni-Bilaspur line.

The Etawah-Katni-Bilaspur line, a most important one, will be about 352 miles in length. It will pass through the Rewah coal-fields and the important towns of Saugor; Garhakotah, where there is a famous cattle-fair and reserved forests; Dumoh, the head-quarters of a district; and Hirapur, once celebrated for iron, as its name implies. It will supply coal to the railways of Central India, to a portion of the Nagpur-Bengal line, will carry food-grain from Chhattisgarh to Northern India, and will have a large pilgrim traffic. The reports are silent on the question of gauge.

Bengal-Nagpur Railway.

The Bengal-Nagpur Railway, connecting Bombay and Calcutta, and passing through a large wheat-producing area, has a coal-field at one terminus—that of Sitarampur—and near the other terminus there are the Warrora Collieries. The coal of Warrora is said to be inferior to Bengal coal. Colonel Hancock reports that at its best three tons of Warrora coal may do the work of two tons of Karhurballee coal, which is nearly equal to English coal. In 1882 the Indian railways consumed 47,892 tons of Warrora coal. The actual cost of cutting and raising the coal is, it is said, Rs. 1-4 a ton, and the price charged is from Rs. 3 to Rs. 5 a ton. It may fairly be assumed that the coal will improve as the collieries are developed. The Rajputana Railway, Colonel Hancock reports, could consume some 20,000 tons annually on the Khandwa-Neemuch section of the line. Mr. Walter Ness, mining engineer, estimated the capacity of the coal-field at 20,000,000 tons of easily workable coal. Ballast, sleepers, excellent building stone, can be obtained in the neighbourhood of this line. It will be on the broad gauge, and the narrow-gauge line constructed from Nagpur to Rajnandgarh, a distance of 149 miles, will be pulled up!

Benares-Cuttack line

The Benares-Cuttack railway will pass through the Palamow coal-fields, and provide a direct route for pilgrims from Benares to Pooree. The reports do not say on what gauge the line is to be constructed; but as it is expected that this line will supply coal to the Oudh and Rohilkhand line, and to the sections of the East Indian line above Moghal-Serai, we presume the broad gauge will be adopted.

As to the gauge to be adopted on the important lines of Cuttack-Pooree and Vizagapatam-Raipur the reports are silent.

It has apparently been determined to construct the railways noted below on the narrow or metre gauge:—

1. Northern Bengal State Railway extension.
2. Assam-Behar.
3. Assam projected railways.
4. Cuddapah Nellore.

5. Bellary Kistnah.

6. Sonthal Railway (2 ft. 6 in. gauge).

7. West Deccan Railway.

Revenue derived from Indian railways.

In the financial statement published in the *Calcutta Gazette* of the 14th March last, Sir Auckland Colvin shows that the net gain on Indian railways during the past five years was £3,270,843. He further remarks that the remunerative character of railway enterprise in India is unquestionable.

The following statement shows the per-centage of net earnings per annum on capital expenditure for each of the Indian railways :—

1	Broad gauge		East Indian	. 8·80
2	,,	Guaranteed	Eastern Bengal	.10·52
3	,,	,,	Great Indian Peninsula	7·29
4	,,	,,	Bombay, Baroda and Central India	5·91
5	,,	,,	Oudh and Rohilkhand	3·07
6	,,	,,	Sind, Punjab and Delhi	2·94
7	,,	,,	Madras .	. 2·30
8	,,	Imperial State	Punjab Northern	0·83
9	,,	,,	Indus Valley, Kandahar	2·01
10	,,	Provincial State	Patna-Gya .	. 5·68
11	,,	Native States	Nizam's .	. 3·08
12	Metre gauge	Guaranteed	South Indian	. 3·26
13	,,	Imperial State	Rajputana, Malwa	5·87
14	,,	Provincial State	Northern Bengal .	5·33
15	,,	,,	Tirhoot .	. 3·94
16	,,	,,	Cawnpore, Farukhabad	3·74

17	Metre gauge	Provincial State	Nagpore, Chhatisgarh	2·15
18	„	„	Rangoon and Irawaddy	4·97
19	„	Native States	Bhavnagar, Gondal	4·24

India cannot furnish the capital required for the construction of railways now urgently needed.

In the construction of railways still so urgently needed in India, it is quite useless to look to India to furnish the capital for the necessary outlay. The amount of railway capital held by native investors is very small. The total number of shareholders in the guaranteed and assisted lines on the 31st of December 1881 was 44,212, of whom 43,945 were registered in England; only 166 natives held shares registered in India. When the Southern Mahratta Railway prospectus was issued, £500,000 out of the £3,000,000 capital were reserved for distribution in India, but only 395 shares, representing £7,900, were applied for. Colonel Stanton, R.E., in the last Railway Administration Report, indeed apologises for this failure to attract Indian capital by saying that, in the instance mentioned, complaints have been made that reasonable opportunity was not given to the Indian public to subscribe, "inasmuch as the time allowed was too short, and the prospectus was not made sufficiently public." He also mentions that several short "branch lines have been put in hand by purely local enterprise during the past year." As regards these local lines, it may be remarked that, regarding some of them at least, provincial governments have been warmly interested; and where this is the case, it is to be expected that resident native capitalists will take shares. Sufficient capital will not be subscribed in India for railway construction.

Mr. Westland, who is possessed of as much financial ability as any Indian officer of the present day, has shown in his recent paper that of 2,131 lakhs borrowed during the last ten years by the Indian Government, only 801 lakhs have been taken up in India. Money, on the average, is much dearer in India than in England. That capital for Indian railways must be raised in London, and not in India, is the opinion even of native capitalists. Recently, at a meeting of the Bombay Chamber of Commerce, there was but one opinion as to this, and as to the impolicy of the break of gauge.

These are the prevailing opinions among those who have thought on the subject, and which we trust will lead ultimately to one gauge and uniformity of action.

Length of railways open in various countries as contrasted with their area and population.

In proportion to its area India is less equipped with railways than any of the more important countries of the world. As compared with Russia, the most backward of all the European States, India, with four times the density of population, has fewer miles of railway open.

Countries.	Miles of railway open on the 1st Jan., 1883.	One mile of railway to square miles.	Population per square mile.
Belgium	2,683	4·0	485
United Kingdom . . .	18,514	6·5	290
Germany	21,672	9·8	213
Netherlands	1,263	10·0	329
France	18,026	11·3	184
Denmark	1,105	12·5	143
United States and Territories	114,412	17·8	14·3*
Austria-Hungary . . .	12,334	19·7	157
Italy	5,800	19·7	247
Portugal	1,000	36·0	114
Spain	4,942	41·0	84
Sweden	3,940	44·0	27
Russia in Europe . . .	14,308	135·8	40
India	10,144	136·3	184

* Including Indian territory.

What the brief survey of the history and system of Indian railways proves.

This brief survey of Indian railways is now completed. It would appear that the following points have been established :—

1st. That India is in great need of additional roads and railways.

2nd. That if the commerce of the country is to be adequately provided for, the railways must be of the standard gauge—5 ft. 6 in.

3rd. That if Indian railways are to be quickly constructed and economically worked, they should be constructed and worked by as many agencies as possible; thus a wholesome competition will be established.

4th. That if the grain trade is to be developed, transit charges must be kept low, and sufficient rolling stock must be provided, and through-booking be introduced.

5th. That some of the rules laid down for the more economical construction of metre gauge State railways are also applicable to lines constructed by guaranteed companies.

6th. That the capital for Indian railways cannot be raised in India, but in England, where also must be the chief control.

7th. That the efforts of the Government of India, and of local administrations, should be strenuously exerted to construct a system of roads for the ordinary traffic of the country, to act as feeders to railroads.

8th. That collieries should not be worked by the State, but by companies as agents of the State.

Improved means of communication along the length and breadth of the vast peninsula of India, bringing its many nations, tribes, and languages, as it were face to face, making smooth the paths of the merchant, scattering abundance where famine had reigned; the science, the civilization, and the religion of the West permeating the darkest recesses of that benighted land, causing the sound of the hammer to ring in the solitude and the desert to blossom as the rose, giving us the most efficient means of repelling aggression from without, or putting down disorder within our border, establishing at once the power and the beneficence of our rule.

Improved means of communication would do more than any other measure that could be devised to give effect to the following gracious and dignified words of the Queen, the future Empress, in a proclamation extending her immediate protection to the millions of India, issued on the 1st of November 1858, by Lord Canning, the first Viceroy of India:—"It is Our earnest desire to stimulate the peaceful industry of India, to promote works of public utility and improvement, and to administer the government for the benefit of all Our subjects resident therein. In their prosperity will be Our strength, in their contentment Our security, and in their gratitude Our best reward. And may the God of all Power grant to Us, and to those in authority under Us, strength to carry out these Our wishes for the good of Our people."

29, Bryanston Square.
June 1884.

NOTE.—All who are interested in India are looking forward with hopeful expectation to the result of the enquiry instituted by the Special Committee of the House of Commons as to the future of railways in that country, and, as essential to their safety and prosperity, to the defence and improvement of the harbours on both sides of the Peninsula.

DEDICATION OF THE SECOND EDITION.

TO

THE HONOURABLE THE COURT OF

DIRECTORS OF THE EAST INDIA COMPANY,

As the guardians of the British Empire in the East, this brochure on the political, military, and commercial importance of railway communication, as affecting the present position and future prospects of that Empire, is appropriately and with much deference dedicated

By their most obedient and

Humble Servant,

THE AUTHOR.

October, 1846.

PREFACE TO THE SECOND EDITION.

When the first impression of "Indian Railways" was on the eve of publication, the despatch of the Bengal Government, regarding the introduction of Railway Communication into British India, was received at the India House, and more recently, the report of the Commissioners appointed by the Supreme Government, to enquire generally into the merits of the question, has been published by order of the Honourable the House of Commons.

That some of the views enunciated in the latter official document, are but little in accordance with those adventured in this pamphlet, was to be expected, and it is a matter of satisfaction to the author, that any of his opinions should be sanctioned and supported by those of the Railway Commission, and he sees no reason why he should relinquish in this Edition, anything advanced in the first.

There is much additional matter introduced in

this impression, in connection with the statistics of India and other subjects having reference to the requirements of that country, for improved internal communication, or to its capabilities of emancipating itself from its primitive, rude, and most inefficient roads and conveyances, achieving by one mighty bound, what other nations have taken centuries to accomplish; and, profiting by the experience of Europe, selecting what has worked well in the several modes of railway administration, such a controlling power might be easily placed in the hands of the Government, without deadening the impulse which private enterprise alone can impart, and effectually prevent the springing up in India of an "imperium in imperio," as has resulted in this country from the laxity or want of foresight on the part of the legislature, and the encroaching audacity of successful enterprise, placing the roads of this great country—the arteries of her vital energy and strength—in the hands of private individuals, with power to tax their fellow subjects, without appeal, to an amount equal to the revenues of a mighty Empire.*

---

* Should the Honourable East India Company grant a guarantee, upon giving a concession, the relation of private enterprise, and the executive of the Government, would of necessity be approximated.

This is not the place to enter into particulars, but it may be stated, that one shilling and elevenpence paid into the

In compliance with the wishes of various correspondents, more detailed information regarding particular projects is supplied. This has been given the more willingly, as the spurious and ridiculous emanations of the ignorant and designing, are brought, by a system of gambling, to rank, apparently, as high in public estimation, as the most feasible and legitimate undertakings sanctioned by scientific and local knowledge.

Severity of comment has been pointed out in the following pages, but those who made this allegation were silent as to injustice. What language can be too harsh, or animadversion too pungent, for those who would palm upon the public the howling wilderness, sullen in primeval solitude, for fields teeming with herds and flocks and rich in husbandry; wretched, isolated villages, as opulent cities, rejoicing in extensive commercial relations.

In one Prospectus, in addition to a number of imaginary towns, a small fort, on the top of a hill 3,000 feet high, is impudently put forth as a populous, flourishing, and accessible city, while, in fact, it is a mere habitable speck in the jungle, and its population, a sergeant's guard!

India House Treasury, would frequently be an equivalent for a 4 per cent. guarantee, and prevent the necessity of throwing open the Calcutta treasury, by making an advance upon goods.

There are those who advocate as the grand desideratum for India, the connecting of the three seats of Government, in utter ignorance of the vast regions which intervene, the extent and nature of the present intercourse, and the little political advantage that would result from such an arrangement with the exception of uniting Calcutta and Bombay.

There are also individuals who love to stand still like ancient land-marks, while the world is advancing around them; they laugh at everything they do not understand, and their grasp of mind, only enabling them to comprehend, or to believe, what is patent to their senses, their risible faculties are frequently excited. The idea of introducing railways into India, was with them a palpable absurdity, on account of physical obstacles; the present roads and embankments of the country, and finally the report of the Railway Commission were appealed to, and set the matter at rest; they now say, although the railways are made, the people won't travel by them; as they are all pilgrims, and the longer time they take in going from one holy place to another, so much the better, the merits of this devotional act consisting in the delays and difficulties to be endured and surmounted. As if the few poor wretches of low caste, who crawl for some hundreds of miles on their stomachs to Juggernauth to gain a profitable reputation for sanctity were to be taken as typifying, by their habits, the distinct castes, classes, and sects of the whole native community. As well might these *stationary* gentlemen term us a nation of fanatics, because we happen to have a few wild enthusiasts among us; or say, that in England we refuse to travel by railroad because certain ancient dames still sigh for the "slow coach" of their youth: nothing can be more ignorant or unfounded than such assumption. Pilgrimages in the East are generally combined with business and other worldly avocations,* and those who can afford it travel on horseback, or in carriages, and the conveyance of pilgrims in India has been reckoned as no inconsiderable part of the traffic for railways, both by Europeans and natives. Colonel Ouseley, Political Agent at Chota Nagpore, remarks, that, "The natives can appreciate well, and better in some cases, as we can, the advantages of rapidity of transit"; and an enlightened, native gentleman, a merchant in Calcutta, expresses himself as follows: "The growing class of intelligent

* An annual fair, is held at Hurdwar in the month of April, at a certain spot on which Krishna stood, at the time Bagirut brought the Ganges stream into existence. The fair disperses immediately after the time appointed for the last purification, and the pilgrims carry with them to their homes the sacred water of the Ganges.

natives would freely resort to it (the railway), and lastly the religious connection between the Hindoos and the holy cities of Benares, Gyah, Allahabad, and others, would alone fill the trains with hundreds of the better class of Pilgrims." These are the sentiments of those acquainted with India and her people.

Notwithstanding the present gloom which hangs over railway property, its gradual development is best proved by the returns, which show a yearly increase of more than one million sterling to the national income, from one thousand eight hundred miles of railway. When this fact is kept in view and the large sums that are lost in foreign loans, and home and foreign mines,* all who are interested

---

* The *Quarterly Review* in one of its admirable articles on railways, gives the following summary:—

"The British capital invested in railroads—expensive if you will—but solid, enduring, vivifying works, is about £60,000,000. The capital risked, we fear, we might say lost, in foreign loans, is computed at not less than £121,000,000, whereas the £60,000,000 invested in our railroads, are not only represented by solid works, a substantial property, but pay on the average 5 per cent., that is, 2 per cent. more than the public securities of the State; to which may be added £6,484,000 of British capital, paid up on *foreign* mining speculations, described in Spackman's *Statistical Tables* (p. 158), as being, with one or two exceptions, utterly worthless, and an entire loss of the capital embarked in them, and also a £4,500,000 paid up in capital on British Mining Companies, designated by the same authority, as not only

in India, cannot but be anxious to see some portion of our superfluous wealth, which is squandered with a prodigal hand both at home and abroad, directed to her shores, to commence a system of transit in that magnificent country, famed through all time for its inexhaustible riches, regarding which, the *Times* of the 25th of September, in its leading article, says: "The wonderful progress of production and commerce in that country (India) encourages us to hope for almost any result. . . . With regard to our East India trade, rashness consists rather in leaving things as they are, than attempting to develop its unequalled, and immeasurable resources," with a density of population in the Lower Provinces of Bengal and Behar, exceeding that of any country in Europe.

The introduction of that mighty engine of improvement, to which England is herself so much indebted, would cause the slumbering spirit of India, to awake from the sleep of ages, the sleep of apathy, superstition, and prejudice, to the knowledge of the value of time, and to assume among the nations an aspect of renovated power. "Her

complete failures, but memorable proofs of the folly and cupidity of British capitalists, on one hand, and of the knavery of their projectors on the other (*Ib.* p. 153), making a total of capital, nearly unproductive, where not entirely lost, of upwards of £130,000,000."

(India) value will then shine forth, and those who consult her interests must rejoice."

To the authorities in the India House, the author's best acknowledgments are due, for the uniform courtesy he has experienced; the liberal access afforded him to valuable official records, has enabled him to place, in a condensed form, much that must be interesting, regarding the resources of our Empire in the East.

He has also to express to many distinguished individuals connected with India his sincere thanks for valuable suggestions, and that encouragement, which has induced him to bestow additional pains on the edition now offered to the public, which he trusts will be found more deserving of approbation than the preceding one.

London, October, 1846.

INTRODUCTORY REMARKS.

WHEN we reflect on the pre-eminence we have attained as a nation, both for political sagacity and an enlarged philanthropy, the neglect with which we have treated, in some respects, our Indian dominions and subjects, cannot but be matter of surprise, if not of indignation; and this surprise is by no means lessened when England is regarded as the great centre of the world's commerce; her sons, wise, brave and humane, and ever in the van of commercial enterprise, with an energy of purpose which secures to them success, whether they pant and toil in the luxuriant fields of a tropical clime, or patiently, as fishermen pursue a precarious commerce in the frozen regions of the north, where the womb of nature is for ever sealed.

We are, emphatically, a money-making and commercial people, and in this character, as merchants trading to the east, with our invoices and bills of lading of our wares, did we first, with anxiety and care, plant our foot on Indian soil, esteeming ourselves happy, if we received permission from the native governments to pursue our thrifty avocations in peace.

Without pausing to note the various phases in our career, till the character of merchant was merged in that of sovereign, we shall merely remark, that for many years our Indian policy has been—if we may be allowed a paradox—that of passive and involuntary aggression, extending only our dominion when we could not avoid doing so, and advancing our frontier as a means of defence. We thus, from the force of circumstances, have had a character thrust upon us not our own; gradually laying aside our peaceful and profitable pursuits, and allowing our philanthropy to slumber, we have acted in the eyes of those little observant of our peculiar political relations in the east, as if we lusted with an insatiable desire for territorial aggrandisement and military renown; but although now our empire is approaching with rapid strides (and, from the portents in the political horizon, will soon attain its natural and obvious boundary) towards the north-west, to be defined, defended, and circumscribed by the Indus and Himalaya, yet, the British empire in the east appears far from having ascended to its zenith; and the time has now arrived to awake to new and other glories, more consonant to our genius as a people, the peaceful triumphs of commerce, from improved intercourse, bringing in its train the arts, the sciences, the literature, the civilization, and religion of the west, causing the barren waste to be fruitful, and the wilderness to blossom as the rose; the sound of the hammer to ring in the solitude, and the gospel of peace to be proclaimed in the darkest recesses of that benighted land.

That the mighty engine of improved intercourse has not received that degree of attention from the liberal and enlightened rulers of India which it demands, is to be attributed, in a great degree, to the expensive wars which have been forced upon them—the delicate political relations with numerous states—the vastness of the territory to govern, and the comparative unacquaintance with some of the provinces, both as to their inhabitants and resources, and many other affairs claiming their immediate regards. By some it is injuriously urged, that the East India Company, acting as trustees for the crown, and from their charter expiring in 1854, have no wish to invest capital in a country which it is possible, although not probable, they may be called upon to relinquish—and as their dividend is limited to 10½ per cent. they can derive no advantage from developing the resources of British India—that this aspersion is unjust, we feel assured—for, although there is much that is anomalous in their authority and constitution, taking their administration as a whole, and making due allowance for the distance of the country governed, its vastness and difficulties, nothing could be more wise and generally beneficent.

If India has had much to complain of—of positive injustice, superadded to neglect, the odium of this injustice rests with us as a people, or rather with our representatives; for have they not, by legislative enactments, treated India more as a foreign country, but little favoured, than as the most magnificent and dazzling jewel of the imperial crown. In times of peace, India and its affairs have been too often treated with an apathy not to be accounted for, till some new victory—some new nation, little heard of before, or if heard of, not known, has bent its unwilling neck to our yoke; when the national vanity is flattered, its curiosity excited, and the Prime Minister of England declares at once the Sovereign's and the nation's voice in applauding and rewarding the victors. But, in bygone times, whenever our connexion with India was not adorned with a remarkable achievement, our ministers and legislators, unmindful of the tide of wealth which flowed from India to our shores, crushed the energies and redoubled the labours of her sons, by unwise and unjustly exorbitant duties on the fruits of those labours, and this gloriously free country held back with all the freezing rigour of despotism the advance of a mighty nation, in whose hands an all-wise Providence had placed its destinies in the career of social improvement, and suspended the development of the inexhaustible riches of its soil, by refusing to open its ports, excepting on the most cruel terms, to its valuable products. While so little reciprocating the nature of our dealings with India—when thus refusing its products—our own manufactures were poured into it, under a small and nearly nominal duty, to the annihilation of the native cotton fabrics once so celebrated, and the total disappearance at last of all local manufacture.

Restraining, with one hand, the free labourer of the East, they encouraged, with the other, the slave owner of the West.

The old sugar duties must be in the recollection of every one. Jamaica sugar, although of superior quality, and produced so much nearer England, paid a moderate duty; while that from India, naturally less rich in quality and coming from so great a distance, was charged with a duty almost prohibitory. These errors are now partially repaired; but time presses onward, and much is still to be achieved by the most enlightened, the most moral and religious government in Europe, to elevate, in the scale of nations, the people of India.

Let the liberality and energy of the future, in peace as in war, make amends for the past. A mighty element of civilization is now coming to our aid—the railway system of communication—the due development of which in India, is, at once, the most gigantic, interesting, and important problem which the genius of the age has propounded to the world.

Its pressing and paramount importance cannot be over-estimated, whether in reference to a great and increasing commerce, or to the consolidation and protection of our dominions, and the many blessings which would flow to the people from improved intercourse; so that now when our sword is sheathed, and the roar of our cannon has ceased to make our enemies tremble on their thrones, the eyes of the soldier, the statesman, the merchant, and the philanthropist, will be alike turned towards the gloomy recesses of Leadenhall Street, where it is hoped that this subject will be discussed with the consideration and promptitude it demands.

For the sake of brevity and distinctness, we now proceed to embody our remarks under separate heads; supporting our own views and assertions by testimony drawn from the best authorities, whether in India or in this country.

POLITICAL AND MILITARY IMPORTANCE

OF

RAILWAYS IN BRITISH INDIA.

The imperious necessity of rapid intercommunication in reference to our Indian possessions, in a political and military point of view, is so obvious, that it would be matter of surprise, were it not for the still more pressing claims on their attention formerly alluded to, that the authorities have not long ere this prosecuted the subject with the assiduous and careful energy which they have only recently begun to evince; but the insult offered to our arms by the invasion of the Sikhs, and the delay which took place before that insult could be avenged, must have effectually demonstrated to all, the impolicy, the impossibility of further procrastination, in summoning science to our aid, to take advantage of the natural facilities of the country—to bring what is distant near—the weak outpost, under the immediate protection of the great station, with its troops and military stores, in its rear. During the late campaign against the Sikhs, nothing could be more apparent, than that our vast resources were for weeks unavailing from the want of rapid transit; powerless to hurl back aggression, we were compelled to suffer, for more than a month, the presence of an enemy within our border, too formidable to be dislodged. It is true that this indignity, offered to the majesty of the British name, is now almost lost in the completeness of the subsequent triumph; but, while we rested on our arms, waiting the arrival of heavy artillery, stores and reinforcements, what might not the enemy have achieved, had he but possessed conduct and enterprise equal to his power. How wonderful the infatuation, that he did not with the first blow he struck, overwhelm Sir John Littler, and then attack in detail our wearied detachments as they came up under the Governor-General and Lord Gough, instead of reserving his strength, till it suited us to become the assailants in those memorable struggles.

A recent Indian periodical* states that, "where it takes three months now, it will take only as many days, to bring distant consignments to market, and the same capital, consequently, which at present can be returned only three or four times a year, may be returned, probably, twenty. A railroad will operate in the same manner, increasing the effective strength of

* Calcutta Review for March, 1846.

the army, by saving the time employed in marches. In the annual relief, infantry regiments are often moved from one end of India to the other, at an average of ten and a half miles per day, halting six days in the month, so that it takes about six weeks to move from this presidency (Calcutta) to Benares. Hence arises the necessity of the concentration at all times of a large force in the neighbourhood of an enemy. There are not the means existing of concentrating troops on a sudden emergency. This was strikingly exemplified in various ways, on occasion of the recent war on the north-west frontier. When it broke out, all officers, whose regiments were in the field, were ordered to join the army. About one hundred, we believe, in the different services—engineers, artillery, infantry, and medical—required to go from this presidency. They were sent at the public expense, and with the greatest despatch. How many do our readers suppose the Postmaster-General was able to send daily? Three!—and as the journey took sixteen days travelling, night and day, few arrived before the war was over. Even this could not have been accomplished at any other period of the year.

"Under the order now countermanded for the establishment of depôts, the regiments stationed in the presidency division were ordered to supply about six hundred men to the depôt, intended to be formed at Benares. The utmost despatch was desired by Government; bullock hackeries, the only kind of carriage ever available here, were put in requisition in the usual manner, but the *garriwâns** had taken alarm at the rumour, industriously and perhaps maliciously circulated, that they were to go to the seat of war. They were consequently obtained with difficulty. Many ran away, and from these causes several days were lost before the march could commence, and a halt of some days more became necessary at the end of the first day's journey. Is this a predicament proper for the Government to be placed in, within a few miles of a great political and commercial capital? Is it just to the great interests involved in the stability of British power, that the movement of troops should depend on native opinion, or on the caprice of the drivers, or owners of bullock hackeries?

"The chief magazine for the supply of military stores for the forces employed in the Lower and Upper provinces, is and must be at Fort William for a century to come. No where else can the vast munitions of war, required on occasions of hostilities, be safely deposited. Their safety is itself a cause of strength, in the impression which the knowledge of it makes on the natives of India. But their use depends on their transport, which, though more easily accomplished by water, than the transport of troops, could be effected with incomparably superior advantages by a railway. The magazines of Allahabad, Cawnpore,

* Drivers.

Agra and Delhi, from which a great part of the Bengal army is supplied, receive all their stores from Calcutta: those of Ajmir, Ferozepore, and Saugor, are also chiefly supplied from this presidency.

"Not only is transport by railroads the quickest, but, if the saving of time is taken into account, it is the cheapest, mode ofconveying troops.

"Sir James Willoughby Gordon, Quarter-Master-General, was examined on this point (before a Committee of the House of Commons), and gave his evidence as follows :—

"'1994. Then, in consequence of the saving of time which is effected, the total cost of the transport of troops is actually less to Government, than their expenses on the road, when they go on foot?—Exactly, perhaps the better way would be, to state one case, which is as good as a thousand. We will take the distance from London to Birmingham; the expenses for marching for one man, being nine marches and one halt, is 10*s*. 10*d*.; by railroad he would cost 10*s*. 7*d*.; therefore, in that distance, there is a saving of 3*d*. on each man.'

"'1995. Lord G. Somerset.—You are now speaking of cavalry ?—No, infantry. Cavalry I have moved by railroad under particular circumstances, which, if necessary, I shall state; but, so far as regards expense, the horse marching costs nothing; he eats the same as he does in the barrack-stable; but when a soldier marches, he costs the public, in addition, 1*s*. 1*d*. per day, of which 10*d.* goes to the publican, and 3*d.* to himself. Then, I should say, that this mode of railway conveyance has enabled the army (comparatively to the demands made upon it, a very small one) to do the work of a very large one; you send a battalion of one thousand men from London to Manchester in nine hours; that same battalion marching, would take seventeen days, and they arrive at the end of nine hours just as fresh, or nearly so, as when they started; by moving the troops to and fro by that mode of conveyance, you could not have done one-tenth part of the work that it was required of the troops to do, and necessarily to do, in the year 1842.'

"'1996.—In the case you have mentioned, for the sake of example, of the conveyance of so many soldiers from London to Birmingham, it is obvious—is it not—that, besides the small difference between 10*s.* 10*d.* and 10*s.* 7*d.*, the soldier was available for nine days' service in this case which he spent in travelling in the other?' 'Yes.'

"'1997.—And over and above that, there is the power of concentration at particular points, the importance of which is hardly to be estimated?' 'Yes; it facilitates military operations to an extent beyond my power to describe to the committee.'

Regarding the superior safety of railroad travelling, as compared with all other modes of conveyance, the same witness made the following statement:—

"'For the last two years, ending December 31st, I

have moved by railroad 130,174 persons; and of those persons a very large number were women and children, and they were moved without any reported accident whatever, which is a degree of security I do not think attached to any other mode of conveyance that has come under my observation, neither by canal, nor by sea, nor by waggon, nor by coach. Perhaps the committee might like to have that in detail, it is a very short paper, and I have therefore brought it.' The witness delivered in the same, which is as follows:—

"'Summary of the officers, men, women and children conveyed by railway in Great Britain, in the years ending the 31st of December, 1842, and 31st of December 1843 respectively.

Period.	Officers.	Men.	Women.	Children	Horses.
June 30, 1842 .	785	28,329	1,884	2,073	
Dec. 31, ,, . .	966	33,683	1,327	1,300	113
Total for 1842	1,751	62,012	3,211	3,337	113
June 30, 1843 .	597	22,869	1,178	1,450	
Dec. 31, ,, . .	905	30,042	1,316	1,470	
Total for 1843	1,502	52,911	2,494	2,920	
General Total 1842 & 1843	3,253	114923	5,705	6,257	113
Total individuals, 130,138					

Horse Guards, 27*th Feb.*, 1844.*' "

* Reports of a Select Committee of the House of Commons on Railways.

In the month of November last this officer gave similar testimony, before the Gauge Commission, as to the economy, safety and adaptation of railroads to military purposes.

He stated that during the three years and a half, ending the 30th of June 1845, 212,000 people were moved by railway, of which 9,600 were women, and above 11,000 children, besides 378 horses, without any reported accident.

The horses came out of the horse boxes, after a movement of 100 miles, just as fresh as when they went into them.

"6325.—Do you imagine, in the event of this country being at war with France, the railways of this kingdom could be advantageously used in the national defence?"

"Certainly. The effect of rapid communication by Railway, speaking militarily, is, that it enables you to do with a small army the work of a large one."

After adverting to the great inconvenience and expense of having large bodies of troops quartered in different parts of the coast, as was the case at the breaking out of the last war, he adds—"Now it would not be necessary to do that; you would probably concentrate them in some central place, and move them from thence by railway."

"6337.—You mean that they would not be concentrated upon any point of the coast?"

"No. At the breaking out of the last war, you had a large division of the army in Essex; you had another in Norfolk; you had an other in northamptonshire, and so on northward. You had a very large one in Kent; you had another in Sussex; you had another in Hampshire; and you had one in Devonshire; all of which were separate and distinct corps, and could not be removed but at great expense of time and labour. Now, in the event of similar circumstances of hostility with France, it would be much better to concentrate all those troops in some central point, such a central point as might be thought best, and from thence they might be conveyed by railway to any part of the coast where their services were most required, to and fro, with very great rapidity and certainty."

"6338.—Taking the great lines as radii from that focus?"

"Yes; the focus might be wherever it might be thought best. You might consider which was best, with a view to ammunition, with a view to proximity to an arsenal, with a view to provisions, and with a view to the troops being quartered; they would go backwards and forwards without difficulty."

The military evidence of Major-General Sir John Fox Burgoyne, K.C.B., Inspector-general of fortifications—lately chief commissioner of public works in Ireland, and also one of the railway commissioners for that country, given before the Gauge Commissioners, contains the following passages :—

"6346.—You are probably of opinion that the fallacy of moving artillery, cavalry and infantry, by railway, might be, in case of war, essentially conducive to the national defence?"

"No doubt of it, of very great importance. I look upon the whole safety of the kingdom to depend upon railways. Looking at the facility there is now for making incursions upon the coasts, with large bodies of men such as the French have, nothing but the power of concentration, which the railways would give, could enable you to resist successfully; and I think you will thus be able successfully to counteract, with the aid of a few other means, the apprehensions of invasion from the power of steam vessels. I quite understand Sir Willoughby Gordon's reasoning about the difference between the present and former time. Formerly the apprehension was always upon the south coast of England, and it was very necessary there to have the troops stationed, so that they could be within reach of every part, by the then mode of communication, which was by ordinary marching, therefore you could not afford to have them above three or four days' distance; but now you would have your troops away 200 miles in the north, and you could bring them down, within twenty-four or forty-eight hours, to any part where there was a threatening; giving you that power, the great advantage of which is well known in military tactics, the power of concentrating upon any given point in a short time. For you could concentrate nearly all the forces of England before the enemy could go through the operation of actually landing 20,000 men; for we know that the operation of landing a large body of men, under every advantage which the British navy affords us, was very serious; it took days and weeks to effect it with all the equipments. I do not believe any other power is at all aware, as we are, of the difficulties of landing troops, because we have tried it over and over again, which they never did; and we have found by experience, that it was attended with very great difficulty, and took a very long time. The whole question of war depends upon the General who can concentrate his troops with the greatest rapidity, and in the greatest numbers, upon a given point of importance; and if you can get down your men from the north faster than the enemy can land them on the coast, of course you have every advantage."

"There is another very great facility that railways give, with regard to military operations, which is in carrying camp equipage. In case of war, camp equipage is of the greatest importance, and the carriage of it by ordinary means is very difficult, but by railway you would carry it with the troops very easily, and you would form an encampment very easily in a very short time."

"Then there is another great advantage in the railways in defensive warfare, which is, that the parties who are defending themselves, who are resisting invasion, have the use of the railway to the last; whereas, if the enemy gets possession of it, it is of no use whatever to him. Now, in the case of ordinary roads, when an enemy got possession of a road, it was of great service to him; he immediately ran along it till he got to the next point of opposition. But, when he gets possession of a railway it is of no use to him at all; he has no carriages and no locomotives; but you have the use of them, on the contrary, till the last moment. I look upon railways to be important mainly for defence, and I think steam generally is chiefly of advantage in favour of defensive power.

"I should expect all the reserves to be a long way in the rear, always having the facility of that rapid communication to various points. I would never trust in the front more than what were necessary for immediate defence.

"The great reserves would all be in the interior.

"Along the outer circumference, troops attempting to assemble, might be met by the enemy and opposed in detail, whereas, from the interior, they have the advantage of concentration on their side, and may direct their masses on inferior forces."

"6336.—Does anything further occur to you in respect to this question?" "I think that the point that Sir Willoughby Gordon mentioned about the security of railways in case of insurrection, is of very great importance. It is one that has always struck me with reference to the danger of having the railways broken up. If you had any apprehension of anything of the kind, you would have a flying corps upon the railway, which would run from one place to another; and anybody that attempted it would get into a great scrape; for you would be upon them before they could be aware of it. They might do partial mischief for a short time, but they could not keep any permanent hold of the thing, or do any such mischief that your own people would not be able to repair in a short time."

That the important advantages of railways for the security and defence of *this* country, so forcibly pointed out by these two distinguished officers, would result from the introduction of this mode of transit in India, must be evident to all, when the greatness of territory, the extent and nature of its frontier, and the numerical disproportion of the army to the population are considered, but only those who are practically acquainted with the country, its people and climate, its roads and conveyances can duly estimate the expense, delay, and annoyances which so frequently accompany the movement of even a single regiment in its line of march; and this, too, in times of peace; but when forced marches become necessary, the carriage seized and retained by authority, even if adequate for the conveyance of camp equipage, is soon thrown so far in the rear as not to be available. The men and officers are consequently, when making two days' march in one, constantly exposed, when in an exhausted state, from the want of their tents, to great heat during the day, and intense cold at night, and such exposure at the very opening of the campaign, deprives the ranks of many an efficient soldier. Railroads would entirely obviate, or greatly diminish, these difficulties, there would be no fatigue experienced, and but little exposure. The same train that would convey the soldier, would also convey his arms, his tent and refreshment, so that an encampment of well supplied and efficient troops might be formed in an incredibly short time, at any point where their services might seem to be required.

The following paragraph we subjoin is from a German paper. "The late affair at Cracow has afforded an instance of the benefits of railways for the speedy transport of troops and warlike stores to the scene of operation; an Austrian corps of 921 men having been transported, on the 3rd instant, from Prague to Almutz, about 160 miles, in fourteen hours and a half; and, on the 5th, a body of cavalry of 1,500 men, with horses and baggage, made the same journey in twelve hours, thus saving from eight to nine days."

Colonel Warren, C.B., Town Major, Fort William, regarding railways in India, expresses himself as follows:—

[There cannot be two opinions upon the subject. For my own part, I regard their introduction as likely to effect such a change throughout the whole country, and to confer such incalculable benefits both upon the government and the public, that no cost (within reasonable limits) could be too great to accomplish the object.

The importance of the undertaking, in a commercial point of view, I presume to be great; but I am unable to give an opinion; but of its advantages, in a military and political point of view, I have no hesitation in stating, that the advantages are infinitely beyond what, on a cursory examination of the subject, might be supposed, and would be cheaply purchased at almost any price.

The practicability of receiving intelligence from distant parts of the country, in as many hours as at present it requires days, and even weeks to accomplish, and of sending instructions, with troops and stores in the same brief period, are considerations which cannot be too highly estimated. Troops could be kept at more distant and healthier stations than at present, and much loss of life from sickness would be by this means spared. Stores would not to the same extent be required at the various depôts, and the loss by decay, and the destruction incidental to the climate which now attains, would also be avoided.]*

* The above extract is from the pamphlet of Mr. R. M. Stephenson, and in all cases where we have availed ourselves of the information contained in the same, the extracts are marked by brackets as above (1846).

Many other officers in India, both in the Engineers and other arms of the service, coincide with the opinion of Col. Warren; but we confine ourselves to a short extract from the letter of Captain Goodwyn, Garrison Engineer, and Civil Architect of Fort William, and Superintendent of suspension bridges and iron roofing.

[To the Government, in the conveyance of military stores, troops, officers and mails, the benefits are really so numerous and of such magnitude, that the merits of each individual case requires more detail than is here necessary. Suffice it to say, that the estimated gains have been entered into, and are enormous, both in a financial and military view; whilst the statistical returns of the number of passengers and of the traffic on the line between Calcutta and Allahabad, of which, I believe, you have the particulars, sufficiently confirm what I have advanced on that head.]

In addition to the facts and opinions which have been stated, drawn from the evidence of the Quarter-master-General of the Army before a select committee of the House of Commons, the more recent testimony of that officer and General Burgoyne before the Gauge Commission, the Calcutta Review, and officers in the service of the Honourable East India Company, we close these extracts on the political and military importance of railways in India, by transferring to our pages the following corroborative testimony of Mr. Williamson, late Revenue Commissioner, Bombay, contained in a printed letter recently addressed to Lord Wharncliffe, as Chairman of the Great Indian Peninsula Railway Company.

"In Europe the importance of a railway as a military work is limited to the speed and comfort with which large bodies of troops may be conveyed to their destination; but in India its value is enhanced by the mode in which it would *spare the health and save the lives* of European troops.

"The saving of human life and the increase of efficiency in the men would of themselves be a sufficient argument in favour of such a mode of transit; but setting aside all considerations of humanity, the mere pecuniary saving would be very great. It is well known, that every recruit landed in India costs the Company one hundred and ten pounds, which sum is considerably increased before he is dismissed from drill and fit for service, so that the saving of every single life becomes a matter of considerable financial importance." *

The cogency of Mr. Williamson's remarks regarding the pecuniary advantage which would accrue to the state by the safe conveyance of troops must be strikingly apparent to all acquainted with the tedious and dangerous navigation of the Ganges.

---

* Pages 11 and 14 of the letter by T. Williamson, Esq., C.S., on the Advantages of Railway Communication in India. (1846).

Three years ago one hundred Europeans perished in this river during a gale, entailing a loss upon the government of upwards of ten thousand pounds.

Leaving these facts to the consideration of those interested in the stability of the British dominion in the East, and merely alluding to the great facilities which the government would derive from safe and rapid transit of their treasure and despatches, the comparative ease with which the present necessarily cumbrous machinery of government might be wielded or reformed, both for the administration of justice, and the collection of revenue in the more distant provinces, the stimulus that would be felt immediately in every department of the public service, by being brought almost into contact with the seat of supreme authority; the active and efficient supervision of which would elicit more fully the highest and best qualities of their servants, improve the revenue, and be a blessing to the people.

Provided with this additional source of energy and strength, should an enemy again be rash enough to threaten our territory, he would find that territory surrounded, as with a wall of iron, bristling with British bayonets, our munitions of war at hand, and our guns in position.

Works so formidable to our enemies, so useful to ourselves, how calculated to impress surrounding nations with the intelligence, the resources, and the power of the paramount authority in India!

SOCIAL AND COMMERCIAL ADVANTAGES

OF

RAILWAYS IN BRITISH INDIA.

"There be three things," says Lord Bacon, "which make a nation great and prosperous, a fertile soil, busy workshops, and easy conveyance for men and commodities from one place to another."

"Railways are, assuredly, next to the invention of printing, the most powerful instrument of civilization that the ingenuity of man has ever devised. It is difficult, if not impossible, to foresee and define the results which they must, of necessity, at some period produce on the fate of nations."*

The knowledge of the value of time, the commercial benefits and social amelioration which flow from improved intercommunication, are now becoming gene-

* Address to the Chamber of Deputies by the French Minister of public works. (1846).

rally known and justly appreciated, and it will not have escaped the observation of the attentive reader of history, that the march of nations in general improvement, enterprise, and the acquisition of riches, has been accelerated, or retarded, in a nearly exact ratio with the means afforded them of exchanging ideas and commodities within their own territory, and extending their relations with neighbouring and more remote countries.

The means of transit besides constituting a chief element in collecting data on which to base a true estimate of the progress of society, operate alternately as the cause and effect of civilization and prosperity. The formation of roads invariably tends to improve the most barbarous district, to evolve its resources and ameliorate the condition of its inhabitants, while the converse is alike certain in result. A country rich in agricultural, manufacturing or mineral wealth, with a people whose energies are awakened to the incalculable benefits which accrue to commerce from the easy and rapid interchange of commodities, demands increased facilities of transit, taxing to the utmost science, experience, and skill to keep pace with its requirements,

The state of internal communication of a country then bears a direct relation to and is co-equal with the progress of its people in general improvement, good roads and other means of transit being the infallible signs—because the certain consequences—of civilization

—as their absence or imperfection proves the reverse in a greater or less degree. "Let us travel," says the Abbé Raynal, "over all the countries of the earth, and wherever we find no facility of travelling from a city to a town, or from a village to a hamlet, we may pronounce the people to be barbarians." Sir Henry Parnell in his admirable "Treatise on the Formation &c. of Roads," makes the following forcible remark—"The making of roads, in point of fact, is fundamentally essential to bring about the first change that every crude country must undergo, in emerging from a condition of poverty and barbarism."

"By this means the village and the city are brought close together in effect, and yet retain all the advantages of their local separation; the port and the manufactory are only separated by the distance, in time, of a few hours, while such distance in space affords room for all the various occupations which contribute to the perfection of either."* A writer on this subject remarks that—"Next to the genial influence of the seasons, upon which the regular supply of our wants, and a great portion of our comfort so much depends, there is perhaps no circumstance, more interesting to men in a civilized state, than the perfection of the means of interior communication."

Although the present mode of transit, when compared with that in use in England some centuries ago

* M.S. Lectures on the Rise and Progress of Internal Communication, by an Eminent Civil Engineer. (1846).

(and which still prevails in Spain, and portions of other countries in Europe, and which is so general in Asia, and may be denominated the pack-horse system), might be regarded as having attained a perfection more than commensurate with the anticipations of its projectors, notwithstanding this, an eminent statist assures us, that we are but in our infancy as travellers. "All railway systems ought to be eminently expansive, and to take what has been accomplished in the past as a criterion of what is to be accomplished in the future, nay, of that which the public will shortly demand, and to found any conclusion on such a narrow basis, would be most detrimental to the public interests. These demand from our engineers (and they will, I doubt not, satisfy the demand) increased power, increased speed, and increased economy. Let us bear in mind that the railway system is but commenced; and, looking at the great improvements which have been made in locomotives, enabling them to accomplish the conveyance of loads double those they could draw some years ago, let us be careful in adopting the present average speed and loads of passengers and other trains, as the speed and loads that will be required some years hence by the public. Let us not devise our future works and arrangements with the idea of 'finality' to cramp our exertions."*

* Principles of Railway Management, by J. Butler Williams, Esq., F.S.S., F.G.S., read before the Statistical Society of London, 16th March, 1846—page 26. (1846).

Vast, and beyond the calculation of the most sanguine, as have been the benefits conferred on this country by railway communication, the introduction of this system of transit into India, must lead to results of still greater magnitude and importance. In England this was only a question of degree; applied to India, it will be one of kind, or a new and vivifying element of social and commercial progression, acting on a population exceeding one hundred millions.* Capital and enterprise, directed by science, have for ages stimulated the industrial energies of our people, and the latent resources of our soil; whilst the extensive and fertile plains of India, teeming with the richest agricultural and mineral products which—when remote from river traffic, from the want of roads—remain to rot on the ground which nourished them, or lie dormant beneath its surface, benumbing the energies and debasing the moral capacities of the inhabitants.

"Great merit is due to the late Lord William Bentinck, for having established a few steam boats on the river, and to the Home authorities for having maintained them. It is ascertained these boats afford a very profitable return; but their number, not exceeding six or eight, so far from being adequate to the

* The entire population of India may be fairly estimated at 150,000,000. (1846).

conveyance of the traffic up and down the Ganges, are scarcely sufficient for the transport of the public stores and troops proceeding to the interior.*

"A reference to the map of India shows that the cotton-growing districts, on the Nerbudda, and those of Nagpoor and Amrowty, in Berar, are remote from Mirzapore, the entrepôt, on the Ganges, lying between Benares and Allahabad; and the mode of conveyance may be thus described:—

"The cotton is brought on oxen, carrying 160 pounds each, at the extreme rate, in fair weather, of seven miles a day for a continuance, and at a price of about five shillings for each 100 miles. If we take the average distance to Mirzapore at 500 miles, each pound of cotton costs in transit above twopence-half-penny. It has thence to be borne by water carriage nearly 800 miles further on to Calcutta, from which port the exportation of such cotton to England at a profit must be looked for in vain. Within the last seven or eight years, a good road, between Jubalpore and Mirzapore, has been formed; and it is satisfactory to know that although 400 carts only passed over in the year after it was built, no fewer than 6,000 went along it in 1838; and this number will daily increase.

* Since the above was written, several fleets of steamers for inland navigation have been established for private enterprise and with abundant success. (1846).

The misfortune of this road, however, as regards the cotton trade, is that it only commences half way between the cotton districts and the entrepôt. The article, therefore, has necessarily to travel 250 miles on oxen's backs, and the contract for conveyance extends to the whole distance; so that, in fact, for all beneficial purposes to the cotton trade in that quarter, this excellent road is almost useless. In order to render it available, it should be completed to Nagpoor and Amrowty. Were this effected, and the transport by carts substituted, as we may be sure it would be, it would diminish the expense of conveyance alone from twopence-halfpenny to less than a farthing a pound. The calculation is simple. An ox carries 160 pounds at the rate of seven miles a day, *in fair weather only*, for a continuous journey of one or two months. In the absence of a defined and good road, a drove of several hundred head of cattle requires to be constantly watched, and prevented from straying on the march: and this leads to the necessity of travelling by day in the hot weather, when the thermometer is seldom less than 100°, and frequently 130° Fahrenheit. These droves are never so few as 100, and often exceed 1000. Every morning, after daylight, each ox has to be laden; and before the operation is over, the sun is already high above the horizon. The cattle have then to proceed at the slow rate of two miles an hour, and seldom perform a journey of more than eight or nine miles per day. The horde generally halts one day in the seven. (Troops, in marching on service, are required to halt once on every third day).* If the caravan is overtaken by rain, the cotton, becoming saturated with moisture, is so heavy as to prevent its transport on the cattle, and the roads, if lying through the cotton ground, are so deep that men even sink above their ankles at every step, and cattle to their knees. It may easily be supposed that, under such a calamity, the merchant and the carrier are both ruined. How different is the case with a cart on a good road. Here the goods, once laden, may be secured from rain, and are never touched during the whole journey. The attachment of the cattle to the yoke does not literally occupy a minute.

"Thus harnessed, the cart can travel by night during moonlight, and morning and evening, in dark nights, at the rate of from fifteen to twenty miles a day; and the cart of the Deccan, awkward and ill-constructed as it is, with two draught oxen, conveys with facility the loads of ten carriage cattle—that is to say, 1600 pounds, and proceeds at the rate of two and a half, or even three miles an hour."†

* In Bengal, in the annual relief, infantry regiments march on the average ten miles and a half per diem, halting six days in the month. (1846).

† "The Cotton Trade of India," by Major General Briggs, F.R.S., 1840.

Since General Brigg's pamphlet was written, the means of internal communication have been extended and improved, but still much remains to be done for developing this essential element of prosperity, power, and civilization.

"Believing it to be generally admitted, that opening and perfecting lines of interior communication (more especially those leading from capitals having, by sea, unlimited commercial intercourse), has ever been found eminently conducive to national improvements, it is deemed unnecessary to offer proof of the assertion, further, than by referring to the prosperous state of Britain and America, where such works abound and are multiplying, compared with that of any country, however superior in natural fertility, in which they have continued neglected, or are unknown."*

That the British merchants resident in India, as well as the wealthy and intelligent members of the native community, are alive to the commercial and social benefits derivable from railroads in India, will be evident from the subjoined extracts.

[The great risk of our rivers in our country boats —the length of the voyage—the want of water a great portion of the year—the strength of the current in the rains, and the periodical monsoons, would all be

* Report on the Rajmahl Canal by General Macleod and Colonel Forbes.

thrown into the scale in favour of railroads, independent of the incalculable benefits the people of India would derive by a rapid and free intercourse all the year round, uninterrupted by causes which impede inland navigation, even when propelled by steam."—ALLAN DEFFELL & Co.

"There can be no doubt, that, as regards the commercial interests of Bengal, and those of the public, any line of railway will be of advantage, and we believe that these are lines the advantage of which would be very great. For instance, from Rajmahl to Calcutta certainly, and probably the longer line between Calcutta and Mirzapore."—COCKERELL & Co.

"Were we to express our views as fully as we feel upon this subject, we should probably exceed the limits of sober calculation. That it will benefit the country by developing her hidden and partially-opened resources—that it will infuse a spirit of enterprise hitherto unknown to her merchants—and that it will increase the consumption of British and other goods where they are known, and create a demand for them where they are not—are inferences which even the cautious must admit."—KELSALL and GHOSE.]

Regarding the probable return to the shareholders on the capital invested, our Calcutta friends are equally sanguine.

[Notwithstanding the difficulty and delay of land carriage, from 19,000 to 22,000 tons of merchandize pass along the military road (per annum?) It has been ascertained that the expense of conveyance by land is equal to between three-pence and four-pence per ton per mile.*

"By water the official returns from the Jungypore toll-house shows that 181,000 tons of merchandize pass annually between Calcutta and Benares, and the districts above that point.

"The expense of the river route, including insurance and interest during the time occupied in transit amount to about two-pence per ton, per mile; on goods of the value of £40 per ton, or somewhat more than the *minimum* charge on a railway.†

"It appears, also, that 435,000 foot passengers pass annually along the military road, and between 30,000 and 40,000 by conveyances of various kinds.

"By the river route the number of passengers in 1840-41 was 58,378, occupying 14,591 boats.

"These returns show a larger traffic, and a greater number of passengers, than were to be found on any of the great thoroughfares of Europe, previous to the introduction of railways; and, the inference therefore, without going into details which are beyond my present

---

* The Bombay estimate is eight-pence to eleven-pence per ton per mile, by pack bullocks. (1846).

† The minimum charge of a railway may be for coals and such rough goods, a penny and even three farthings per ton. (1846).

limits, is, that such works would answer better there than they have elsewhere, especially if they can be constructed, as I believe, for £5,000 per mile, instead of from three to four times that sum as in Europe.

"I am satisfied, indeed, after very careful enquiry and minute attention to the subject, that no country in the world has ever offered so tempting a field for the investment of capital in railways, as the valley of the Ganges, from one extremity to the other.

"The physical impediments are much less than those upon the line of any large railways I have ever examined."—G. ASHBURNER. (Firm of MACINTYRE and Co.)

"If an industrious and thriving population, numbering about 100,000,000—a large, active, and daily expanding internal traffic—cheap land and labour, with most of the necessary materials for construction on the spot, at prices equally low—and perfect security for person and property, are elements that will command success, then it is certain that a more promising field than Bengal for the investment of railway capital, could not be found.

"I speak exclusively in a commercial sense. The military question, so intimately connected with this subject, I am unable to offer an opinion upon. The revenue that would arise from the conveyance of troops and stores, however, I should think would be very large.

"In fact, the more I look at this subject, the more

satisfied do I feel that the introduction of a well-organised system of railway communication into Bengal, would prove not only highly advantageous to the presidency itself, but also to the shareholders, by yielding them a liberal and steady return for capital.

"The above is my deliberate opinion, formed after much careful consideration of the question."—MUTTY LOLL SEAL.]

The following sentiments and anticipations regarding the moral influence of improved intercourse on the people, emanating as they do, from an intelligent and enterprising native merchant of Calcutta, Baboo Ram Ghopaul Ghose, cannot but be interesting.

[We are aware that the people of this country are generally poor—that the natives of Bengal are not a travelling people, and that the religious prejudices would interfere to some extent to prevent the Hindoos resorting to these conveyances. While we admit that the majority of the people cannot afford to travel in a railway train, we maintain that the number of those who can, are by no means small. The social relations between the Upper and the Lower Provinces is almost *nil*, but the mercantile relations are extensive and extending; and so far as mercantile pursuits are concerned, the up-country people are noted travellers.

"The growing class of intelligent natives would freely resort to it; and, lastly, the religious connexion between the Hindoos and the holy cities of Benares, Gyah,

Allahabad, and others, would alone fill the trains with hundreds of the better class pilgrims. This brings us to consider the extent of religious prejudices. As a native of the land, the writer feels some confidence in stating his opinion, that he believes they may be overcome by a few simple arrangements. Let there be three divisions of the people—namely, Mahomedans and high and low caste Hindoos. If any female passengers offer, let them be accommodated in separate carriages. And do not let the travellers be required to make a run of more than twelve hours at a time (which, of course, would never be necessary).

"We feel sure, with these easily effected arrangements, railway travelling would be generally and eagerly availed of by all classes of men—except, perhaps, by a few, a very few, old, antiquated Hindoos, who look upon every innovation with feelings of horror. The only serious objection would be on the part of the females; but even this stronghold of native prejudice we hope to see successfully undermined by the civilising influence of steam."—KELSALL and GHOSE.]

The above opinions and hopes coincide with our own, although they are not those generally entertained. It must be allowed that there are many native gentlemen of considerable fortune resident in Calcutta, Moorshedabad, Patna, Benares, Delhi, &c., and a numerous and increasing class of mahajuns* in those cities, Mir-

* Merchants.

zapore, and elsewhere, who would soon find it to be for their convenience and interest to travel by railroad, whether in the pursuit of business or pleasure, and the natives of the Upper Provinces, naturally given to travel, would speedily adopt the new system were their prejudices duly consulted.

Prior to the introduction of locomotives on railways in this country, opinions were entertained precisely similar to those generally expressed regarding the relative value of passengers and goods traffic on Indian railways, the principal portion of the estimated profit being grounded on the latter.

"When the first projects for railways to be worked with locomotive power were discussed and brought under public notice it was anticipated that the chief source of profit would be found in the conveyance of goods and merchandise.

"The unexpected and extraordinary increase in the number of passengers, however, produced by the economy of time and money, rendered the passenger traffic more immediately and evidently profitable; hence it naturally engrossed the attention of the managers, whose entire energies were engaged to provide greater accommodation, combined with speed, safety and regularity.

"Of late the old established lines have increased the facilities for the carriage of goods, and provided accommodation apparently more commensurate with the demand. So far as the experiment has been carried, it has shown generally that the net revenue from the goods traffic has been increasing in a quicker ratio than the net revenue from passengers.

"On the London and Birmingham, Grand Junction, and Great Western Railways, the income from the goods traffic now ranges from 25 to 40 per cent. of that derived from passengers; the increase in the revenue from the goods traffic having been within twelve months about 30 per cent. on each of these great trunk lines.

"On the York and North Midland, the Paris and Rouen, the Paris and Orleans, and similar lines, the goods traffic now produces a revenue about equal to half that produced from passengers, the increase having been in the same period about 30 per cent.

"Late arrangements made by the South Eastern Counties for the more economical and regular carriage of goods have caused an increase of revenue from that source of upwards of 100 per cent.

"Important as these facts are to show the advantages of a movement in the right direction, I am convinced that they do not represent, even approximately, the vast increase in the goods traffic which must follow upon a liberal management and more extended accommodation.

"But the most important field of all, because the most exhaustless, remains to this time almost unoccupied. I refer to the conveyance of agricultural produce and bulky materials, which are either conveyed by canals or common roads, or too frequently remain confined in districts where their value cannot be turned to the best public or private advantages."*

The concluding paragraph of the above extract is in an especial degree applicable to India; and we now close this section with a few remarks on the general traffic of the country.

[The enormous traffic already existing, and constantly on the increase, the almost incredible number of passengers of all descriptions, who now travel by the tedious and insecure means of hackeries and bullock carriages, would most assuredly avail themselves of the security, rapidity, and comparative economy, with which they would be conveyed by railway.† The planter and merchant in Central and Upper India, whose goods are now consigned to the dangerous, crazy boats, which navigate the rivers, at enormous risk and decided uncertainty of their arrival at their destination

* The Principle of Railway Management, by J. Butler Williams, Esq., F.S.S., F.G.S.

† A Calcutta merchant, desirous of visiting Benares, distant 428 miles, incurs an expenditure of forty pounds, loses more than a month on the journey, there and back, if he goes by steam vessels, and if he goes by Dâk (post) the amount will be fifty pounds, and he will have eight or ten days incessant travelling; by railway the time occupied to and fro would be under twenty-six hours, the cost ten pounds, seven pounds, four pounds ten shillings, or so, according to the class or train selected. (1846).

in a marketable condition, would hail with joy the means of transporting their indigo and cotton with the certainty of obtaining the price of the day, and the security afforded to the merchandize by the rapidity of the conveyance."

H. GOODWYN,
Garrison Engineer.]

The official records at the India House prove that the annual exports and imports of Calcutta exceed £16,500,000 sterling.—The chief portion of this great and still augmenting traffic, is either received from, or conveyed to, the interior, by a most vexatiously slow and expensive mode of transit.* Without adverting to other products of the soil (eighteen million acres being under cultivation in the north-west provinces), we may mention that to the north-west of Calcutta, there are upwards of half a million acres devoted to the cultivation of the sugar cane, and in the year 1844 there were received in Calcutta from the interior nearly 140,000 tons of sugar, which exceeds the estimated

* By river craft, moving at the rate of twelve miles per diem, the charge is two-pence per ton, per mile, including insurance and interest. By land, moving at about the same rate, four-pence per ton, per mile; this is nearly double the average charge for heavy and bulky goods on the principal lines in England, and great reductions are still in progress. (1846).

import for the current year from the whole of our West India possessions, by 15,000 tons.*

---

* "The estimate I (Lord John Russell) now hold in my hand, I consider extreme, and by no means likely to be realized. It first states the amount of colonial and free labour sugar in the warehouse:

		Tons.
Colonial and free labour sugar in the warehouse, April 5th, 1846		40,000.
Estimated import from April 5th, 1846, to April 5th, 1847 (Customs' letter):		
West Indies	125,000	
Mauritius	50,000	
East Indies	80,000	
		255,000
Calculated amount of free labour sugar admitted from foreign countries		20,000
Making in the whole		315,000
Probable stock, April 5th, 1847, stock being notoriously low		45,000
Available for consumption		270,000

(Lord G. Bentinck) "His noble friend (Lord J. Russell) had also calculated the importations from the East Indies, during the year 1846-47, at no more than 80,000 tons. Now he (Lord G. Bentinck) had reason to believe, from enquiries he had instituted, that importations to the amount of 109,000 tons might be expected, during the year from Bengal alone, independently of the importations from Madras. The exportations from Madras for the first three months of the last year, did not exceed 600 tons; but the exportations from that presidency during the first three months of the present year had amounted to 3,500 tons. He

The general commerce of the Ganges is estimated at from one million, to one million two hundred thousand tons per annum; and supposing that one half of this should be taken up by a railway at Rajmahl it would, at one penny per ton, per mile, with the usual deduction of forty per cent. for working charges, give a net return of twelve and a half per cent on an estimated capital of one million and a half, which might be required for the purpose of uniting Rajmahl with Calcutta, exclusive of passengers, troops, government stores, and the conveying of the mails.

That the commercial traffic of India is susceptible

---

believed there was every reason to anticipate an importation of 15,000 tons of sugar from Madras this year; and if this were the case, the defalcation in the supply occasioned by the drought in the West Indies would be amply compensated by the increased supply from our East India colonies. The Right Hon. gentleman, the Chancellor of the Exchequer (Mr. C. Wood) seemed somewhat incredulous; but he would only direct that Right Hon. gentleman's attention to the enormous increase in the production of East India sugar which had taken place within the last few years. In 1836 or 1837 the differential duty which had previously been maintained between East and West India sugar was removed, and the duty on sugar produced in those Colonies was equalized. In 1836-37 the production of sugar in the East Indies for importation to this country did not exceed 13,000 or 14,000 tons. Ten years of protection had, however, so far encouraged the growth of sugar in the East Indies, that he believed our importations of that article from Bengal alone, during the present year, would amount to 100,000 tons."—*The Times*, July 21st, 1846.

of great expansion is demonstrated by the following statement contained in the Bengal and Agra Guide and Gazetteer for 1842:—

"It may be remarked that the inland trade in general has received a new impetus from the abolition of the transit duties in 1836. The tolls collected on boats at Jungypore, previous to that year, amounted to fifty thousand rupees; the year following the amount was one hundred and thirty thousand rupees. This branch of the service has progressively increased."

During the last year the Accountant General of Bengal has been publishing in the Calcutta Gazette a comparative register of the receipts and charges of the Bengal Government for several years preceding 1844-45:—

	Receipts.	Expenditure.	Surplus.
1839-40 .	Rs. 7,19,41,586	Rs. 2,19,56,352	Rs. 4,99,85,234
1842-43 .	8,75,84,546	2,62,75,151	6,13,09.395
1844-45 .	9,52,21,640	2,79,42,677	6,72,78,963

The above has reference to the finances of the lower division only of the Bengal presidency, and by the authority of state papers we have thus a net revenue, after deducting the charges of the collection, the cost of production, the maintenance of public establishments, of more than six millions sterling.

This account, however, does not include the expense

of the troops stationed in Bengal and Behar, and other important items. If we estimate these charges at two millions, there will remain a surplus of income over expenditure, of more than four millions sterling.*

We feel that we could not close this very essential

---

* In the charges of this presidency, there is one small item of 18 lacs of rupees, or £183,000, put down as Nezamut charges, and we are anxious to fix attention on this sum as the origin of that extraordinary prosperity which the revenues of these provinces now exhibit. "This is the sum paid annually to the family of the Nizam of Moorshedabad, the former Viceroy of Bengal and Behar. Those who are conversant with the history of British India, will remember that Lord Clive, on his first visit to Bengal, conquered those provinces from the Mahomedans, but left the administration of the revenues and of justice with the Nabob whom he had set up. On his second advent, he was induced, by a view of the mischief of the double government to simplify and improve the administration, by taking it out of the hands of the Moorshedabad Durbar. The Nabob was accordingly pensioned and his occupations confined to the innocent pursuit of his own pleasures.

"The management of the country was placed in the hands of government, which was responsible to the parliament and people of England for the wise and conscientious discharge of its duties.

"For several years after this great organic change, the wisdom of it was rendered extremely doubtful by the inexperience and the brutality of the European agents who were employed. But under the influence of those high principles and endowments which were successively imported from England, the system of administration worked itself pure, and reached a degree of efficiency which formed a gratifying contrast to the early and disreputable history of our government. The result of this system we may sum up in a single sentence: under the ablest of the Mahomedan Viceroys, portion of our subject, in a manner more satisfactory to our readers, than by giving a paragraph from the able and lucid exposition of the state of the revenue in some of the provinces of the Bengal Presidency, contained in the money article of the Times of the 12th of May last. (1846).

"Some very copious information respecting the finances of the lower division of the Bengal Presidency has been furnished by the last arrival from India. The great sources of revenue in the Lower Provinces, which embrace the Soobahs, of Bengal and Behar, and the districts of Cuttack, are six in number—namely, the land revenue, the excise on spirits, the stamps, the salt, the opium monopoly and the customs. The receipts for the land revenue, in the financial year 1844-45, are stated at 3,71,00,000 rupees. The amount in the year 1841-42 was about the same, but more than an eighth of it consisted of the arrears of former years. For the last four years the income from this source has varied very little, and the permanent rent-roll is assumed to be about 3,70,00,000 rupees,

---

the revenues of these provinces never exceeded two millions and a half. It is important to keep the eye steadily fixed on the fact, that all this stupendous improvement is owing to the measure of giving the Viceroyal family money enough for the purposes of amusement, for the Harem and the Menagerie, and assuming the entire control of the administration ourselves."—*Calcutta Paper*. (1846).

which is about £500,000 sterling more than it was sixteen years ago. At the same time the expenses in collecting this revenue have been greatly diminished. The excise on spirits, commonly called the 'abkaree,' was more productive in the last three years, than during any previous period, having risen to 23,69,000 rupees from 21,70,000 rupees, the amount in 1841-42; the cost of collection having been also diminished. Stamps have not fluctuated, but the salt revenue, from some unaccountable cause, has steadily and progressively decreased. The profits of the opium monopoly, on the other hand, have steadily and progressively advanced from the year when Commissioner Lin accomplished his celebrated work of confiscation and destruction, which has resulted in giving the Chinese a keener appetite for the drug. In 1837-38, two years before that bold act, the profits had risen to the sum of 143 lacs of rupees, or nearly £1,500,000 sterling. The Chinese Commissioner at once reduced the receipts from this branch of revenue to £1,000,000 sterling, but since the settlement of the Chinese affair, a re-action has commenced, and last year the amount of revenue was above £1,750,000 sterling. The customs' revenue gradually increases. In the year 1836-37, the first since the abolition of the transit duties, the receipts were 36,04,000 rupees, and in 1844-45, they were 66,41,000 rupees, with less cost of collection. The receipts generally, 1844-45, amount to 9,77,86,119 rupees, and the expenditure to 3,59,80,958 rupees."*

---

* If we assume two millions sterling as the amount chargeable on the revenue for troops, home department, &c., &c., there will remain, as formerly stated, a surplus of income over expenditure of four millions sterling. "These two provinces of Bengal and Behar, which are by far the most opulent and productive in our possession, thus furnish nearly one half the income of the whole British Empire in India; and all the resources by which that Empire has been extended, consolidated and improved. The maintenance of our dominion in the East, and the encouragement of those grand and useful undertakings which are necessary to the improvement of the Empire, depend almost entirely on maintaining unimpaired the revenues which are derived from the provinces under the Governor of Bengal."—*Calcutta Paper*. (1846).

Note to Second Edition. (1846).

THE first edition of this little work had passed through the press before the publication of the Report of the Railway Commission, composed of Mr. Simons, C.E., and Captains Boileau and Western, Bengal Engineers, and prior to its perusal by the writer; and there does not appear to be, after attentive consideration of that official document, any reason for withdrawing, or modifying, any opinion expressed or conclusion arrived at, in those portions of the text, which described the merits or demerits of particular projects, or which had reference to the proper mode of introducing railroads into India, with the view ultimately of establishing an efficient and comprehensive system. The Report does not apply to the other sections of this pamphlet.

EAST INDIAN RAILWAY,

FROM

CALCUTTA TO MIRZAPORE.*

THIS great trunk line, which is destined ultimately to connect the seat of the supreme government with its most distant provinces, will, it is understood, commence at or near Calcutta (*most probably at Howrah*, on the opposite bank of the Hooghly), and proceed by Burdwan, through the hilly country, and crossing the Soane river, terminate, for the present, at Mirzapore.

---

* Length of line	448 miles
Extension to Delhi	452 ,,
Line with extension	900 ,,
Capital (original)	£4,000,000
,, For extension	4,000,000
,, In reserved shares	2,000,000
,, Total amount of	£10,000,000

(1846).

So far as Burdwan is concerned, the project is feasible enough, this much of the line being easy of construction, and the mineral and other traffic holding out a remunerative prospect; but as the proposed line from Calcutta to Rajmahl can supply the requisite accommodation to the collieries at Burdwan, we think that the East Indian, or as it is called in India, the political line, should, for various reasons, devote its energies elsewhere, as the best mode of fulfilling its ambitious hopes of being, as the Ganges is now, the great highway of India, and break ground at Mirzapore, instead of Calcutta, and crossing the Jumna, proceed by Cawnpore* to Agra and Delhi. A direct line from Calcutta to Mirzapore must have difficulties to encounter amongst the hills,† to say nothing of the Herculean labour of crossing the Soane‡—there are

* The largest and most important military station in India. (1846).

† "The summit of the country at or near the Dhuuwa Pass, where a very rapid descent occurs from the westernmost range of hills in Bengal to the plains of Behar." "And although steeper gradients will have to be here introduced, to overcome this natural barrier we do not expect, from the levels we have taken, they need be greater than can be worked by assistant power when the trains are heavy."—*Report of Railway Commission.* (1846).

‡ "The river Soane is a formidable obstacle to the cheap construction of a railway, being two miles and three furlongs in breadth, and the foundation or natural substratum below (at present) an unknown depth of sand. The erection of a viaduct across this great river, is, however, a matter of expense only,

no considerable towns or stations to accommodate—the population is scattered, it being estimated that, in the route for a distance of two hundred miles, the population does not exceed one inhabitant per mile, and the country generally but little productive—and although it should have, as its upper terminus Mirzapore, the great central commercial mart of India, we do not think the through traffic, on which it must be dependent, would answer the expectations of the promoters, as it would be in direct competition, not only with the usual river craft on the Ganges (which has ever been the great commercial artery of the country), but the several powerful and influential companies for the inland steam navigation, intimately connected as they are with the principal merchants and capitalists, would be most formidable rivals, keeping up as they do, by their numerous steamers, a constant communication between Calcutta, Patna, Benares, Mirzapore, Allahabad, and the other great cities and towns on the river, proceeding at the average speed of fifty miles per diem; and this rate of progression, an eminent merchant informed us the other day, would soon be

---

there appearing no difficulty in the case that perseverance and ingenuity will not overcome."—*Ibid.*

To build a bridge as great in all its dimensions as the Blackwall Railway, and the foundation below "an unknown depth of sand," no difficulty! A bridge without a foundation! "A matter of expense only!" (1846).

doubled from their steamers being enabled to continue their course by night as well as by day. Thus we should have a line not free from difficulty, a poor part of a rich country, and a formidable opposition, without advancing the seat of government to any great extent towards the frontier, as the steamers have gone for many years to Allahabad, forty-three miles higher up than Mirzapore. Another objection to the selection of this, as an experimental or preliminary portion of the trunk line is, that terminating at Mirzapore, or Allahabad, it leaves the travellers or goods at the very point where the real difficulty begins, the Ganges, above Allahabad, from its ledges and shallows being closed to steamers, and, excepting for a few months in the year, the navigation even for country craft is very precarious, and the Jumna, from the sharp and angular rocks which rise from its bed, is still more dangerous and difficult.*

The above are the reasons why the grand trunk line should not be commenced at Calcutta to go to Mirzapore, and we shall now proceed to give those reasons which induce us to desire to see it commenced at the latter point, or rather at Allahabad, and pushed on with vigour to the imperial city of Delhi.

---

* The quantity of water used for irrigating the increasing extent of cultivated land on the banks of the Jumna is annually diminishing the volume of its waters and its capacity for navigation. (1846).

We have visited most of the countries in Europe, and in Holland witnessed with much interest the mode of constructing railways in that kingdom, which from the nature of its soil and surface resembles in some respects, the alluvial plains of India. We have also travelled much in the latter country, and have proceeded by slow marches from Calcutta to the Himalayah, and have seen no large portion of territory present the like facilities for the introduction of a railway, as from Allahabad to Delhi. There is no natural difficulty of any description, no river to cross of any magnitude, as the line would traverse the Dooab, having the two great rivers one on either side, the country presenting as nearly as possible a level surface, its average inclination cannot be more than one in five thousand, and yet it is comparatively free from inundation, and the soil is in consequence more solid than in the lower provinces.* This line would have no rival, for

---

* The towns of Lahore and Umritsir are, according to Burnes and Gerrard, 900 feet above the level of the sea, and 1,000 miles distant from it. The average slope of the country along the banks of the Indus, may be estimated at less than 11 inches per mile, and on comparing this with the valley of the Ganges, we infer the general inclination of the country towards its mouth to be even still more gentle (after making due allowance for the smaller volume of water in the Ganges compared with that of the Indus, from the sluggish nature of the stream, and the tidal influence extending above Calcutta, while in the Indus it ceases below Tatta, 25 miles nearer the sea than the former. (1846).

the river steamers, instead of competing with it, would form a powerful basis, and keep up a continuous commercial and general communication between the railway and Calcutta; and our great military stations and magazines at Allahabad, Cawnpore, Agra and Delhi, would be all in close communication with each other, and by means of the steamers have a free and rapid access to Calcutta.

This line of all others for testing the railway system of communication as applicable to India, on an extended scale, is, in our humble opinion, incomparably the best, and should it solve the mighty problem, in the solution of which, the whole civilized world will soon take an enlarged and deepening interest, in a manner at once satisfactory to the government and the proprietors, as we are confident it must do beyond their most sanguine hopes, it would then be in a position to advance to the Sutlej, or to execute a retrograde movement towards Calcutta.

Having performed a great part of its mission in binding our great military stations and magazines in Central and Upper India in intimate relations, and having appropriated to itself the through and local traffic of that portion of the country, it would thus have a commerce and basis of its own which would at once nourish and support the extension of the grand trunk line, or enable it to throw out tributary feeders, in fact, empower it to advance in any direction the exigencies of the state, or the claims of commerce might seem to demand.

While the railway was thus ministering to the public service, by concentrating the largest and most important military and civil stations, and the most populous and magnificent of the native cities, there would be ample time allowed it, to develop and mature its plans without any apprehension of a rival claimant springing up in its rear, for no other company seeing the best, the easiest portion of the trunk, already appropriated, would be disposed to fill up the chasm between Mirzapore and Calcutta, and encounter the rivalry of the already established steam companies supported by the monied and commercial interests of Calcutta, to whom the several fleets of steamers on the Ganges belong.*

---

* It was far from our wish when discussing the merits of the East Indian Railway to detract an iota from those of its projector, Mr. R. M. Stephenson, whose exertions in connection with the introduction of railways in India we duly appreciate. We have always thought, and recent events have more strongly impressed upon us the opinion, that the great desideratum was, to connect Calcutta with the N. W. Frontier. We only differ as to the mode of doing this. (1846).

Note to Second Edition. (1846).

* Our opinion remains unchanged, notwithstanding that the Railway Commission have enunciated propositions, and proposed projects in exact accordance with the views entertained by the East Indian, or Mirzapore Railway Company; but which they have failed to demonstrate, not even supplying the requisite data on which to found the demonstration of the plans and propositions proposed and enunciated by themselves—we say that our opinion remains unchanged as to the impolicy of *commencing* the railroad system by an attempt to supersede the river navigation, where it is comparatively free from obstruction, and is always available for steam navigation, as is the case between Rajmahl and Allahabad. The former is situated at the head of the Delta of the Ganges, and the latter at the confluence of the Ganges and Jumna, the distance between the two towns, by the river route, being 500 miles. *But should a line be determined on for this portion of the country, an extension of the Rajmahl line up the Gangetic valley to Mirzapore and Allahabad. would have many advantages over the direct route indicated by the East Indian, or Mirzapore Railway Company* These advantages we shall notice in detail when we come to review the Report of the Railway Commission. It may, however, be mentioned now, that although the actual, or lineal distance between Calcutta and Mirzapore by the valley of the Ganges, would be 100 miles longer than by the direct route, yet taking the difference of gradients into account (assistant power being required on the latter, and pro rata to the power required so is the distance) the gain in time by the direct line would not be more than three or four hours, which would be too trivial to be an element in any calculation of the comparative merits of the two lines, in a country where time occupied in travelling is estimated by months instead of hours.

GREAT NORTH OF INDIA RAILWAY,

FROM

ALLAHABAD TO DELHI.*

THE object of these pages is to describe projects, not companies, so that while discussing the merits of the East Indian Railway, we dealt with it as a whole, and had regard not only to its immediate objects, but to its future and ultimate extensions; we merely recommended a departure from the order of progression laid down, and not an abandonment of any one of its objects.

---

* Length of line, 400 miles. Capital of Company, £4,000,000.

"They would then have a great length of line for a reasonable average outlay. The lower half from Calcutta to Mirzapore, costing considerably above that average, and the upper half from Mirzapore to Delhi as much below it."—*Vide paragraph* 84, *Report of Railway Commission.* (1846).

The East Indian line we have seen, was to proceed from Calcutta to Mirzapore, and eventually to Delhi and the N. W. Frontier, selecting for a first effort the poorest, the most thinly peopled, and the most difficult portion of the line, reserving what was of easy and rapid attainment for the future. The Great North of India line, on the contrary, knowing that the communication between Calcutta and Allahabad (the great entrepôt for passenger and commercial traffic), forty-three miles above Mirzapore, was already provided for by the Inland Steam Navigation Companies, commences at Allahabad, where, as we have already stated, the chief difficulties in the river transit begin, and will form a great trunk line between that city, Cawnpore, Agra, and Delhi: "but as the completion of comparatively short lines is the best mode of introducing railways into any country," it is proposed to complete this undertaking section by section. Should this plan be adhered to, we would recommend as a first step, the connecting of any two points, between Cawnpore and Delhi—for example, a line from Cawnpore viâ Etawah or Mynpooree to Agra,* or from Agra by Muttra, and Allyghur to Delhi:† the traffic

* Length about 166 miles.

† Length about 104 miles.

The Company propose, and the Railway Commission recommend, as a preliminary section, that portion of the line between Allahabad and Cawnpore, in length 133 miles. (1846).

on the road above Cawnpore being much greater than below that station, and the ground being, if anything, still better adapted for a railway. The Great North of India proposes a continuation of the line from Allahabad to Mirzapore, and from Delhi to N. W. Frontier. In the preceding section we have dwelt so minutely on the advantages and importance of a line from Allahabad towards the N. W. Frontier, that we do not think it necessary to make more than these general remarks. The East Indian and Great North of India lines must inevitably amalgamate, and thus adjust their rival claims; the one has the prestige of priority, the other that of the more judicious selection of a starting point.

GREAT WESTERN RAILWAY OF BENGAL,

FROM

CALCUTTA TO RAJMAHL.*

The next design which merits attentive consideration at our hands, from the immediate facilities which it would give to government and commerce, is the line from Calcutta to Rajmahl. This railway claims priority of registration, although from untoward circumstances connected with its birth, it was only second in the field. It was ushered into life under the auspices of a Company denominated the Great Western Railway of Bengal, and from the capitalists and merchants of Calcutta extending to it their patronage and support,

---

* Length of line, 180 miles. Capital, £4,000,000.

The amount of Capital appears disproportionately large to the length of the Line, but it is the intention of the Company to extend the main Line, eventually, to the N. W. Provinces, by the Gangetic valley, as far as Allahabad. (1846).

Note.—This Line was supported by the late Dwarkanauth Tagore. He was sole Trustee to the company for the above project from the time it was constituted. (1846).

it is known in India as the "commercial line," in contradistinction to the East Indian, or the "political line." The Great Western Railway of Bengal for the present confines its attention to connecting Calcutta with the Ganges,* via Burdwan, Berhampore, Moorshedabad, at Rajmahl,† where it would receive the

* This line, like the Mirzapore project, will either commence at Howrah, to save bridging the Hooghly, or proceed on the Calcutta side of the river by the great military station of Barrackpore to Pulta Ghāt, or opposite to Ghireety Ghāt, and then proceed by Chinsurah Hooghly, &c., to Burdwan. At or near Burdwan, seventy-five miles from Calcutta, will be the point of divergence of the Mirzapore and Rajmahl lines. (1846).

† Rajmahl, once the capital of Bengal, is situated at the head of the Delta, on the rock-bound and unchangeable bank of the Ganges, and has a population of upwards of 30,000. In the vicinity, there are large and rich deposits of coal and iron: the amphitheatre of hills in the rear of the town is covered with a variety of excellent timber: stones fit for building purposes are also abundant in this locality.

The facilities thus afforded, as far as materials are concerned, for the formation and working of a railway, from having the four important elements essential to its construction and efficiency, at one of the termini, need not be dwelt upon. It may, however, be pointed out that from its position and resources, especially when connected with Calcutta by a railway, Rajmahl will naturally become the great station for the numerous fleets of steamers engaged in the inland trade.

Below Rajmahl the Bhaugerruttee and Jellinghi rivers (the present uncertain and tedious channels of communication between the Ganges and Calcutta) run from the great Ganges and uniting their streams at Nuddeya, constitute the Hooghly, which flows past Calcutta to the bay of Bengal. (1846).

concentrated commerce of India, traversing the most fertile and densely-peopled portion of our dominions; it will form the only link wanting in the chain of communication between the two great channels of commerce, the main Ganges and Hooghly. It is already ascertained to be of easy construction, having been carefully surveyed by the orders of the local government, for the purpose of making a canal to unite the two rivers already mentioned, and is agreeable to the recommendation of the authorities in Leadenhall-street, with reference to the introduction of railways in India.

We shall now quote from the Indian periodical (the *Calcutta Review*,) formerly alluded to, which appears, notwithstanding a disavowal of such intention, anxious to make out a case against the Rajmahl line. The writer in so respectable a journal cannot be a Mahratta ditcher (a Calcutta cockney) unacquainted with what takes place in the interior of the country which he inhabits! He certainly does imply that the Rajmahl line would pursue the old and beaten track of commerce, but avoids mentioning the possibility of its co-operating with the river steamers on the main Ganges; indeed, while discussing the merits of this project, he shuns allusion to such vessels being in existence, insists that the railroad would be opposed to the river traffic, and yet the steamers belong to the same parties with whom this line, by his own showing, is so popular, viz., the Calcutta merchants and capitalists.—But to the extracts.

"In justice to this company it must be admitted, that it would accomplish all the objects of the canal. On the eastern side of the Ganges, from Patna downwards and along the Bhaugerruttee, the country is a rich alluvial soil, the proprietors of which carry on the cultivation of indigo and sugar, chiefly with capital advanced by the banks, merchants and agents of Calcutta. The produce is abundant, and of great value, and much, or most of it, is brought down by native craft on the Ganges, Jellinghi and Bhaugerruttee, the navigation of which rivers is at all times, from causes varying with the seasons, tedious and difficult, and often dangerous. The passage of cargo boats takes between twenty and thirty days from Rajmahl to Calcutta. The losses are great, and the insurance as high as from England. To supersede the river navigation, or take its place, is the object of the Great Western Railway—and as it would be eminently useful to the capitalists of Calcutta, it is popular with them. This point of view, however, is not a comprehensive one. It includes the consideration of commercial traffic alone, and has no reference to the wants of Government, nor to the principles on which grand trunk lines are now constructed in England. The road would have the river parallel with part of its course, and in direct competition with it."

And yet the navigation "is at times, from causes varying with the seasons, tedious and difficult, and often dangerous—the passage of large boats takes between twenty and thirty days from Rajmahl to Calcutta. The losses are great, and the insurance as high as from England!" This needs no comment. "To supersede the river navigation, or take its place is the object of the Great Western." Quite the reverse—it is to facilitate it, by co-operating with the river steamers on the main Ganges, and saving them the expense, delay, and danger of the Nuddea rivers and the Sunderbunds. "As it would be eminently useful to the capitalists of Calcutta, it is popular with them." Yet these gentlemen are the proprietors of the several fleets of river steamers to which river the railway is to be opposed. "This point of view, however, is not a comprehensive one." If you turn the small end of a telescope towards the dome of St. Paul's instead of a great and majestic structure, you would see a thing like a tea-cup turned topsy-turvy, or the top of a muffineer (pepperpot) presented to you, and you might well exclaim, "This point of view, however, is not a comprehensive one!" "It includes the consideration of commercial traffic alone, and has no reference to the wants of Government." In connexion with the steamers on the main Ganges, it would establish a safe, rapid, and certain communication between Calcutta, Allahabad and the upper provinces. That a communication between Calcutta and Rajmahl was in accordance with the wishes of Government, we prove from the statement in the preceding page of this writer. "Many years ago, a canal from Rajmahl to Calcutta was proposed by Colonel Forbes, an eminent engineer officer, who ascertained the levels and projected the details. The construction of it was authorised by the Court of Directors, and prevented by the Affghan war, which exclusively occupied the attention of Government, and exhausted the funds set apart for the purpose." (This, we are assured, is not the case—the amount still being on the books of the Calcutta Treasury). "On the restoration, however, of peace, after the Gwalior campaign, Lord Ellenborough, as he himself declared, sent to the Board of Control a strong recommendation of the canal, and probably it would have been commenced, but the plan of the East Indian Railway Company appeared at this period. The idea of a railway to Rajmahl was merely an accidental transition from the previous design of a canal, and led to the formation of the Great Western Railway Company. In justice to this company, it must be admitted, that it will accomplish all the objects of the canal"! and yet we are told, "that it has no reference to the wants of the Government,"! although one of their own eminent engineer officers ascertained the levels and projected the details of a canal which "led to the formation of the Great Western Railway Company. In justice to this Company, it must be admitted that it will accomplish all the objects of the canal,"! the construction of which was authorised by the Court of Directors, funds were set apart by the local Government for the work, and the Governor-General sent home a strong recommendation on the subject to the Board of Control and yet we are told "that it has no reference to the wants of the Government"!

Is this a fair and manly mode of treating a subject in which not individuals or companies, but nations, are interested, in which the onward progress of the natives of the soil, in all that humanizes or elevates man above his fellows is so deeply involved? Is it worthy of a philanthropist and patriot to come to the discussion of a subject which takes within its scope the performance of sacred duties to those subjected to our rule, and the defence and consolidation of the greatest empire ever established in India, with a mind so biassed or imperfectly informed, that one sentence in the same paragraph contradicts the other?*

---

* *The Bombay Times*, in speaking of the article in question, says—"It is an ill-concealed attempt to puff Mr. MacDonald Stephenson's Calcutta and Mirzapore line, and to run down its rivals. The opinion of the writer seems to be, that it will be inconvenient to abstract large amounts of capital from England at a time, and that, consequently, one line should be finished before another is commenced—Government settling the question of priority. Now if this principle be adopted, it is clear that a 'heavy blow and great discouragement' will be inflicted on many existing projects, and that much of the benefit which was expected to be

This is the more remarkable, when contrasted with his liberal views and benevolent aspirations, when he treats on the subject of improved intercourse generally; and when he brings under review designs, with slender claims to public confidence, although they may have been expanded by eloquence, and honoured with banquets, to such he is but too forbearant. As we proceed, we shall comment on several of these schemes *seriatim*, and in the mean time we return to our immediate subject.

---

derived from the *early* and *general* introduction of railway communication will be altogether lost. But we hardly think it possible that Government can contemplate a course of procedure so suicidal, so fatal to the best interests of India. If railways are desirable at all, the sooner we have them, and the more generally they are established, the better. Government may, perhaps, more readily grant its assent to a line which promises to be useful in a political point of view, than to one which is calculated merely to promote public convenience and commercial profit; but we do not see why, approving and permitting the construction of the former, it should dream of offering any objection to the latter, provided, of course, the projectors be willing to accept the terms and conditions it desires to impose. It is the duty of the state to guard the national interests, and make proper provisions for the public safety, but where neither are in jeopardy, but the reverse, it would surely be an act of inexplicable folly for it to withhold its sanction from projects of improvement in which capitalists are anxious to engage, on the shallow plea that the capital they wish to expend cannot be conveniently abstracted from the home circulation.—*Bombay Times*, May 9th, 1846.

By means of the Rajmahl line acting in concert with the several prosperous and influential steam navigation companies established on the Ganges, Calcutta will have quick and easy access to the north western provinces, through the heart of the indigo, opium, sugar, rice, cotton and silk districts, with a saving (for nine months in the year, when the smaller rivers between the Hooghly and Ganges are closed) of upwards of 300 miles of distance, by avoiding the tedious and perilous labyrinth of the Sunderbunds.

The report on the celebrated Rajmahl canal by General Macleod, late chief engineer, and Colonel W. N. Forbes, has the following paragraphs.

"Bearing in mind that the Ganges receives in its course through 1200 miles of the central and infinitely improvable plains it fertilizes, eleven rivers, several of them equal to the Rhine, few less than the Thames, and that when it has reached the head of the Delta at Rajmahl, its *distance from Calcutta* does not exceed 200 *miles,* and further having in remembrance, that during a great portion of the year, the only passable channel for boats drawing five feet water, between the latter *city* (the capital of India) and the station named, makes a circuit of 528 miles, this chiefly through the perilous labyrinth of creeks, and wood-encumbered straits, forming the wilderness called the Sunderbunds, it will readily be acknowledged, that amongst the good effects of opening a direct line of permanent navigation between deep water in the Hooghly above Calcutta, and the great river at Rajmahl, there would be the highly important one of its affording the means of conveying safely, cheaply, and speedily to the Ocean outlet, *increased* quantities, and ultimately improved qualities of the agricultural and mineral produce of the entire regions traversed; nor this alone, as by inevitable commercial reciprocation, the same line would immediately serve for supplying those regions with augmented amounts of the sea-borne products or manufactures of other countries."

"The Committee appointed in 1831 to report whether there be any and what prospect of keeping the Bhaugerruttee river open,—or, of *essentially* improving the navigation of it by any means at the disposal of government, after arriving at the conclusion that there *was not*, and that the certain result of forming a cross channel between one of its upper reaches and the Ganges, would be the early filling up of this channel by shoals of alluvium, similar to those annually deposited in the Bhaugerruttee itself,—recommended the construction of the Rajmahl canal, or of the one immediately under consideration, expressly, on the ground that 'no cut running nearly east and west, therefore generally at right angles to the main discharging branches of the Ganges, will ever be found *permanently* favourable for navigation.' Yet such rectification of the Bhaugerruttee has not infrequently been proposed as the means of improving its navigation; and were the Canal levelling sections of no other value, they would be useful in demonstrating that an outlay of money on attempts by such cuttings, *to improve the communication through the bed of the Bhaugerruttee could* only terminate in making it (if possible) *worse.*"

The report goes on to state that by means of a canal, during that portion of the year when the rivers are full, " most of the time lost in contending with the then rapid and ever tortuous Bhaugerruttee would be avoided, as also the risk, in the latter, annually leading to numerous wrecks and total losses of large amounts of property." Regarding the traffic, after having adverted to circumstances in their former reports, the Canal Committee make the following observations in paragraph 47 :—" And amongst them the fact that at one time, when *two* of the *Nuddeah Rivers* were only passable for dinghees, (or the smallest description of country boats) and that whilst at the same period* the third was only navigable for the minor class of cargo boats, the annual collections in the form of toll at the rate of one rupee per one hundred maunds, on the total tonnage passing through these channels, amounted to one hundred and fifty thousand rupees, assuredly prove that if the comparatively safe and

* The dry season.

direct line by the canal were once opened and fairly established, the total amount of tonnage daily passing through it would not fall short of three thousand tons; which (at twenty-seven maunds to a ton) would make the *total number* of boats passed in a day (each averaging six hundred maunds burthen) one hundred and thirty-five; and if (as proposed in our former reports) the toll levied was at the rate of two rupees per one hundred maunds, it will be seen that the annual income derivable from the work would be upwards of five hundred and eighty thousand rupees."*

"The *localities* in which, within accessible distances, stone or minerals adapted for building, are to be met with, have been pointed out in our previous reports, as *have* also *those* of beds of iron ore, and of coal (the latter since experimentally brought into use), which the canal would either intersect or closely approach."†

"In justice to this Company, it must be admitted,

---

* Or 14½ per centum on the expended capital. With reference to a railway from Calcutta to Rajmahl, the traffic has been taken by an eminent Calcutta merchant and the managing director of an inland steam navigation company, and estimated to give, after all deductions, a net return of 12½ per cent. per annum. (1846).

† Report on the Rajmahl Canal, by General Macleod and Colonel Forbes. Plans occupying fifty large sheets of drawing paper, exclusive of one hundred and fifty square feet, containing the topographical survey, accompanied this report, and are now deposited in the India House. (1846).

that it will accomplish all the objects of the canal."—*Calcutta Review.*

We have dwelt thus minutely on the merits of the Rajmahl line, conceiving it to achieve everything that the merchant could desire, and taken in connexion with the fleets of river steamers on the Ganges, the wishes of the Government to approximate the metropolis of British India, with the upper provinces, may with ease and celerity be carried out; while the Grand Trunk Line, *viâ* Mirzapore and Delhi, is slowly and steadily advancing towards the north-west; and besides, an eminent authority, General Macleod, late chief engineer in Bengal, has stated in a letter published in "The Friend of India," of March last, that the Great Western Railway of Bengal is, in his opinion, the best for India, and has recently joined the London Board of Direction.* The report of the railway committee on this line is as follows:

Para. 19.—"A permanent point, however, on the banks of the Ganges, exists at or near Rajmahl, which might be suitable to receive the great traffic of the River, and be connected with the Trunk line a little northward of Burdwan,† and be found advantageous

* Since the above was written, General Macleod has become Chairman of the company for the above project. (1846).

† *Where we predict it the trunk line will pause for a season in its course to Mirzapore.* (1846).

to the general trade of the country, in like manner as the proposed canal of Lieut.-Colonel Forbes would certainly have been if that important work had been carried into execution. Such a branch railway would in no point be removed very far to the westward of the projected line of the canal in question."

36.—"The first branch should be from a point near Burdwan to Rajmahl, along the district of country selected many years ago by Lieut.-Colonel Forbes, for the Rajmahl canal; such a railway will, in future, supersede the necessity for the canal, which, however, would have conferred great benefit on the trade of the country, if carried into execution when he first proposed it; the fact that such a canal had been for many years a desideratum, proves the same thing in favour of the more modern mode of intercommunication.

37.—"Besides the accommodation of the trade of the Ganges, it will give accommodation to Purneah, Malda, Dinagepore, Rungpore, and the country in that direction through which it may possibly hereafter be found desirable to extend this refined mode of transit.

38.—"After all that has been stated from time to time in favour of Lieut.-Colonel Forbes's important work, nothing more need be added in favour of a branch railway in that direction."

As it is more than probable that the East Indian or Mirzapore line will, from physical obstacles, and the absence of traffic, decline advancing for the present beyond Burdwan, the Great Western or Rajmahl line has every prospect of being the Grand Trunk Line for connecting Calcutta with Central and Upper India.

It is worthy of remark, that although the Rajmahl line is treated in the report as a mere branch, yet its intrinsic merits are so great that the possibility is hinted at of this line becoming the great stem from which branches will proceed to supply some of the richest districts in India.

DIAMOND HARBOUR RAILWAY

AND

DOCK COMPANY.*

THE above Company some years ago made a feeble attempt at existence, but not having attained even to the transition or chrysalis stage, died without a flutter, and was speedily forgotten by all but its disappointed projectors. Last year, when the mania was at the hottest, it was re-hatched and came out under the wing of some of the most influential gentlemen connected with the shipping from London to Calcutta, whose interests would be materially promoted by the success of this two-fold undertaking. How it is re-

---

* Also known as the Calcutta and St. George's Point Railway and Dock Company. (1846).

garded in India may be gathered from what follows, taken from a recent Calcutta periodical.

"Diamond Harbour is a part of the river about half way between the sandheads or sea and Calcutta. Above it is the very dangerous shoal of the James and Mary, where many valuable ships have been injured and stranded. To enable the shipping to avoid this peril, and to stop short in a very dangerous river navigation, is the object of this company. It is only the larger ships and more valuable and less bulky cargoes, and those which take steam and go insured, which probably will use the railroad. They will effect a saving of about a half per cent. in the insurance, and perhaps one day's steaming; but this is doubtful; probably the cost of conveyance by railroad and the incidental charges of the merchant will exceed this saving. A railroad to Gravesend, without the advantage of any considerable number of passengers, and with the interest of the Catherine Dock and other docks opposed to it, would present to our English readers a fair comparison to the Diamond Harbour Railroad."

"We should much distrust the scheme."*

Whatever the public utility, we might expect the most determined resistance from the merchants† and

---

* Calcutta Review, for March last, p. 228. (1846).

† They have numerous steam tugs on the Hooghly, from which they derive a handsome profit. (1846).

owners of house property in Calcutta, and other influential parties, to a project which would necessarily create a perfect revolution, subverting all existing arrangements; creating a new town with all its appendages, in a most unhealthy locality, putting the Government to an enormous expense for erecting new Custom-houses and other offices, without any corresponding advantage to the public service. This company therefore cannot expect much favour or support at the hands of the home and local authorities. Supplying one want, certainly in an improved manner, it would leave to others the labour of meeting a hundred inconveniences, resulting from so great an innovation and disturbance of the present distribution and investment of capital.

In the opinion of a practical Engineer, intimately acquainted with the locality, the making of docks at Diamond Harbour and keeping them in a *state of efficiency* is beyond the reach of art, and the railroad without the docks would be of little benefit to any one.

NORTHERN AND EASTERN RAILWAY.

A VERY brief notice will suffice for this impracticable project; we say impracticable advisedly, for we have what we esteem the highest authority for saying so, without reference to our own personal knowledge of the country. It is a good *office* line, that is, it looks well on the map to a person not acquainted with the country, and the nature of the rivers in its route. The Northern and Eastern proposes to start from a magnificent terminus in the city of palaces, and in the true spirit of direct communication, in spite of natural obstacles, which in these scientific days it very properly disregards, plunging into a net work of Nullahs (small rivers), skirting the banks of large streams, which overflow every year, it dashes boldly onwards to somewhere on the Ganges, it says Bogwangolah, but as this is a shifting village, changing its local habitation, if not its name, every year to the extent of some miles, according to the caprice of the river, the upper terminus with its warehouses, &c., will no doubt have wheels, and be as migratory as Wombwell's Menagerie. They intend afterwards, we believe, making an extension to China, (tunnelling the Himalayah) and other neighbouring and accessible countries, making Bogwangolah the great central terminus for railway communication in the East; and the Indian Direction is worthy of these majestic designs, for it rejoices in Princes and Rajahs.

The Calcutta Review after having given very cogent reasons for the controlling power of Indian Railway Companies being vested in a London Board of Directors, and the Calcutta or local management being merely their agents, and amenable to the authority of Home direction, from whom their power ought to emanate, regarding the direction of this line expresses itself as follows. "In one of the Companies* whose scheme is before us, there seems to be a departure from these principles. If we were asked our opinion beforehand, we should say that a pompous array of Presidents, Vice-Presidents, Chairmen, Princes, and Rajahs, would inspire our distrust, as utterly alien to the principle of responsible and economical management. In the Company to which we refer, the Calcutta Board is more numerous than the London; is evidently meant to have

* The Northern and Eastern.

original powers; and not to be accountable. It would be impossible to prescribe to such a list the duty of agents or servants. It consists of a singular mixture of natives, lawyers and merchants. Perhaps the variety is supposed to realize the principle of representation. We think it does not, but the principle itself is inapplicable. Nor is it such a selection as would be made by any prudent person, or body of persons, having proprietary interests, and caring only for the profit to be derived from the intended operations. With the most perfect respect we say it—that Princes and Rajahs are mere ciphers in a Direction. It is no disparagement of them to say that one good Bunniah,* who is also an honest and respectable man, would be worth dozens of them. As for the lawyers—to be directors of banks and trading companies is not within their proper province; nor in England are they ever seen in such a situation."†

* Shopkeeper.

† Calcutta Review for March 1846, p. 231.

MADRAS AND BOMBAY DIRECT RAILWAY.

HAVING disposed of those projects intended for the improvement of the principal Presidency of Bengal, to which we deem allusion necessary, we now turn to the dependent Governments of Madras and Bombay, and are at once attracted by a great undertaking which has its proposed termini in the Capitals of those Presidencies; annihilating the intervening space it would bring into close approximation those widely separated and important localities. This the last, and most transparent of those railway visions which we shall draw attention to, has but recently seen the light, and is denominated

"The Madras and Bombay Direct Railway," its advent having been announced with a magnificent flourish of trumpets, the echo of which still vibrates in our ears, Princes, Ministers, Dignitaries of State hailing its birth as if it had been a beautiful and illustrious babe, instead of a crude and singularly ill-timed abortion,—the last effort of a dying and maniac spirit of gambling which had already spread desolation and misery enough, without giving us to endure any additional infliction. The promoters of this fiction are no doubt honorable men, but on looking at the list of directors, they are only remarkable for the smallness of their number, and the entire want, with the exception of one or two gentlemen, if we remember aright, of any apparent connection with the vast and distant region they have selected for the scene of their labours.

They probably propose the railway from benevolent feelings towards the government letter carriers, to save them their tedious and toilsome journeys. Traffic on this route, no one ever heard of, and for hundreds of miles there is no made road, however indifferent, but we suppose that they, if they make the one, think that providence will send the other, and no doubt it would come in time.

In the Prospectus, allusion was made to the Sikh invasion, with much propriety, as showing the necessity for railways to meet or repel danger from the north-west frontier, and the sequitur flows naturally, that for this purpose, Madras and Bombay should have railway communication, not towards the frontier, but with each other! Bombay being distant from the recent point of attack at Ferozepore one thousand miles, and Madras about sixteen hundred miles, Bombay being seven hundred and sixty-three miles to the north-west of Madras.

This railway, should it be able to emerge from the Ghauts, would lose itself in almost interminable jungle, redolent of malaria, and replete with noisome reptiles—a land without inhabitant, and where it would only startle the tiger as he crouches in his lair—we have no hesitation in saying, that the Madras and Bombay Direct, is a direct absurdity.

Note to Second Edition, 1846

In this Edition, when describing approved projects, minute information regarding capital, distance, &c., has been supplied in foot notes, in compliance with the wishes of those desirous of becoming acquainted with such details; but deeming the Madras and Bombay Direct, and the two schemes which immediately precede it, to be wholly impracticable, such supplemental matter could neither be interesting nor useful so far as they are concerned.

THE MADRAS RAILWAY,

FROM

MADRAS TO WALLAJAHNUGGUR AND ARCOT.*

MORE modest in its ambition than the one which we have just now so freely animadverted upon, the Madras Railway Company only contemplates, for the present at least, a line of seventy miles in length, and which, after careful and accurate surveys, was approved several years ago, as of easy and cheap construction.

The Company for the prosecution of this most legitimate enterprise, is supported both in this country and in India, by the Civil and Military servants of the East India Company, as well as, by some of the leading members of the commercial portion of the community.

This line has all the requisites for an experi-

---

* Length of line 70 miles.

Capital (shares £20 each), £500,000.

The other companies have £50 shares. This latter division of capital appears to require revision. (1846).

mental railroad; the distance is moderate, not exceeding seventy miles, and the country between the termini, may be taken for all practical purposes as a dead level, the rise in seventy miles not exceeding six hundred feet; there is at present a substantial raised road for carts upon the line, which has successfully proved the capability of such a work to withstand the peculiar sources of destructive action enumerated in the Court's minute, as operating against the railway system in India. The termini, are both places of great commercial importance; a large traffic in goods, passengers, troops, and military stores already exists upon the road, and it passes through a fertile and very populous country.

"The construction of a railroad on the Great Western line of communication, between Madras and Bangalore, attracted attention so long ago as the year 1832; in the year 1836 a line in this direction, as far as Wallajahnuggur, was surveyed by an eminent officer in the Madras engineers. The subject was subsequently taken up by a member of the Board of Revenue at Madras, and the construction of a line for the sole purpose of the conveyance of salt from the sea coast, where it is manufactured, to Wallajahnuggur, where the greatest part of the produce of the country westward from Madras is brought upon cattle, which take salt as a return load into the interior of the country, was pressed upon the attention of the local government for its adoption. At a later period, more detailed surveys of this line have been made, and two of them very recently, by officers of engineers who were fully acquainted with all the varieties of construction of railroads in this country, and in America.

"The surveys and estimates of these officers contain the minutest details of the cost of construction of a single line of rails, upon a principle which has been found to be perfectly efficient in America.

"But it is considered, that, however desirable such a construction may be for the feeding lines that connect the thinly peopled and less cultivated tracts of the country; with the main trunk lines, upon which the largest portion of the traffic must always pass, a more substantial method of construction, and one more approaching that found to answer best in Europe, will be required upon the trunk lines, of which that from Madras to Bangalore, is the most important within the Madras territories. The country from Madras to Arcot, however, is so singularly favourable for the construction of a railroad, that the cost of a single line with rails of the dimensions generally used in this country, will not exceed £5,000 a mile; and by fixing the available capital at £500,000, it is considered, that a sufficient fund will be provided to meet all the possible contingencies that can attend the construction of the proposed line.

"The present population of the territories included

in the Presidency of Madras, exceeds 14,000,000. The population of Madras itself, the terminus of the railway, now exceeds 600,000. The line which is now proposed, will pass close to the populous town of Conjeveram, at a distance of forty-five miles from Madras, and through a densely peopled and fertile country the whole way. The principal article of traffic towards the interior, will be salt, for their supplies of which the population inland is entirely dependent on the coast. From Wallajahnuggur the line will communicate with the great cotton and indigo district of Cuddapah-Bellary, and the country towards Hyderabad on the North and West, it will afford facilities for the transport to the coast of the produce of Mysore and North Arcot, consisting of sugar, coffee, betel-nut, lac, potatoes, wheat, oil-seeds, grain of various kinds, charcoal and firewood. Towards the West and South it will facilitate communication with the cotton districts of Salem and Coimbatore; and towards the South with the fertile countries of Trichinopoly and Tanjore. The best cotton that is raised in India is produced in the Madras territories; all that is required to enable it to compete successfully with American cotton is, increased facilities for bringing it to the shipping port of Madras,* in good condition,

* The projected pier at Madras will be a great boon to commerce, and can only be duly estimated by those acquainted with the present expense, delay, difficulty, and danger of landing and shipping goods, from the violence of the surf. (1846).

and at a moderate rate of transport, which can only be effected by a railroad*. The natural capabilities of the Mysore country for the production of the finest sugar and coffee are unlimited; and a cheap and commodious system of transport, is all that is required to develop its resources.

"At present there exists a traffic on this line, of goods alone, amounting to about thirty thousand tons a year, and a hundred and fifty thousand passengers in each direction, which would make a fair return upon the capital. It is impossible to calculate the returns to be expected for the transport of troops, military stores, treasure, and the conveyance of the mails on account of government, but the amount must be considerable. The same consequences must follow the introduction of railroads in India, that have followed elsewhere; and already the results, in every instance, have far exceeded the expectations which the most sanguine speculator would have ventured to form before the opening of the Manchester and Liverpool railway. The system is now but in its infancy in Europe, and its progression hereafter, no one can calculate. The same results must follow, in every instance of the introduction of railways into countries possessing a fertile soil, a

* The Madras rate for conveying government stores by carts, is fivepence-halfpenny per ton per mile. The Madras Railway estimate is twopence per ton per mile. (1846).

good climate, and a numerous and industrious population; and at this moment, there is, probably, no portion of the globe where the introduction of railways will ultimately produce more important results, than the British possessions in India.

"Should the success of the first line which it is contemplated to undertake, warrant the extension of the railroad system throughout the Madras territories, it is the intention of this Company to raise the additional capital that may be required, to proceed in the direction of Cuddapah-Bellary and Hyderabad, North: Mysore, Salem and Trichinopoly, West and South: and to connect the remote provinces with the trunk lines, by branches of less expensive construction, throughout the Madras territories."*

We have no doubt of the ultimate result being favourable, and dismiss the project, wishing it every success.

There is no other scheme connected with Madras, that we are aware of, worthy of notice.

---

* Papers relating to the Madras Railway Company, printed 20th August, 1846.

Some conception of the resources of this portion of the "Golden Peninsula," may be formed from the military means which the single state of Mysore was able to accumulate, under the pressure of a long war. At the peace, the treasure of Tippoo was calculated at eighty millions sterling; he had six hundred thousand stand of arms, two thousand cannons, with a regular force of artillery, cavalry and infantry, of one hundred thousand men, besides hordes of irregular horse. (1846).

GREAT INDIAN PENINSULA RAILWAY,

FROM

BOMBAY TO MHOW, HOSUNGABAD, SHOLAPORE, &c.*

We now proceed to present to our readers' consideration the only railway which Western India boasts of. The presidency of Bombay occupies a most influential position, whether we view its political and military bearings, or estimate its commercial relations; and it has only been for the sake of having some regard to the methodical arrangement of our subject, that we have postponed till this period the mention of a railway, which has for its primary object, the accommodating of Bombay and its subject provinces.

In the magnitude of its ulterior designs it is second

---

* Length of lines, 1,300 miles.

Capital of Company, £6,000,000.

Railroad to be constructed on American plan at an estimated cost of £3,000 to £4,000 per mile. (1846).

to none, and is supported both here, and at the presidency, by gentlemen of wealth and consideration.

However favourably we may be disposed to a great and interesting undertaking, we see it almost at the outset beset with obstacles of no common magnitude. We borrow from Mr. Chapman's* statement the following extracts: "from Bombay to Tannah, at the north-east corner of the island of Salsette, the ground has been carefully examined by Mr. Clark, who is now at Bombay, and whose experience as a railway engineer in England justifies reliance on his opinion. The length of this portion of the line is twenty-eight miles: the ground favourable, and the earth-works light. At Tannah a river of about four hundred yards wide is crossed to gain the main land. So far, there is little choice of the route to be taken, and little of any kind to remark; but from this point the direction to be taken by the main line, must be matter of anxious consideration, and can be finally determined only after careful and extended enquiry."†

"Everybody knows, that at a small distance inland from the western coast of the Peninsula of India, a

---

* The Manager of the Company. (1846).

† "I am able," says Mr. Clarke, "upon actually measured data, to state, that the lines from the foot of the inclined plane to Sion, and I believe I may add to Bombay, a distance of seventy-eight miles, is on the whole favourable."—*Letter by the Local Committee to the Governor of Bombay, June*, 1846.

range of rugged and precipitous mountains, improperly, but generally called the Ghauts, buttresses and defines the table land of the Deccan; between this range and the sea, is a strip of land, called the Concan, low and flat in the valleys, but much intersected, and encumbered with transverse offsets from the great range. The highest points of the Ghauts rise to the elevatino of above four thousand feet, and the face of the range towards the sea, presents little but precipitous walls, or impracticable slopes. In a few places, however, the crest is cleft down to the level of the inland plain, that is, about two thousand feet above the sea, and a transverse spur at the same place, jutting westward into the Concan, affords the means of ascending to it, though commonly not without considerable difficulty and labour."

"The ascent of the Ghauts is always spoken of as the great difficulty on this line, and the chief objection to it. The description of the Malsejee Ghaut* just given from official papers, may properly serve to diminish the force of any fears on the subject: nevertheless, the climbing of these celebrated heights by mechanical means, will still remain a most interesting practical problem. If it can be accomplished by means already in use, and suitable to the circumstances of the case, it will be better to do so, than to incur the cost,

* See Mr. Chapman's printed statement. (1846).

risk, and delay of new contrivances; if, however, such be not at our disposal, I do not speak by guess in saying, that the requisite devices will not be wanting."

From the top of the Ghaut to a considerable distance the country is open and level, although as we proceed, the cultivated fields are displaced by jungle, and the villages are far apart, and in some instances deserted.

But the soil is naturally rich and admirably adapted to the cultivation of cotton, the great staple of this portion of India. The people are most industrious, and only want efficient roads to enable them to send their goods to market, to make the elevated region of the Deccan vie with the rich plains of Bengal in productive power. At present, this portion of India is alike discreditable to the British and the native rulers. From the feeble, and almost bankrupt government of the Nizam, only formidable to its defenceless peasantry, nothing can be expected but that its provinces should gradually, from the grinding exactions of its officials, return to the deadly and primeval wilderness, and that its deserted villages should be tenanted by noxious reptiles and beasts of prey. But the wretched government of the Nizam is fast drawing to a close, when the fields will be regenerated, and the voice of man heard again in the villages, under a rule at once strong and beneficent. This has ever been the case on a transfer from Native to British authority, with the exception of that portion of the Deccan already in our possession, and why we have held back our hand from extending the usual blessings of our rule and opening the resources of the country, by some attempt, however imperfect, at improving the means of communication, is to be sought for, in the great difficulty of making roads in the Deccan from the nature of the soil, men and horses sinking knee deep in its black and slimy loam.

The Bombay government have frequently projected roads, but as the revenue of this government sometimes falls short of the expenditure, the balance being defrayed from the surplus revenue of Bengal, the reason is obvious, why beyond protection to life and property, we have little at present to offer the refugees who cross our border. With moderately good roads or a railway, we should reclaim fertile fields from the jungle, clothe and feed a disheartened and most industrious people, reaping in return a more prosperous revenue, and additional security to our possessions. Duty, true policy, beneficence and self-interest the strongest plea of all, we fear, centre for once in one point, and urge upon us the necessity of improved intercourse in the west of India. The hardship which the poor people of the Deccan suffer in bringing their cotton to market, is scarcely to be credited, and is graphically described by Mr. Williamson, late Revenue Commissioner, Bombay, in his second letter to Lord Wharncliffe. This letter, and another by the same gentleman, we strongly recommend to the attentive perusal of all interested in the welfare of India, confining ourselves to an extract or two.

"But there is *one* mode of promoting internal improvement which has been tried more or less in most provinces in India, and which I will venture to say has in no single instance been found to fail—I allude to the improvement of internal communication. As far as my experience in India goes, no road has ever been constructed without an immediate, and almost magical effect on the prosperity of the town with which it communicates, and yet the extent of the new road annually opened in the whole of the Western Presidency of India, is not beyond what would be deemed requisite in a single county in England.

"The consequence is, that the cotton which might travel the whole distance to the sea-coast, on carts along the made road, at the rate of six bullock loads on a cart drawn by two bullocks, twelve miles per diem, now creeps the greater part of the distance six loads on six separate pack bullocks, only eight miles per diem. As a proof on this new line of the effect of improving roads I may mention the instance of the Bhore Ghaut.

"When this pass was first made practicable to wheeled carriages about the year 1828, the tolls realised between £400 and £500 a year. Twelve years ago a speculator was ruined by farming them from government for £1,000. They now annually let at £3,000 or £4,000 per annum, so that in four years, besides providing for the expense of annual repairs, the tolls now more than cover the original cost of constructing the road."

This line is proposed to be made cautiously according to the encouragement held out, and should it advance so far as Nagpore, 508 miles E.N.E. of Bombay (close to Kamptee, the most central military position in India,) it will proceed either to Calcutta, or what is more probable, join the great East India trunk line at Mirzapore, which is 890 miles E.N.E. of Bombay.

This latter arrangement would give us our intelligence from Upper India and Bengal a week earlier than at present, and in conjunction with the trunk line from Calcutta to Delhi, would enable the combined armies of the two presidencies, to concentrate their powers on almost any point of our dominions that could by possibility be threatened. This enterprise will for the present curb its ambition, till it has solved the difficult problem of climbing the Ghauts.* This would of itself be a great achievement, and of incalculable advantage to the presidency.†

* The Americans have ascended the Alleghany mountains, a height of 1398 feet, and at a very moderate cost, by means of fixed engines. (1846).

† A letter, under date June, 1846, addressed by the Committee in Bombay to the Governor of that Presidency, has the following

The Directors of this project will, we have no doubt, watch over the interests of their shareholders, and secure to them, if a concession be obtained, such a guarantee, as shall preclude the possibility of loss. We do not think, however, that it will be one of the first lines authorised to be made, for its success in a

---

extract from the Engineers' Report of the actual ascent of the Malsej Ghât.

"The whole plane will be in length 31,000 feet, and its total descent 1,718 feet; giving an average gradient under one in nineteen, which average is obtained very nearly throughout, and never exceeded to a greater extent than one in fifteen. The plane has two curves, one 7,400, the other 16,900 feet from the summit; each is in length 800 feet, and of 5,000 feet radius. The plane, therefore, may be considered practically as straight. The earthworks required, will be chiefly tunnelling and open gallery. It is difficult to draw the line exactly between the two, but in round numbers it may be stated, that there will be 10,400 feet of tunnelling in eight lengths, and 5,100 feet of gallery, passing rather close to, or within from ten to thirty feet of the face of the slopes. The excavations are in excess of the embankments and are conveniently placed for their formation. The lead throughout will be trifling. The material to be excavated is either rock or moorum; the former is much fissured; the latter soft and easily worked. Both, however, there is reason to believe, to be sufficiently firm to stand in the tunnels without artificial support. The masonry will be light, and composed almost wholly of culverts. The quantity of water that will flow under the line during each rainy season, is considerable; but owing to the scarred and broken character of the ground, the water-courses are very numerous, and the force and volume of any one stream not considerable." (1846).

commercial point of view is certainly problematical in comparison with the Great Western of Bengal, or any portion of the great trunk line between Allahabad and the Sutlej. We, however, heartily recommend the Great Indian Peninsula to the protection of a wise and paternal government.*

Having passed in review before us, the various schemes for railway communication in India, and having given our opinion, founded, as we conscientiously believe, on sound data, or upon what we have seen, or known ourselves—we feel, that we have discharged the grave and onerous duty which we proposed, and we now resume for a few moments our general remarks.

---

* "Should an arrangement at any future time be concluded for the passage of troops through Egypt, the importance of the Great Indian Peninsula Railway would be vastly increased, for, as a glance at the map will show, it would then form a portion of the steam communication by which our troops would be most speedily conveyed from England to almost any part of India. And even with our present limited means of transport through Egypt, officers joining their regiments, might often save many weeks in reaching their destination. This becomes a point of immense importance in any emergency, such as has twice occurred within the last four years, when all officers belonging to the army in India, and absent on leave in Europe, were by one order required to join their regiments without delay."—*Letters addressed to The Right Honourable Lord Wharncliffe by T. Williamson, Esq., C. S., late Revenue Commissioner, Bombay.* (1846).

SUGGESTIONS

AS TO THE

MODE OF INTRODUCING THE RAILWAY SYSTEM INTO INDIA.

It has been stated, we think without due consideration, that "it cannot signify to the government (who must derive considerable benefit from the measure under any circumstances) which line may be first completed." From this opinion we entirely dissent, as it is obviously the interest of the Government, as well as that of the people, and the Shareholders, that the first line opened should be the one of all others, possessing the highest political and commercial advantages combined with the greatest facilities for construction, the most moderate expenditure, and the best adapted for being an integral portion of a great whole. Railway experience and expenditure at home, will point out the propriety of having, before a single sod is turned, a general outline of the system which is hereafter to pervade India, laid out and defined, and thus guard against the disappointment and confusion which would necessarily ensue, from the injudicious selection of an isolated scheme, having reference only to a particular locality.

But even when the general outline of this system has been, after mature deliberation, decided upon, we repeat, that it is the interest of all parties, that the first line or section opened, should be the one of all others possessing the most important advantages, combined with the greatest facilities for construction and the most moderate expenditure, for it is obvious, that according to the success or otherwise of the first line, so will the general introduction of railway intercommunication into a new country, be accelerated or retarded. "But besides as a railway is so superior to all other means of communication, that it must necessarily supersede them, and confers the greatest advantages on the localities through which it passes, it becomes of greater consequence that the lines for railways should be wisely selected, and that railway companies should not be suffered, by any injudicious choice, to inflict injury, either on the public in general, or on the owners of property. That these subjects were not at first sufficiently attended to in this country, can hardly be a matter of surprise, when we reflect on the ignorance with respect to the nature of the change about to be effected by the new power thus brought into action, which then generally prevailed."*

Confident, from the successful result of the first experiment, the Government would have no difficulty in extending its patronage and support to new undertakings, and capitalists would eagerly contend for the prize of gain in the vast and magnificent fields of the East. Instead of losing their money in foreign loans, or enriching with railroads, Holland, Belgium, or France, by their superfluous wealth transmitted to India, under the guarantee of their native government, they would at once enrich themselves, ameliorate the condition of their distant fellow subjects, and indirectly, but surely, add to the dignity and wealth of their own country; giving to the mechanic and labourer of India, such employment as would speedily open up new markets and outlets for the products of the industrial energies of our home artisan, and add incalculably to the security and strength of our Eastern dominions. Thus the two countries would act and re-act upon each other to their mutual benefit.

Much depends upon the character of the line first completed.

Suppose, for example, a long line to be selected, no matter how direct, or how great the mart it led to, for

---

* Railway Acts.—*Second Report.*

the result will be effected by what it goes *through*, and not by what it goes *to*.* Suppose such a line for one-half of its course to traverse a barren country, in many places covered with almost interminable jungle and totally uninhabited, beset with physical difficulties of the most gigantic description—there could be but one result, and that result fraught with disappointment to the government, the entire loss of the capital embarked, and the postponement for an indefinite number of years to India, of the inestimable boon of improved intercommunication.

Unacquainted with India himself, the English capitalist looks to those placed in authority and acquainted with the country, to act with a just and discriminating vigilance in making the first move in the right direction; and those in authority will not disappoint this reasonable expectation. It might have been hoped that the railway commissioners would have cleared the way to a satisfactory decision on this subject, with an authority derivable from the soundness of the views

---

* Mr. Peto states in evidence before Mr. Morrison's committee, that the experience of Belgium furnishes a striking corroboration of the soundness of these views, as it has been proved by the report of M. Desart, in whose hands the Belgium government placed the whole of its railway statistics, that in a given population, the traffic of the small towns and villages along a line is proportionally greater than the traffic between two large cities at the termini."—*Railway Acts. Second Report.* (1846).

enunciated, the variety of new and interesting data—the prestige of office and acknowledged ability. But their report, beyond giving an official sanction to railroads in general, sheds no new light on the question at issue; long, without being comprehensive, elaborate, without supplying any data to arrive at practical results, giving no estimates of cost, or specifications, or traffic tables, even leaving to private enterprise the decision, (with one exception) of whether this or that line should be ultimately adopted. The commissioners instructed "to suggest some feasible line of moderate length," the principal portion of their report is devoted to recommending the adoption of a railroad of four hundred and fifty miles in length, through the most difficult, most unproductive, and most desolate portion of a country, elsewhere easy, fertile, and densely peopled.

The grand object, both for the government and the merchant to attain is, to connect Calcutta with the N. W. Frontier, and there can be no great difference of opinion as to the direction of the line from Mirzapore through the Doab to the banks of the Sutlej; this at once disposes of nearly two-thirds of the entire length of the grand trunk line; but as to the best mode of connecting Calcutta with Mirzapore, there are two, if not three, opinions enunciated, and it is to be borne in mind that this portion of the line, besides commencing at the metropolis of British India, traverses the provinces of Bengal and Behar, the revenues of which we have already shown equal those of the whole of the remaining British territories in India, yielding a surplus of £4,000,000 annually, a portion of which flows from India to our shores, and the rest enables us to improve, consolidate and defend other and more remote regions in the East, naturally less productive. It also ought to be borne in mind with regard to the vast descending trade of the Ganges, that but a small proportion of the produce brought from the interior of the country comes from above Mirzapore. Notwithstanding these facts, the railway commission recommend a direct line, merely because it is a direct line. They state that the summit level of the country gives a rise of eight hundred feet, and that assistant power will be requisite to work the trains, the Soane river will have to be crossed by a bridge, the foundation to be sought for, below "an unknown depth of sand." This bridge, or viaduct would equal in all its dimensions those of the Greenwich Railway. The natural barriers to be surmounted are composed of primitive, transition, and secondary rocks, generally of the most obdurate and impenetrable class: such as granite, greenstone and basalt.

But even if the direct line was not beset with almost every variety of physical obstacle, it would be inexpedient from the poverty of the country, diversified at long intervals by a little cultivation, and scarcely animated by human beings.

The report in para. 43, states that a great part of the country in its route—till very lately—"was abandoned to the beasts of the forest."

It is obvious that reliance is placed on the exploded theory of through traffic being the chief support of a railroad, and it is equally obvious to those acquainted with railway statistics that nothing can be more fallacious than such reliance. M. Desart, Inspector of Belgian state railways, has reduced the rates of traffic to a system, and proves that the large return expected from connecting by a railway two great commercial cities, is not realized if they are beyond a certain distance; but is absolutely certain to be drawn from a line binding together a succession of minor towns and villages, and we have no doubt but that this mode of calculation will be found of universal application.*

---

* "The statement worked out from the government traffic returns, established beyond all doubt the following principle, viz.: That the number of passengers between two towns connected by a railway does not depend only on the population or commercial importance of these towns, but most materially on the distance between them. Thus, the number of passengers will be greater on a line connecting a succession of small towns and villages, situated as they generally are in England and Belgium, than on a line of equal length connecting two large towns."—*Extract from the Half-yearly Report of the Directors of the West Flanders Railway, July 3rd,* 1846.

For further information, see the work of M Desart, the government engineer and divisional inspector, recently printed. (1846).

The branches of such a direct line would be crushed and paralyzed in a vain rivalry with the steamers and river craft in their efforts to divert to a new, and to nearly all the important seats of commerce, circuitous route, the great descending trade of the Ganges, and as the chief portion of this trade proceeds from points below Mirzapore, it would certainly not ascend the stream to arrive at that terminus; so that the trunk line would remain for many years unproductive to the shareholders, and useless to the state, with occasional exceptions, for nearly all the emergent movements of troops and stores take place in the Upper Provinces.

The second mode of commencing the railroad system in India indicated to us, is from some point on the west bank of the Hooghly to Monghyr on the Ganges. This line is declared by competent authority to be perfectly practicable, and as it would leave behind it a much smaller portion of the valley of the Ganges, and therefore take up much more of the trade brought down to the Ganges by the great rivers flowing from the lower ranges of the Himalayahs, it would from this cause and the comparative cheapness of its construction be much more likely to be commercially remunerative: but this line, although superior to the former in cheapness of construction, in shortness and in traffic, would still be an expensive line, the summit level not being less than 800 or 900 feet, having to avoid in its route hills higher than any of those in England or

Wales, and to bridge from 30 to 40 streams of various dimensions. This line is not calculated to be an integral portion of a great and harmonious system; as a trunk line it is neither the most direct nor the easiest route to the N. W. Frontier, nor that possessing the greatest through traffic; and taken *per se*, it gives nearly 300 miles of railroad, without supplying a single town or station of the least magnitude, if we except Burdwan, between its termini; and for many miles having to encounter the difficult, pestilential, jungle covered hills of Rajmahl and Bhaugulpore; so that the Monghyr line is at once deficient in all the requirements of an experimental line, either for introducing internal communication on an extended scale, or meeting the wants of a particular district; like the Mirzapore direct line, it shuns the city and withdraws from the rich and populous plain, to cultivate the wilderness, and stimulate its scattered, squalid, and poverty-stricken inhabitants to agricultural, commercial and locomotive activity.

The line from Calcutta on the Hooghly to Rajmahl on the Ganges appears to us to possess every requisite claim to immediate selection by government—the ground has been surveyed with great minuteness by their own officers, it follows the old and beaten track of commerce,* through a rich and densely-

* It has been observed in every age, that when any branch of commerce has got into a certain channel, although it may be

peopled country, and completely outflanks the Rajmahl and Bhaugulpore hills, its upper terminus at the lowest practicable point on the river, and close to where the navigation is at all seasons either difficult or dangerous, and for nine months in the year most vexatiously circuitous, the advantages of this line are fully admitted in the report of the Railway Commission, and were minutely detailed by us on a former occasion. But in treating the subject generally as in this section, it is important to recollect that when comparing the merits of different projects, that a railroad having Calcutta for one terminus and some point on the Ganges for the other, the traffic will be in an inverse ratio to the length of the line, that is, the further a line is carried up, before it debouches upon that great commercial artery, the less would be the traffic.

---

neither the most proper nor the most commodious one, it requires long time, and considerable efforts, to give it a different direction." *Historical Disquisition regarding Ancient India, by G. W. Robertson, D.D., F.R.S.*

"It will be found that all the successful railways in England are on those lines where communication existed before."—*Report on the Application of Railway Communication in India, by Captain Western, Bengal Engineers, published in the Calcutta papers in March*, 1843.*

---

* This able officer is now a member of the railway commission in India. (1846).

The line from Calcutta to Rajmahl, besides being unexceptionable, *per se*,* is a line that must be made, if railroads are to be made in India, either as the principal trunk, or as the most important branch that any trunk can possess; its merits in the latter and subordinate capacity, are, as just stated, fully admitted in the report of the railway commissioners. But the published report of one of those commissioners in 1843 is decidedly in favour of a trunk line to Mirzapore, by Rajmahl and the Gangetic valley, and the opinions of eminent mercantile and scientific men transmitted from India by the very last mails, are in favour of the Rajmahl line being gradually extended up this great, fertile, and populous valley.

We have already stated our decided preference for

---

* "That this line of country affords every facility for forming a railway, will, I think, be allowed by every one acquainted with it. It is only necessary to state, that from Calcutta to Rajmahl, a distance of two hundred miles, it passes through the Delta of the Ganges, and that in the survey undertaken under the superintendence of General Macleod and Major Forbes, with a view to construct a canal from Rajmahl to the Hooghly river, it was ascertained that the fall in the distance of one hundred and twenty-eight miles proposed for the canal was only fifty feet, as will be seen in the report by those officers of the 15th February, 1841; and as there are no difficulties in the way of high lands for the canal to contend with, none need be anticipated for a line of railroad."—*Report on the Application of Railway Communication in India, by Captain Western* (1846).

that plan of commencing improved transit, which would only supersede the river navigation where it was most defective, and co-operate with it where it was always available, *i.e.* a railroad from Calcutta to deep water in the Ganges at Rajmahl—from this point, river steamers to Allahabad, at the confluence of the Jumna and Ganges, where deep water ceases—and a railroad from Allahabad to Delhi and the Sutlej.

This would itself be nearly one thousand miles of railroad, exclusive of branches, traversing the easiest, the richest and most densely-peopled portions of our dominions where the river transit is either dangerous or tedious, as by the Nuddeah rivers and Sunderbunds, or only applicable to the smaller country craft, and closed entirely to steamers, as the great rivers are beyond Allahabad. Above this point it is impossible, by land or by water, to move military stores or merchandize, in any quantity, beyond the average rate of twelve miles per diem. No Eutopian ideas of a railroad system starting at once into complete perfectibility, should divert enterprise and capital from so fair and inviting a field, with such feeble rivals, (as the native carts and smaller river crafts) to compete with steamers accomplishing fifty miles per diem, and they will soon nearly double that rate, when a railroad relieves them from the Nuddeah rivers and Sunderbunds.

"If such a rail be established, the steamers instead of starting from Calcutta, will start from its Northern terminus, which will thus become in fact the steam port of Calcutta. The narrow and often angular streams in the Sunderbunds, and lower Bengal will thus be avoided, the necessity of a double vessel will cease, single vessels of larger dimensions and engines of greater power may then be employed, by which a large saving of time and money will be effected.

"The advantages of such a line in every point of view are sufficient to recommend it to public favour."*

---

* *Friend of India, 19th February,* 1846.—"The Friend" alludes to the Bogwangolah line, which, on account of its terminus, being a shifting village (as stated in the First Edition of this Pamphlet) has been reported against, the preference being given by the commissioners to Rajmahl, some miles higher up the river, because it was stationary, and this being settled by authority, no doubt the Friend will give his voice also in favour of a fixed port, instead of a migratory one. Some of the companies have for their passengers and goods, a flat in tow of the steamer, this explains what the Friend means by two vessels. In his paper of the 14th of May last, the Friend informs us, that a splendid new steamer, the "Patna," will make the voyage by the Sunderbunds from Calcutta to Allahabad in ten days, provided she does not stick in the Sunderbundes, which would be at the rate of a little more than a hundred and eighteen miles daily; the whole distance being 1,186. The distance from Rajmahl to Allahabad being only five hundred miles, the same steamer travelling at the same rate, would reach the latter station in four days and a quarter. The two land journeys being six hundred miles, would, at a very moderate rate of railway speed, be performed in twenty-four hours—thus allowing nine hours at each terminus, viz.; Rajmahl and Allahabad for the removal of passengers' baggage and goods,

After having supplied the regions indicated, the two lines might gradually approach each other as circumstances rendered it desirable or necessary.

It now remains to state the comparative merits of the two modes of completing the trunk line by filling up the interval. The more direct from Burdwan to Mirzapore has been already described and objected to, the other from Rajmahl by all the various populous cities in the fertile valley of the Ganges we describe in the words of the railway commissioner, Captain Western :—"from Rajmahl along the banks of the Ganges, with the exception of one point where a shoot from the Rajmahl hills extends into the Ganges at Siclygully, no difficulty occurs; indeed the only engineering difficulties at all would be the passage of the rivers, and these I trust would soon be shown not to be insurmountable, for it has already been proposed to build bridges over the rivers Jumna and Ganges at Delhi, Agra, Allahabad and Benares; and plans and estimates for a masonry bridge across the Jumna at Delhi were in preparation when I was at that station; besides, the bridges could be built of sufficient width to allow of the construction of another road alongside the portion marked off for

---

which is surely more than sufficient for every purpose, the entire distance from Calcutta to Delhi may be accomplished, according to "the Friend," in six or seven days. (1840).

the rails, for the passage of the ordinary traffic of the country."

The table at the foot of the page,* carefully prepared from the *dâk* (post) routes, shows the relative distances by the two lines. The actual length of the line to Mirzapore by the valley of the Ganges would be about one hundred miles more than by the direct route, but to make the latter of any commercial utility it would require several branches of great length, which would act as feeders to the trunk line, but fail to accommodate the great intermediate traffic, and it will be seen that going to any intermediate point, Patna, for instance, the difference is very trifling, while the

---

* DIRECT LINE TO MIRZAPORE.

		Miles.
Calcutta to Burdwan		75
Burdwan to Shirgotty		216
Shirgotty to Chunar		137
Chunar to Mirzapore		22
		450
Add for Branches—		
Burdwan to Rajmahl	120	
Shirgotty to Patna	80	
,, to Raj. Ghat. (on the Ganges opposite to Benares)	17	
		217
Total		667

GANGETIC VALLEY LINE.

	Miles.
Calcutta to Rajmahl	178
Rajmahl to Monghyr	105
Monghyr to Patna	102
Patna to Benares	138
Benares to Mirzapore	26
Total	549

(1846).

facilities for constructing the line by the valley would be great, as it could be commenced at all the stations simultaneously, the river being available for carrying the material of the road to so many points; the internal traffic also between the various towns on the route would form no immaterial portion of the receipts of this line.

Another very material point would be the difference in expense of the two lines—On the direct line we are assured the summit level gives a rise of eight hundred feet at several points, while the other, for all engineering purposes, is a level almost throughout. Those well entitled to give an opinion, state that the cost of the one would be, per mile, twice as much as that of the other.

The railway commissioners have reported in favour of the direct Mirzapore line, the principal commissioner not having seen, or at all events not having surveyed any other, but it would be much to be lamented, were there to be a postponement of the court's decision till there was a fresh survey, as there can be but one opinion regarding the Rajmahl line, and the one from Allahabad to Delhi, and the comparative merits of the two routes to Mirzapore can be tested while these are in progress of construction.

Although the direct Calcutta and Mirzapore line shows a gain of about one hundred miles in its lineal distance over that of the Rajmahl and Gangetic valley, considering the relative distance in a mechanical point of view, we shall find that but a very slight difference really exists.

We are informed by the commissioners in the 27th section of their report, that the gradients on the former line will be so steep as to require assistant power to work the trains, and we know from the undulatory nature of the country between Burdwan and Mirzapore that a heavy working line will necessarily occur, requiring a considerable expenditure of power to maintain a given velocity: whereas the line by the valley of the Ganges, outflanking the hills, will have no difficulties to encounter, if we except a portion of the route between Rajmahl and Bhaugulpore—the inclination of the country being about twelve inches per mile; of necessity, therefore, the line will approach nearly to a level. If we suppose the gross weight of load propelled on both lines to be the same, and we take the amount of power expended in travelling over both lines to maintain a given velocity; and if, then, the relative amounts be spread over a level plane in both instances, we shall find that the increased expenditure due to the more steep and undulatory line from Calcutta to Mirzapore would produce an equivalent line of level nearly equal to that of the more level line by the Gangetic Valley, hence the mechanical distance and the comparative time occupied in making the journey on either line will be nearly the same.

The gain in time by the shorter line, if any, would be too inconsiderable to be taken into account in a country where time occupied in travelling is estimated by months instead of hours, or to be a just compensation for so great an amount of expenditure.

Before concluding this important section, we return for a few moments to the projects intended to carry out the grand desideratum of connecting Calcutta with the N.W. Frontier, when it will be seen which are the best adapted to achieve this object with the smallest expenditure of time and money.

The East India line (from Calcutta to Mirzapore) declining all co-operation with the river, would do this in a slow and most expensive manner,* if allowed to carry its plans into effect, and be entirely dependent on the through traffic between the termini.

The Great Western (from Calcutta to Rajmahl) and the line from Allahabad to Delhi passing many towns and villages, and taking advantage of the river navigation where it is available, (instead of superseding, would stimulate corresponding improvements in the river) would, at half the cost, and in one quarter of the time, supply this now indispensable desideratum.

---

* "The lower half, from Calcutta to Mirzapore, costing considerably above that average (the average cost of the railway from Calcutta to Delhi), and the other half, from Mirzapore to Delhi, as much below it." *Report of Railway Commission*, para. 64. (1846).

By adopting the river from Rajmahl to Allahabad the average cost of construction would be reduced one-half, as that portion between Burdwan and Allahabad which comprises all the difficulties, would not be included in the general estimate for a complete communication between Calcutta and the Sutlej, and the outlay would be saved for making four hundred miles of railway through a barren, desolate and difficult country.

On the whole, then, it is our conviction that the Great Western of Bengal (from Calcutta to Rajmahl) and the line from Allahabad to Delhi, co-operating with fleets of river steamers, from Rajmahl to Allahabad, would at once be not only the most judicious, the easiest, the least costly, the soonest constructed, and in every other point of view the most advantageous mode of introducing the railway system into India—but most probably the only practicable mode that is at present before government.

The subjoined extract from a letter of General Macleod, late Chief Engineer, Bengal, published in the "Friend of India" of March 19th, 1846, stamps our views with real and solid value.

"I think the line proposed from Calcutta to Rajmahl a vast improvement and a very rational scheme. The soil is excellent the whole way, and the surveys of that part of the country already so minutely taken as regards levels, and eveyrthing else required, that they may commence making their plans at once.

"I should certainly take a great interest in the line, as I do think it the most eligible that could be thought of, and one that would form a most important benefit to the country. The next best line in my opinion will be that from Allahabad to Delhi.

"I do not know that I can afford the Directors any great extent of information, but I shall be glad to give them all I possess."

It has been already stated that this eminent and experienced engineer officer, is now Chairman of the Great Western of Bengal Railway Company, whose project is to connect Calcutta with Rajmahl.*

---

* "We know of no measure more calculated to strengthen the power of the British government in India, or more likely to exercise a beneficial effect over the people of Hindostan than the introduction of railway communication. In Europe the invention of steam power has been attended with the happiest results to large masses of people, and it is generally observed that indications of progressive improvement are no where so visible as in those places which are accessible to the immediate influence of steam communication. Thus, as in times of yore by the application of the philosopher's stone, it was supposed that all things would be turned into gold, so in the present day, by the happy introduction of steam, it is found that barbarism becomes converted into civilization, barrenness into fertility, poverty into wealth. What then may the philanthropist not hope for the people of India, when he learns that the Court of Directors are about to investigate the applicability of railway communication to this country? For this purpose, they propose associating two or three eminent engineers, who are to report upon the subject, and who are to suggest some feasible line of moderate length as an

experiment. If this trial should prove successful, we may expect in a few years to see lines of railroads traversing the whole country; but if, on the other hand, it should prove a failure, India will sink back into lethargy still greater than that in which it now sleeps; and the march of civilization will be retarded instead of advanced. It is, therefore, most important, that the first trial should be made under such circumstances as would most probably insure success; and too much care cannot be taken in selecting that line which holds out the greatest political advantages to government, and which promises the best return to the capitalist." —*Delhi Overland Gazette.*

In addition to promoting internal communication, the introduction of railroads may be easily made to subserve agricultural purposes, by the formation of tanks where ground is required for embankments, and by the conveyance of water along the different lines; thus irrigation, the *sine qua non* of farming in the East, might be greatly extended, and those frequently recurring famines, in particular districts, arising from the want of water, would be either averted, or much alleviated.

Besides, annihilating the hopes of the farmer the deprivation or diminution in the supply of this necessary of life in the scorching climate of India, is the frequent and immediate cause of dreadful misery and mortality.

The author has to thank Mr. Williamson for a copy of his letter on this subject, and the courteous note which accompanied it.

For further information see *Letter on Irrigation, by T. Williamson, Esq., late Revenue Commissioner, Bombay, addressed to Lord Wharncliffe.* (1846).

GENERAL MANAGEMENT

AND

TERMS OF CONCESSION.

THREE propositions suggest themselves as to the policy to be adopted, and agencies to be employed in the formation of railways in a new country.

1st.—That they be, with certain restrictions and provisions, left to unfettered and unaided private enterprise, as has been hitherto the case in this country.

2nd.—That the government itself should project and define a great and comprehensive system, as well as execute and work the lines most apparently conducive to the common weal as in Belgium.

3rd.—That the government should grant concessions or leases of various sections, or particular projects, to private companies on such terms as might be mutually advantageous: the latter to have the execution of the works, and the management of the traffic of the lines, under the direct supervision and control of officers appointed by the government, as has been practised in France, and more recently in Belgium.

Judging from the confusion which has arisen in this country, by giving the reins to speculative enterprise, the crude and angular manner in which railways were commenced in France, and the harmonious and beneficent manner in which the Belgium system has resulted, there appears to be little doubt but that it is the most effective and rapid mode of introducing railways into a country. We would, however, from financial considerations, deviate so far from this example as to give, after defining the line, the concession to a private company, for Belgium had to borrow money at five per cent. to make railroads, which did not till very lately yield more than two and a half per cent., and Pennsylvania, which in 1824 was bitten with the improvement mania, "believed, and truly, that a system of inland communication by means of canals and railroads would tend to increase her prosperity. She believed that the annual income of these public works would not only pay the interest on the first cost, but would leave a liberal overplus for public purposes." What was the result? The state, after having spent millions, wisely gave away the works in an unfinished condition to companies of private individuals, on condition that they would finish them. "In addition to this, the favouritism and peculation inseparable from government patronage and expenditure, served to swell the costs of these works to a most disastrous extent. The consequence was, that in 1841 or 1842 the state was forty millions in debt. State lines can neither be worked with the same economy, nor can they have imparted to them, that impulse which the spirit of private enterprise alone can give."

Regarding the management of the different companies it has been suggested that an amalgamation of the lines would be recommended or enjoined by authority. An amalgamation of interests we think essential, so as to remove all fear of competition, which would, at present, be both premature and injurious, and by allotting to each of the companies (their priority and claims to public confidence being duly considered) a certain portion of the several approved projects, all tending to produce an uniform and harmonious system, they would mutually co-operate and stimulate each other to bring their respective tasks to a speedy and satisfactory conclusion;* and when concluded, the different managements would be a check upon each other and a mutual aid by their several ex-

* The Great Western of Bengal might be required to complete the line to Rajmahl, and the East India and Great North of India to proceed conjointly with the line from Allahabad to Delhi and the Sutlej. (1846).

periences; by a friendly rivalry they would endeavour to meet the requirements of the government, the accommodation of the public, and the interests of their shareholders; while the different boards could, by acting in concert, either by exchanging directors, or amicable adjustment, establish a uniform tariff for passengers and goods, so essential to the working of a continuous line of railway; the proceedings of all the boards being under the supervision and controlling power of officers appointed by the India government.

It is now generally admitted that although, theoretically, unity is strength, yet that the practical effect of amalgamation carried beyond a certain point, is rather detrimental than otherwise to the management of working railroads, and that all the benefits derivable from unity of action are secured to the public, by the clearing house system of the bankers of Lombardy transplanted to this country and elsewhere, and now applied with as perfect success to the interchange and re-adjustment of railroad carriages and trucks, as to bank notes and cheques. Should it, however, be considered that the traffic in India, so simple in its nature, and likely to continue so for many years, would be in any degree retarded or encumbered by having several boards of Directors, it must certainly be conceded that there ought to be both in London and in India a separate management for each presidency, but all acting under a common code of laws and regulations to be settled by authority, and when the three distinct systems of Bengal, Madras and Bombay begin to approximate and interlace, then the exchange of directors or the formation of a sub-committee, composed of the chairmen of the three companies, would answer the purpose of imparting a uniformity of action to all. The latter mode would facilitate and simplify the necessary correspondence with the authorities, or officers appointed by them to supervise the proceedings of the several railway companies.

That the Boards in London should consist of those acquainted, and in some degree, identified with the particular Presidency they propose to traverse with railroads is evidently most desirable, and that they should receive the active co-operation of capitalists and merchants of acknowledged status and business habits, is equally apparent.* On this point Mr. Arbuthnot

* "In surveying the vast extent of territory embraced by the British dominions in India, with a view to the introduction of railroads into that country, it would appear obvious, that the local demarcations which have been found convenient in the administration of the Indian government, should be kept in view. In raising the capital required to carry these undertakings into execution, it will be necessary that the directions of the companies which may be formed in the country, should contain a large proportion of gentlemen possessed of local knowledge and experience in that part of India which is to form the scene of their operations; and in this view of the case, it seems natural that, for the more efficient working of such projects, a separate board should be

makes the following judicious observations. "It appeared farther to those parties who took an interest in the subject here, that the conduct of associations for introducing railways into the different localities required in India, would be much more efficiently discharged, were they to be undertaken by parties personally conversant with the different localities, aided by the co-operation of gentlemen in this country more conversant with English modes of transacting business, than gentlemen who have passed a great part of their lives in India can be expected to be."*

The local knowledge of the one would guard against an injudicious selection of a line, and the known wealth and business habits of the other would impart to the association strength and efficiency; with such a combination the English shareholder would feel assured that his capital was judiciously and safely embarked,

---

formed in this country, for the organisation of railway operations within each of the presidencies of Bengal, Madras, and Bombay, to act in conjunction with local committees at the Indian Presidencies; each of such boards in England to contain such a proportion as may be thought desirable of parties qualified by residence and local knowledge of the different Presidencies to afford useful advice and correct information upon the subjeets brought before them."—*Prospectus Madras Railway.*

* Letter of J. A. Arbuthnot, Esq., Chairman of Madras Railway Company, to the Chairman and Committee of the Chamber of Commerce, Madras.

and turned to the best account that the circumstances of the undertaking admitted of.

That the energies of capitalists require the guidance of local knowledge is very apparent, from one powerful company having identified itself with a project generally believed now to be impracticable on account of the vast outlay necessary to carry its designs into execution, and the appearance of another association, still more powerful, formed for the purpose of making a railroad to a shifting village, which, every now and then transplants itself to the extent of some miles, according to the caprice of the river. This latter scheme (the Northern and Eastern) has been formally condemned by the Railway Commission in Para. 19 of the report; nevertheless the prospectus has been published in Calcutta, and we are informed that the promoters are only biding their time to take the English capitalists by storm.*

---

* "All the objects, as appears to us, of the Northern and Eastern are, or may be, comprised in the larger views of the Great Western Company. And probably it (The Northern and Eastern) will have to alter its plan as respects its Upper terminus (Bhogwangola) as the course of the river hereabouts is so uncertain that one year the company might find itself, rails and godowns (warehouses), in the bed of the river; another year, some miles distant from the channel where the craft would have to unship their cargoes,"—*Calcutta Review for March*, 1846.

"The great mart at Bhogwangola is of so unfixed a character,

The representatives in India of the different companies, having a deputed authority should always remain subordinate to, and removable by the London Boards. The propriety of this is universally admitted in India; the organisation of its society, its state of transition, and the experience of the past, appear to render such an arrangement indispensably necessary. On this point the Calcutta Review of March last remarks, "We regard it as a principle universally applicable to all proprietary institutions, that those who supply the capital should have either the management or an effectual voice in the management, and this principle has generally been acted upon; even Indian companies scarcely possess an exception. The affairs of the East India Company itself, when it was merely a commercial body, were exclusively managed by the directors in England. The Oriental and Peninsula steam company, one of the most successful concerns connected with India, manages the Indian branch of its great business by means of an agent selected on the ground of personal confidence in him, and he is strictly

---

from the extensive and continued changing of the bed of the Ganges, that unless its continuation Northward and Eastward be considered desirable, it would appear that a branch to Bhogwangola, simply to accommodate the trade that now passes along the Ganges to Calcutta by the Sunderbunds route, will not be found to answer as a commercial speculation,"—*Report of Railway Commission.* (1846).

governed by the orders or instructions of directors in England."

It remains to say a few words on the conditions and stipulations, which, in justice to the government and the shareholders of the successful companies, ought to be observed in the concession.

The successful company will be incorporated by a charter, granted by the supreme government, and the court of directors will concur in applying for a similar charter from the crown, conferring on the railway company the requisite powers.

It is to be expected that the government will include in the concession, or grant, all the land necessary for the railway, and afford the necessary protection to the works till their completion.

The proceedings of the company ought at all times to be open for the inspection of government.

That the government should have the use of the line on payment of an equitable remuneration, and induce companies to have a large stock of trucks, platforms, wheels and axles, which in case of emergency any common carpenter could raise a superstructure upon, and thus place many additional carriages adapted for the conveyance of troops at the disposal of government.

The general rates of conveyance to be fixed by mutual agreement between the government and the company. Of course there will be other clauses beyond these just hinted at, touching penalties for non-fulfil-ment of contracts, and as to whether or not the line should, on settled terms, become eventually the property of the State. These and such like stipulations demand serious consideration both from the government and railway companies.

We take it for granted, that no company would be rash enough to undertake a work of such magnitude, and at so great a distance, as a railroad in India, without such a guarantee from the government as would enable the directors to call up their capital without difficulty or hesitation on the part of the shareholders, the majority of whom, being in England, are necessarily but imperfectly acquainted with India and its resources; indeed, were the Directors of a company disposed to act otherwise, they would soon discover that the entire change which has taken place in the public mind regarding speculative enterprise, would render such attempt abortive, irrespective of the merits of the undertaking, and thus nullify the wishes and the hopes of the government and the people of India.

In considering the amount of the minimum rate of interest to be guaranteed on the expended, or paid-up capital of a company, some regard ought to be had to the prevailing rates in India, both as to government securities and private investments, as well as those ruling in this country. By recent accounts from Calcutta, the banks paid 6 per cent. on deposits for three months, and charged 10 per cent. on loans at short date, although secured by deposit of government paper; and the bazaar rates ranged considerably higher. In England the capitalist can command at present 5 per cent. from railway companies in actual operation, and to this amount the opinions of bankers and merchants in the City, whom we have consulted, converge as the proper amount for a minimum guaranteed rate of interest for Indian railways.* This would be merely a nominal guarantee, so far as government is concerned, if the lines be properly selected, as the statistical data show a goods traffic, to more than twice the amount;† and if the principle of low charges, as laid down by Mr. J. Butler Williams, deduced from the practical working of English lines, be applied to India, the return would, we feel assured, be enormous.

---

* Should there be no limitation as to the exact amount of capital to be guaranteed, or no clause in the concession involving forfeiture to the state of part or whole of the capital actually expended, in the event of non-completion of the contract on the part of the railroad company, of course a smaller per centage would suffice even for the first project to be completed, the guarantee of the East India Company being equivalent to that of the Royal Government, and given with the sanction of the latter. Should the charter not be renewed in 1854 the territories of the Company lapse to the crown, subject to their debts and liabilities. (1846).

† The Rajmahl Canal Committee prove, from the existing traffic of the country, that, "the total amount of tonnage daily passing through it (the canal) would not fall short of 3,000 tons."—*Report on the Rajmahl Canal, para.* 47. (1846).

But we would rather appeal to the wise and beneficent government of India, on other and more generous grounds, and take leave of this topic in the words of the Irish Commission, men alike distinguished for learning, ability and enlarged patriotism. "Thus, although a railway itself, as a mercantile speculation, might not, at once, fulfil the sanguine expectations of the projectors, it would be an invaluable source of general wealth and prosperity."

COST OF CONSTRUCTION, &c.

According to the Report of the Railway Commission in India, the country generally presents from the evenness of its surface, remarkable facilities for the ample development of the new system of inter-communication; from this circumstance, and the abundance, and cheapness of labour and materials, the cost of construction will be much less than in our most favoured lines in England; and besides, the government having the power of taking at a small valuation the land necessary for public roads, there will be no refractory landowners to deal with, nor any protracted and expensive parliamentary contest, to fritter away the funds of the companies.* This arrangement, besides its economical

* The expenses of English railways may be divided into:—Parliamentary—Land and compensation—Works—Permanent way—Engineering—Law charges—Land valuers—Stamps for debentures—Office expenses, &c. Applied to India, one-half of these items may be struck out. (1846).

effect, will have others of a highly beneficial nature; the natives would be generally impressed in favour of an undertaking thus sanctioned and supported by the government whose mandates they revere.

The two physical difficulties which have weighed most, with those acquainted with India, and which are peculiar to the country, are, we believe, now entirely set at rest: *viz.*, the periodical inundations and ravages of the white ant.

As to the former their effects have been experienced and provided against; there can be no ground for apprehension on that head.

Regarding the destructive ravages of the white ant, the injury to be apprehended has been much exaggerated, we do not anticipate any bad effect from this insect, further than attacking temporary wooden sheds, or buildings; we have no recollection of the white ant making an impression on anything which was liable to motion, concussion or vibration. The insect protecting itself under a covered way of earthy matter, which it throws out as it advances, we imagine that the disturbing, tremulous motion given to the sleepers by the advance of a heavy train, would effectually deter its attack, or, if not, speedily dislodge the enemy by destroying his covered way; besides stone or Reynolds' cast iron sleepers might be used for sleepers instead of wood, or the latter might be fortified by means of one of those recent patent inventions, which have been found successful in imparting to timber preternatural hardness and durability.*

Timber of excellent quality is plentifully distributed over the country, and may be had at a cheap rate; in some places, almost for the expense of cutting. Teak, Saul, Sissoo, Soondree, and Babool, (a species of Mimosa) from their resisting the white ant, their durability and their abundance, will probably be selected for sleepers.†

The soil being admirably adapted for making bricks, they may be commanded to almost any extent in almost any locality.

With the coal and iron already noticed, as occurring in many parts of India, we also find stone well adapted for building purposes.

A reference to the Appendix will show the cheapness of labour and materials in India.

---

* Sir William Burnett's invention preserves wood against rot and the ravages of insects. (1846).

† Teak is well known for its solidity, hardness and durability as the most valuable timber of almost any country—but it is expensive. Sissoo also commands a high price in Calcutta, and has, although not so frequently as teak, been used for ship building. It is dark, coarse grained, and possessed of great tenacity.

Saul is less expensive in Calcutta than the former, is coarse grained, a degree less hard and tenacious than Sissoo, but bears exposure rather better. It is very abundant in the broad belt of forest at the base of the Himalayah, and in the hilly regions in other parts of the country where it may be obtained for almost a nominal price. (1846).

The average cost of railways has been

In England, per mile . . .	about	£31,000
In Scotland, "	"	22,000
In Ireland, "	"	22,000
(Vide "Porter's Traffic Returns" Statistical Journal, vol. vii., p. 176.)		
In Belgium "	"	18,000*
(Vide "Report of Statistical Bureau," Delaveleye, Brussels, 1844.		
In France "	"	14,000
(Vide Claudel's "Aide-Mémoire des Ingénieurs,' p. 455. Average of five metropolitan lines).†		

Soondree is peculiar to the Sunderbundes and the Upland district to the west of Calcutta, and excels all the forest trees of India in the density of its fibre, in toughness, in durability when exposed, in strength or resisting power, and its acidity gives it a perfect immunity from the ravages of insects. It never attains a great size and is occasionally contorted, but sticks adapted for railway sleepers, *i. e.* of 8 or 9 in. scantling are to be had in any quantity at a cheap rate; it makes good buggy shafts, but English workmen object to it, as it turns the edge of their tools. A large quantity of this wood may be seen at the London Docks, or at Messrs. Roberts and Mitchell's, Old Jewry Chambers. (1846).

* The cost of the West Flanders lines will not amount to one half of the average cost of the state lines per mile. Second half-yearly Report of the Directors of the West Flanders Railways, July 3rd, 1846.

† Principles of railway management by J. Butler Williams, Esq. F.S.S, F.G.S. (1846).

In Germany, according to Legoyt .		£10,940
In America . . .	from £1,600 to	9,400
Average for the rougher sort, including stations for a single line		2,812*
Estimates for India, according to Vignoles	7,500 to	10,250†
„ Captain Goodwyn, exclusive of plant .		3,000
„ Captain Western (incomplete „ .		4,400
Estimates for Great Indian Peninsula (exclusive of plant) on American plan . .		3,000

It is stated in the report of the Irish commission that railways might be constructed in that country at the rate of £10,000 per mile. "The Board of Trade in their report on the South Western District, in 1845, states that the lines proposed to be made in that part of the country might be constructed for about £12,000 per mile; and the estimated cost of the mass of new railways projected during the last two years, ranges

---

* For the mode of constructing railways in America—*see* "*Weale's Ensamples of Railways.*" (1846).

† The line from Calcutta to Mirzapore, if executed in the manner proposed by the Railway Commissioners, may be estimated at . . . . £20,000 per mile

From Allahabad to Delhi . . 8,000. „

From Calcutta to the Sutlej it would be an average of From . . . . . £12,000 to 15,000

And would require a capital of, about . £18,000,000.

(1846).

with few exceptions, between £25,000 and £10,000 per mile."*

Mr. Butler Williams declares that the opinions of engineers and statists agree in establishing the conclusion that the lines to be henceforth constructed, will on the average approach more nearly to the lower than the higher standard.

It must be borne in mind that no just idea can be arrived at, of the cost of a railway, from the gross amount per mile, irrespective of other circumstances. The difference in the value of land and house property and the magnificent ideas of our engineers, forcing us to raise monuments to their genius and taste in our termini and stations, are important elements of cost. On the Liverpool and Manchester line, thirty miles in length, the buildings cost £280,000. The Euston extension of the London and Birmingham railway, little exceeding one mile in length, cost £255,722, the gateway alone costing an enormous amount.

The court of directors have wisely ordered their railway commission in India, to refer for information and guidance as to the construction of railways to the experience of America as well as Europe.

We think it highly probable that by eschewing what is only ornamental, and improving upon the American

* "Defects of the English system of Railway Legislation," by James Morrison, Esq., M.P. (Longman, 1846. Page 13.)

system, we might effect an extensive railway development in India, at much less cost,* and better adapted

---

* Take for example the Rajmahl line which has been minutely surveyed, "the earthwork in the line proposed would be very little, and I think, I may safely say, that the earthwork and ballasting for the rails, will be much the same as the construction of the Great Trunk road in India, which consists of an earthen road thirty feet wide, on an average three feet high, with a portion sixteen feet wide metalled, the metalling being one foot deep; the cost of the trunk road including the small bridges, but exclusive of the bridges over the large rivers, and Engineer officers' salaries is under 2,500 rupees a mile. The fencing, which must be strong enough to keep out cattle, will cost 1000 rupees a mile. The large bridges will be a heavy item which cannot be estimated without a proper survey of the line, but if laid down at 2,500 rupees a mile, will, I think, include every large bridge required over the Ganges, Soane, and all smaller rivers—making altogether 6,000 rupees a mile for works.

"The permanent way, meaning the sleepers and rails, cannot be estimated to be done cheaper in India than in England. The sleepers will require to be kyanised, (but if kyanising is not found to resist the white ants, it will be necessary to use stone blocks, or perhaps to use Reynold's cast iron sleepers) and the cost will be two rupees each, and as 3,520 are required in a mile of double line, the cost of these will be 7,040 rupees a mile; the rails should be of the full weight of sixty-five pounds to the yard, and the cost will be £12 or 120 rupees a ton, making 24,600 rupees a mile; then the chairs, pins, and wedges for fastening down the rails, and labour in doing so, about 6,000 rupees a mile, making a total of 37,640 rupees a mile.

"The remaining item of Engineering and surveying would be very small, and might be put down as 360 rupees a mile, thus making for the total cost of the railway:—

to the rougher work it would be subjected to—than by attempting to transport a Birmingham or Great Western, with all their grandeur and complicated arrangements, into Hindostan.

Works	6,000 rupees per mile
Permanent way	37,640 ,,
Engineering and surveying .	360 ,,
Total	44,000 rupees per mile"

Report, by Captain Western.

Add to above	Rupees 44,000=	£4,400
Termini, stations, and buildings		300
Land and compensation		100
Working stock		1,000
Superintendence, &c. for three years . . .		200
Miscellaneous		500
	Total	£6,500

Allowing an ample margin for contingencies, say, per mile £8,000

(1846).

CLASSIFICATION OF PASSENGERS, &c.

It may be interesting to compare in some particulars the working of our railways with those of Belgium, the only country in Europe, besides our own, in which such works have hitherto been carried on as a system, and where the results have been published.

At the end of 1842, there were in operation in that kingdom, 282 miles of railways, the average cost of construction of which was £17,120 per mile, while the average cost in this kingdom has been £34,360,* or just double the cost in Belgium. This difference results from a variety of causes. In the first place, the works being undertaken by the government, there

---

* Those lines principally used for transporting coals and minerals are not included in this average. (1846).

were no expensive parliamentary contests, no opposing interests to be bought off, no unreasonable compensations to be paid for land; and from the nature of the country, there were comparatively few engineering difficulties to be overcome. Besides these circumstances there has been much present saving effected in the manner of executing the works, which have been performed in a less perfect manner than would satisfy the magnificent ideas of our engineers.

The number of passengers conveyed along the various lines in Belgium, in 1842, was 2,724,104 or 662 for each 1,000 of the population, the proportion in the United Kingdom having been in the year ending 30th of June, 1843, 879 for each 1000 inhabitants, or 33 per cent., greater than in Belgium.

The proportions using various class carriages were:—

	In Belgium.	In the United Kingdom.
1st class,	9 per cent.	19 per cent.
2nd	25	51
3rd	66	30
	100	100

The receipts from passengers during the year, were, in Belgium £187,372 or one shilling and fourpence halfpenny per passenger, against two shillings and twopence three farthings in the United Kingdom.

The proportions in which the receipts were contributed by the three classes of passengers were :—

	In Belgium.	In the United Kingdom.
1st class	23	45
2nd	25	42
3rd	52	13
	100	100*

It will be seen by the preceding tables that the majority of travellers in the United Kingdom take the second class, and in Belgium the third class; the actual receipts for the third class in Belgium, being more than equal to that drawn from the first and second classes combined; and we are convinced, that, although any payment is beyond the means of the artizan or labourer of India, yet (as we have elsewhere stated,) there is a large and thriving population of merchants and smaller traders in the great cities of India, that would avail themselves of these classes of carriage, were even the average English rates of conveyance adhered to. Mr. Laing computes the average

* An examination of the returns made by the various railway companies of the United Kingdom, with respect to their traffic, during the year ending 30th of June, 1843. By G. R. Porter, Esq., F.R.S. Treasurer of the Statistical Society of London.—(*Journal of the Statistical Society of London, for June* 1844).

distance travelled by each passenger in this country at thirteen and one-eighth miles, for a fare of two shillings and two-pence three farthings, while in Belgium the average distance travelled, is stated to be, seven and three quarters leagues, or about nineteen miles, for one shilling and four-pence halfpenny.

Regarding the arrangement of the different classes, and the relative fares to be charged, we must be guided in our calculations by the peculiar state of society in India—we should have five distinct sets of carriages, divided as follows :—one, appropriated to the conveyance of Europeans, the Civil and Military Officers of the State —two, that is, a first and a second class, for the Mahomedans, and the same for the Hindoo portion of the people, with due provision for the conveyance of their females, the carriages suitable for the natives could also be made available for the conveyance of troops, both European and native.*

With the exception of troops, there would be scarcely any European travellers but those going by the first class carriages, and as these would be public servants,

* Although it would be necessary and proper on the first introduction of a new mode of transit to consult the prejudices of the native community, we are persuaded that the minute subdivision of the people recommended above, would soon be quite unnecessary, as at present, all castes, classes, and sects make no scruple to cross the rivers in the same ferry boats, without reference to the caste status or religion of their fellow passengers. (1846).

proceeding or returning on duty, or on leave of absence, there would be little probability of reduction in the fares greatly augmenting their numbers.

The charge should have reference to the expense of travelling by *dâk* (post), by steamers, by budgerow, and marching, and it is to be borne in mind that to this class time is in reality money. For instance the staff, and command allowances of the staff and regimental officer, determine on the day on which he is relieved of the duties of his office, and re-commence on the day on which he reports his arrival at the Head Quarters of his division or regiment. Take an every day case of a Lieut.-Colonel or a Medical Officer, arriving from England, when his regiment is some 800 miles up the country; for every month which he occupies in marching or proceeding by water, to join his regiment, he loses :—

Lieut.-Colonel, per mensem . Rs. 430=£43

Regimental Surgeon . . Rs. 300=£30

A daily loss of one pound eight and eightpence and one pound respectively.

So that they could afford to pay a very high fare, and yet be gainers, and escape exposure to the climate and fatigue.

The very opposite principles apply to the other classes. After having made every arrangement for the safety and comfort of all, we should hold out by the moderation of the fares, every inducement to the natives to abandon their unsafe and tedious conveyances, for one offering them every facility, combined with economy; making a sufficiently wide difference, to define the distinction between the native nobleman or rich merchant, and the petty trader, and the fares for these classes, particularly the last named, should be made as low as it is practicable; bearing in mind that profits accrue in an exact ratio to the masses conveyed, whether the masses be passengers, live stock, minerals or merchandise, *e.g*:—a line with a traffic of 750,000 tons per annum, (that of Liverpool and Manchester) could carry goods with as much profit at a penny per ton per mile, as a line (the Paris and Orleans), with a traffic of 150,000 tons, at three pence per ton per mile.

CONCLUSION.

WITH our Calcutta Review friend we have broken a lance on one or two occasions, and we shall be, with all courtesy, happy to do our *devoir* again, if he persists in looking through the wrong end of his telescope. His essay was a preliminary one, we shall expect to see his views more decidedly in favour of legitimate undertakings and opposed to crude absurdities. His local knowledge ought to qualify him to apply the scalpel, and lay bare, for the benefit of the English public, the real merits of the candidates for their favour; and transferring the closing remarks of our friend to these pages, we wish him for the present adieu. "In parts where the permanent settlement has been established, the revenue will be more easily collected; in other parts, the land will be at an improved rent, as it will necessarily be improved in value. A railroad in this point of view will be a more valuable acquisition than Sindh, or the ceded Sikh Provinces. We believe it is impossible to form too high an estimate of the manner in which it would develop the agricultural capabilities of the country. In the Report on the Ganges Canal, which was intended to run from Hurdwar to Allahabad, we find a contrast drawn between the evils which the canal would mitigate or prevent—such as famine—and the malaria which it produced, occasioning sickness, and disease in the contiguous population. No malaria attends a railroad: it pretends not indeed to prevent a failure of crops, but it does better, it facilitates commerce, multiplies the power of capital, and pours a supply wherever there is a demand, and enables charity to perform its object and mission."

"The natives of India are concerned in it." (railway communication). "The undoubted effect would be in a constantly augmenting ratio, to unfold the unknown mineral resources of their world-famed land—vastly to enhance in value the products of its prolific soil—widely and cheaply to diffuse the objects of personal comforts, and refined social enjoyment—and annually to save the lives of thousands that must otherwise perish from the hazards, the fatigues, and the exposures of the present rude and semi-barbarous modes of travelling. The merchants of England, and of every realm within the empire of civilization are concerned in it.

"Philanthropists of every name are concerned in it." (railway communication). "Its tendency would be to save the time and strength of devoted labourers, in visiting different and widely distant spheres of usefulness—more speedily and economically to concentrate the material means and instrumentalities of improvement in favourable localities—and more rapidly and successfully to multiply those radiating points, whence the light of science, and art, and true religion may emanate all around.

"The mighty impulse which it would impart to the development of the exhaustless treasures of so highly favoured a region, and to the awakening energies of so multitudinous a people, could not fail to make itself felt on the shores of the Baltic and Mediterranean, in the mines of Cornwall, and the back woods of America, in the dockyards and harbours alike of the Atlantic and Pacific, and in every seat of manufacturing industry throughout the commercial world. The honour, the dignity, and the glory of imperial Britain are concerned in it. The complete permeation of these 'climes of the sun' by a magnificent system of Railway communication, would present a series of public monuments vastly surpassing in real grandeur the aqueducts of Rome, the pyramids of Egypt, the great wall of China, the temples, palaces, and mausoleums of the Great Moguls—monuments not merely of intelligence and power, but of utility and beneficence, which would for ever wipe away the fiercely indignant reproach, that, 'were we to be driven out of India this day, nothing would remain to tell that it had been possessed, during the inglorious period of our dominion, by anything better than the ourang-outang or the tiger.'" A reproach more undeserved we believe was never heard, and could only have been uttered (one would imagine) by some canting orator, the paid champion of liberty and equality, and the slave of party.*

Were we driven out of India to-morrow, we should leave behind us glorious monuments of our rule in the temples reared to the God of the honest, brave and

---

* The Eastern Sage Desh-u-lubun Ocharik in writing to one of these hollow declaimers, says:—

"Nothing of good can originate with them; (The East India Company) they have erred you would make out, from their very first illegitimate birth in good Queen Elizabeth's virgin time, up to the present portentous era of free trade and political economy. Thus they have blundered and bungled on, from step to step, into the lamentable, undisturbed possession of one of the largest and finest Empires in the universe; their very pre-eminence in the East—the quiet peacefulness of their subjects—the unobtrusive and simple machinery of their local governments—the silently progressive amelioration of the population committed to their charge, and the extensive diffusion of education and useful knowledge—the numerous institutions for the sick, the indigent, and the uninformed, embracing every class, Hindoo or Mussulman—their delicacy towards ourselves (more, I may venture to say, than they exhibit towards their own European servants, civil or military) and scrupulous regard for the protection of the lands, religion, ordinances, and feelings, of the millions they govern. Nay, the merciful *Feringee*—in fields reclaimed from the wilderness—desolate hearths restored—ruined cities and towns rebuilt—instead of anarchy, rapine, and spoil—protection, contentment and peace!

"Inglorious period of our dominion!" We almost blush to imprint upon our page so foul a stigma, while the sands of the Sutlej are still red with the blood of our enemies, while the voice of Europe declares that our bravery in the field, is only to be equalled by our generosity to the vanquished; at home our victorious chiefs have been equally awarded the laurel crown and civic bay—we admit, however, that we have left much undone for the people of India, and in nothing have

---

very state itself of the government, which obtains loans from us at half the interest for which the traders of Calcutta can procure money;* these and every other just and honourable characteristic of our present rulers, are misrepresented, vilified, decried.

"No one acquainted with our ancient history and government can deny, that however many of us may complain of the loss of dignities and immunities formerly, but precariously possessed, the mass of our people have derived many substantial advantages from British connection, which has not only rescued us from the numerous evils which we suffered, under our native rule, but has gradually led to our incorporation as a part of the British Empire, to the diffusion of literature among us, the introduction and promotion of a knowledge of the sciences, and the benefit of equal laws, and a distribution of justice similar to that enjoyed by the parent state." (1846).

---

* "During the Burmese war, the East India Company borrowed money at five per cent; while the most respectable merchants and agents of Calcutta were paying ten."—*Letter of Desh-u-Luban Ocharik, of Calcutta.*

we been more culpable and impolitic, than having neglected for so long a period the means of communication.

The Romans of old, and the Czar of the present day, attended to roads, as an important element of policy and power: and the ignorant serf of the north enjoys under the iron despotism of the Black Eagle of Russia, facilities for trade and intercommunication, which are withheld from the intelligent subjects of the wise and generous England.

We will not speculate on the momentous results with which this subject is fraught to millions yet unborn, how it speaks of a quickening and pervading civilization, remunerative labour, amelioration to the many, and the removal of superstition and prejudice; and what accession will it not bring to us of riches, power and glory by developing the resources of a mighty empire, hitherto almost without roads, by stimulating the industry of its inhabitants, whose natural intelligence has been either lost in apathy, or chilled by the petrifying influence of caste, while, by the easy and rapid concentration of our troops, our power must become irresistible,* and the glory would be ours of having done our duty to the hundred millions of our brethren committed to our charge, attaining at

* A friend of the writer's heard the Governor-general of India state, that with railways our army would at once be doubled in effective force. (1846).

once a more assured and consolidated empire, a vastly augmented revenue, with a more industrious, and therefore, a richer and a happier people.

While the foregoing sheets were passing through the press* the despatch of the Bengal Government, regarding the introduction of railways into British India, has been received at the India House.

The sentiments of the local Government, will, we feel assured, be in accordance with the recommendation of the railway commission, and will give those projects† for connecting the seat of supreme government with the N.W. Frontier that prominence and consideration which their pre-eminent, political, and commercial importance demands.

---

* In the month of July last. (1846).

† Great Western of Bengal, (Calcutta to Rajmahl) and the line from Allahabad to Delhi. (1846).

APPENDIX TO SECOND EDITION.

1846.

MODES OF TRAVELLING IN INDIA AND FARES.

The natives of the lower provinces generally go by water as there is less fatigue attending this mode of transit, but the Up-country people generally prefer travelling on horseback or in carriages.

An European or a wealthy native going by *dâk* (post) from Calcutta to Benares, a distance of 428 miles, will incur an expense of one shilling per mile besides buckshees (presents) to the bearers about one shilling per stage, making in all about £25 for one journey, which he will be five days in accomplishing (exclusive of halts). If by Palkee with eight bearers, going fifteen miles per diem, he will have to pay £12 10*s*., besides £2 10*s*. for a banghy,* and will consume nearly a month on the road. This mode of travelling, besides the loss of time, is attended with danger from robbers. The journey is accomplished in sixteen days on horseback. By water, by budgerow from £15 to £25—and forty days occupied on the journey if going up the river.

By steamer for the above journey the fare will be much the same as by budgerow, and the time occupied may be about ten days for three months in the year, and nearly twenty for the remaining nine months.

---

* A banghy wallah, or bearer of two light boxes.

By Gharry, (native carriage drawn by oxen) the cost will be £10, and travelling at the rate of twelve miles per diem.

Infantry regiments move at the rate of ten and a half miles per diem, halting six days in the month, so that it takes about six weeks to move from Calcutta to Benares a single corps.

"The cost then of a detachment of 300 men, proceeding by water to Allahabad, would be as follows:—

Boat allowance to one Field Officer (say a Major) for two and a half months, at	Rs. 360	Rs. 900
Boat allowance to three Captains, for two and a half months, at	180	1,350
Boat allowance, 10 Subalterns, at	100	2,500
Ditto ditto 1 Surgeon, at	180	450
Twenty-five, 600 maund boats for men		3,375
		Rs. 8,575

And if to this is added the boats for the accommodation of the sick, row boats and store boats, the amount will be considerably increased, without taking into consideration the extra establishments proceeding with such a detachment, whereas the cost of conveying such a detachment by the railway, at a penny a head per mile for 600 miles, would only be £750 or 7,500 rupees.

"The cost of extra establishments, with European troops marching, I cannot so accurately state, but it will be found, I think, to exceed the cost at which they could be transported by railway."*

Small parties or individuals marching or proceeding by water move at a quicker rate.

* Report in 1843, by Captain Western.

CLEARING HOUSE SYSTEM AS APPLIED TO RAILWAYS.

The ultimate effect of the extension of a uniform railway system is still more clearly shown in the operations of the clearing house.

We are fortunately enabled to furnish an account of this interesting and valuable institution, from a pamphlet* lately printed for private circulation by its ingenious author, Mr. B. Morison.

It appears that soon after the opening of the continuous lines of railways between Liverpool and London, it was found that travellers would not be content with the mere acceleration of speed, but required to be carried through at one charge, and if possible by one conveyance. The same demand was made for goods. This arrangement was carried into effect; but although the public were better served, the accounts of the companies interchanging fell into sad confusion. Each company had charges against those which ran over its lines, and in like manner owed money to those lines, giving rise to an interminable affair of cross accounts. Then, as railways increased, some were prosperous, and some were poor.

---

* The Origin and Results of the Clearing System which is in operation on the narrow gauge Railways.

The prosperous were well supplied with carriages, waggons, trucks, and all that comes within the meaning of "railway stock," the poor companies had as little as they could help, and made up for the deficiency by unacknowledged borrowings; so that, altogether, the interests which should, for mutual and public good, work most harmoniously, clashed in a manner that could be pleasing only to the lawyers of the disputing companies. The solution of the litigious maze was found in a plan derived from that of the city clearing house, which was carried into effect under the auspices of Mr. Glyn and Mr. Hudson.

On the 2nd of January, 1842, the system of the Railway Clearing House came into operation on the railways extending from London to Darlington in one direction, and from Manchester to Hull in another. It was adopted, at subsequent periods, by the companies whose railways extended from Darlington to Carlisle, Sunderland, Hartlepool, and Scarborough; and from Birmingham to Gloucester, Birkenhead, Liverpool, Fleetwood, Lancaster and Manchester. And in a few months it will be in force in all the railways included in the area defined by a line passing from London through Gloucester, Liverpool, Fleetwood and Glasgow to Edinburgh; and returning by Berwick, Newcastle, Scarborough, Hull, Yarmouth and Cambridge, to the metropolis; or, in other words, in all the narrow gauge railways in Great Britain lying north of the Thames, with the exception of the few short lines which are beyond the limits of the area just described.

The main principles of the system thus widely diffused, are first, that passengers shall be booked through at all principal stations, and conveyed to their destination without change of carriage; that the horses and cattle shall likewise be sent through without change of conveyance, and that goods shall, in the same way, be carried through without being either shifted or re-assorted. Secondly, the companies respectively shall pay a fixed rate per mile, for such carriages and waggons not their own property, as they may use; and a further sum per day by way of fine or demurrage for detention, if kept beyond a prescribed length of time; and lastly, that no direct settlement shall take place between the companies in respect to any traffic, the accounts of which have not passed through the railway clearing house.

In order to work out the clearing principle, there are sent daily from each of the clearing house stations (including all the principal booking stations of every line, forming a part of the railway union),

1st. A return of the passengers booked through.

2nd. A return of the horses, private carriages, and cattle booked through.

3rd. A return of the parcels booked through.

4th. A return of all the carriages, waggons, &c., which have arrived or been discharged either loaded or empty.

From these returns the accounts of what is due to and owing by each company is made out at the clearing house, and after being examined and approved by each company, the final settlement of the accounts is effected by the railway clearing, paying, or receiving the balances, as the case may be, through the hands of the bankers, who act as agents to the several companies. In this way all the transactions of one company, with all other companies, amounting frequently to many thousand pounds a week, are cleared weekly by a sum seldom exceeding a few hundred pounds.

The means which the clearing house possesses for having each vehicle reported from the moment it leaves the parent line until it returns to it, and the plan adopted of charging mileage for stock used, and demurrage for stock detained, have put an end to the practice before referred to, of borrowing from neighbours to supply an improper deficiency in carrying vehicles.

From these returns, for the year 1845, we find that 517,888 passengers were each conveyed through an average distance of 146 miles—the average length of the lines travelled over being forty-one miles, so that each passenger travelled over four railways on an average, and must have passed three junctions or points of conveyance—to accommodate these passengers, 59,765 railway carriages and 5,813 trucks, carrying private carriages, were sent through. There were also sent through in the same year, 7,573 horse boxes, 2,607 post offices, and 180,606 goods waggons, besides waggons conveying minerals, of which no record is kept at the clearing house.

There are other circumstances connected with the clearing house, which render it a most valuable institution. The control is vested in a committee, composed of all companies who form part of the union. Their meetings tend to produce harmony and also uniformity in their respective arrangements, and to impose a check on the disposition to introduce diversities of system, which, for some motive or other, railway managers have so often evinced.*

* Mr. Morison's pamphlet on Gauge Evidence. Vide also the work, by Mr. Samuel Sidney, on the same subject.

PRICE OF LABOUR AND MATERIALS IN INDIA.

Average amount of Wages and Prices of materials on the spot.

Masons or bricklayers, per day	£0	0	6
Carpenters ,, ...	0	0	6
Labourers (able bodied) ,, (three of whom are equal to one European)	0	0	3
Ditto ,, per month . . .	0	5	0
Cost of excavating to an average depth of twenty feet, and removing the earth to a distance, for every five hundred and seventy-four cubic feet, or twenty-one and three quarters cubic yards .	0	2	0
Cost of one hundred cubic feet of masonry . .	1	8	0
Ditto ditto of arched masonry . .	2	0	0

MATERIALS.

Bricks—11 inches—per thousand . . .					0	7	0
Ditto ,, ,, for arching .					0	13	0
Chunar stone (Calcutta price) each eighteen inches square and two inches thick, per score . .					0	16	0
Tiles, eighteen inches, per hundred . . .					0	4	0
Ditto ,, ,, (pan or roof) .					0	2	6
Lime per cart load (14 cwt.)					0	4	0
Sand (washed) per hundred ferrahs . . .					0	14	0
Timber (rough) teak per ton .	£3	0	0	to	5	10	0
,, Saul ,, .	2	0	0	,,	3	10	0
,, Sisso ,, .	1	0	0	,,	2	10	0
Teak, in plank six inches thick (Calcutta price) per ton . .	4	10	0	,,	5	10	0
Piles per hundred					15	0	0
Cost of conveying materials by land, per ton, per mile					0	0	3
Ditto by water, exclusive of loss of interest and insurance					0	0	1¼

COST OF BRIDGE OF THIRTY FEET WATERWAY, EXCLUSIVE OF TOWING PATH.

From report on Ganges Canal, 1845. *Page* 56.

	L	*B*	*D*	*No.*	*Cub. Con.*	*Cos. Rs.*	
Piers	18	6	20	2	4,320		
Arch	42	2	18	1	1,512		
Counter arch	39	1	18	1	702		
Wing walls	36	1½	15	4	3,240		
Cornice	120	2	½	2	240		
Parapet	120	1¼	3	2	900		
Pillars	4	4	6	4	384		
Ditto superstructure	3	3	3	4	108		
Towing path foundations	30	3	6	2	1,086		
Ditto superstructure	48	3	6	1	864		
Foundation curtains	30	3	4½	2	810		
Spandrils	12	3	1½	2	108		
Flooring between pier and towing path.	18	3	1	1	54		
Total cubic feet					14,328		
Deduct							
Foundation of pier in rear of towing path	18	6	4	1	432		
Grand total cubic content of masonry					13,896		
Of which say, 1,512 cubic ft. of arched masonry at 20 Rs. per 100 cubic ft. Rs.						302 6 4	
12,378 ditto plain ditto 14 Rs. per ditto						1,732 14 9	
Total cost of the bridge . Rs.						2,035 5 1	£203 10 7½

PRICE OF LABOUR AND MATERIALS IN ENGLAND.

	s.	d.		s.	d.
Common excavation, per cubic yard . .	0	5	to	0	8
If basketed	0	6	,,	0	9
If wheeled	0	8	,,	0	10
Ditto and staged, for every run, viz. 20 yards add	0	1½			
If carted, or otherwise removed a distance not exceeding 900 yards, add . .	1	0	,,	2	6
(If beyond the distance, add proportionally.)					

NOTE.—If in tunnels, allowance must be made for the sinking of shafts and haulage of excavation in proportion to the depth of shaft and length of tunnel; also in excavating for bridges or other buildings, allowance must be made for working room and sustaining slopes, as well as for any other contingency that may arise in excavation or formation and the subsiding of banks.

	s.	d.		s.	d.
Unsoiling, per super. yard, without carriage .	0	1½	,,	0	3
If wheeled, per run of 20 yards, add .				0	0¾
If removed 900 yards, add . . .	0	4	,,	0	10
(If beyond that distance, add proportionally.)					
Soiling slopes of embankments or cuttings .				0	3
Forming surface level of road for ballast .	0	1½	,,	0	3
Forming face of cuttings and embankments for soiling	0	1½	,,	0	4
Forming drains each side of roads in cuttings, per yard lin:	0	3	,,	0	6

BRICKWORK.

NOTE.—The following prices are calculated at £14 per rod, taking the bricks at forty shillings per thousand, delivered at the works, including profit. For every shilling more or less, add or deduct per cube yard, fivepence halfpenny.

	£	s.	d.
Brickwork, in mortar, per cubic yard . . .	1	4	9
Ditto, in Roman cement	1	10	1
Ditto, if worked camber, per foot superficial . .	0	0	1
Ditto, if circular	0	0	1
Ditto, face pointed, in ash mortar . . .	0	0	2
Ditto, in cement	0	0	2½
Brick-on-edge coping, in cement, per foot run .	0	0	5
1½ brick ditto ditto . .	0	0	8
NOTE.—Cement, asphalte, or hydraulic cement, laid over arches, per yard superficial, from one shilling and ninepence to	0	2	9
Clay, well puddled, and laid over arches 6 inches thick, per sup. yard	0	2	8

The average price of stone in England, fit for building purposes, may be estimated at four and sixpence per cubic foot when in the rough state.*

* For the above particulars the author is indebted to the courtesy of Mr. Weale, 59, High Holborn, who furnished him with some of the proof sheets of a work now in the press—entitled "*Engineer's Pocket Book for* 1847."

TRANSVERSE STRENGTH OF WOODS.

A valuable article has appeared in the military repository, embodying in a table the results of a series of experiments performed on this subject, (transverse strength of woods) at the gun carriage agency Kásipur (Cossipore). The woods selected were Bengal Sundria, (Soondree) Murany Sál, (Morung Saul) Gorakpur Sál, (Gorukhpore Saul) Rangoon Teak, Java Teak, Pegu Teak, Bombay Teak, Murany Tun, (Morung Toon) Bengal Deal, Norway Deal, and American Ash. The pieces experimented on were each seventy-two inches in length, two inches square, and sixty inches between the points of support. Amongst other results it appears that the Bengal Deal, though unseasoned, was equal to the Norway, each breaking with seven hundred and twenty pounds, and with a deflection of two and a half inches. The great range in the strength of Teak is one of the most curious and valuable of the results. The extremes are Rangoon and Bombay or Malabar 1175 and 591 pounds giving a ratio of 2 : 1. Both woods were seasoned. The highest value of Bombay Teak was 889 pounds,*

---

* British oak ranks next to Rangoon Teak in transverse strength. The iron-wood of Arracan is approved of by the Railway Commission for sleepers, but little is said as to its qualities, and nothing as to quantity or price. (1846).

Bengal Súndri (Soondree) is the strongest wood tried, and required 1384 pounds to break it. Murang Sâl (Morung Saul) is the next, 1319. It appears in general that the woods are stronger for being seasoned; in the case of the Sundri (Soondree) the difference was remarkable, 1384 and 992 or 75. The greatest range of Sâl Chaokars (Saul Chowkers), and Daokars (Dowkurs) was 1319 to 1179, when seasoned; unseasoned it did not go below 1085—Murang Sal Battis (Morung Saul Batties) gave only 787. Tún (Toon), not seasoned, 667, and American ash 483.*

* Gleanings in Science, Calcutta, March, 1829.

RELATIVE POPULATION OF BENGAL AND BEHAR.

PER SQUARE MILE.

Year.	Square miles.	Population.	Relative Pop. Per square mile.
1793	144,762	24,000,000	165
1843	144,762	48,007,061	331*
Rate of increase per cent. in fifty years .			100

* Population of Great Britain, by last census, per square mile, was 240. (1846).

STAPLE ARTICLES OF COMMERCE OF BENGAL.

Estimate of the quantities of some of the staple articles of commerce annually imported into Calcutta from the country West of Rajmahl for exportation and local consumption, from the best informed Mahajuns (native merchants) engaged in the trade.

	Tons.	Cwts.
Indigo . . .	3,214	5½
Sugar . . .	89,285	14
Saltpetre . . .	21,428	11½
Cotton . . .	7,857	2½
Wheat . . .	12,500	
Gram . . .	16,071	8
Dholl and pease . .	16,071	8
Oats . . .	1,785	14
Barley . . .	71	8
Opium . . .	628	11
Linseed . . .	7,142	17
Mustard seed . .	1,785	14
Teel seed . . .	178	11
Ghee . . .	178	11
Total Tons .	178,199	15½

N.B. Besides the above there is an innumerable variety of other imports that cannot possibly be estimated, such as Mirzapore carpets, cashmere shawls, scarfs, coarse piece goods, &c., but which constitute a large and valuable trade, yearly increasing.*

* The above statement is compiled from the valuable pamphlet of Mr. R. M. Stephenson, and by recent advices from Calcutta, it is estimated by English merchants that upwards of one hundred tons of grain, besides other kinds of provisions, and live stock, would be conveyed daily by the Rajmahl line for the Calcutta market. (1846).

TRAFFIC ON JUMNA.

Total traffic on Jumna downwards, taken at Allahabad Bridge, of boats, during 25 days of April, 1841.

36,024	Bags of salt	at	12 Bags per Ton	3,002		
52,080	Bales of cotton	,,	8 ditto ,,	6,510		
828	Bags of saltpetre	,,	12 ditto ,,	69	Tons.	
2,000	Hides	,,	50 ditto ,,	40		
	Add for 5 days	..	.. ..	1,924		
					11,545	

Jumna traffic upwards.

13,119	Bags of rice	at	12 Bags per Ton	1,193		
2,240	Ditto cocoa nuts	,,	12 ditto ,,	170		
2,347	Spices	,,	12 ditto ,,	195		
2,815	Miscellaneous	,,	12 ditto ,,	234		
	Add for 5 days	..	.. ..	358	2,150	
						13,695

TRAFFIC ON GANGES.

Total traffic on Ganges downwards, taken at Allahabad Bridge, of boats, in April, 1841.

Quantity	Item		Rate		Tons	Subtotal	Total
54,700	Pieces of Kurwah cloth	at	500	pieces per Ton	109		
1,004	Bags of mustard seed	,,	12	,,	84		
6,305	Ditto saltpetre	,,	12	,,	525		
7,162	Bales of cotton	,,	8	,,	895		
12,250	Hides	,,	120	,,	102		
4,450	Miscellaneous	,,	12	,,	371		
13,700	Horns	,,	120	,,	114		
						2,200	
	Ganges traffic upwards.						
1,348	Wine chests	at	12	pieces per Ton	112		
1,013	Bags of cocoa nuts	,,	12	,,	84		
7,394	Ditto rice	,,	12	,,	616		
4,189	Ditto spice	,,	12	,,	349		
4,940	Iron and tin	,,	10	,,	494		
						1,655	
	In addition to this, 94 boats containing passengers and goods not counted, and may be estimated at 40 tons each					3,760	
							7,615
	Total amount of traffic on Ganges and Jumna in April, 1841						21,310

TRAFFIC ON GRAND TRUNK ROAD.

Statement of the amount of traffic along the Grand Trunk Road as kept at Futtehpore, under the superintendence of conductor Tuceffe, *during the month of April*, 1841.

Futtehpore, 1st *May*, 1841.

Hackeries.	Bilies.†	Camels.	Elephants.	Bullocks.	Tattoos.	Mules.	Horses.	Buggies.	Carriages.	Palanquins.
West 636	407	64	23	106	162	51	19	8	2	48
East 441	428	159	21	189	133	7	19	5	3	55
Day 1,077	835	223	44	295	295	61	38	13	5	103
Night 419	113	197	6	50	33		72	19		58
Total 1,496	948	420	50	345	328	61	110	32	5	161

† Native Carriages.

COMPILED BY PERMISSION OF THE AUTHORITIES, FROM OFFICIAL RETURNS IN THE INDIA HOUSE.

Statement showing the Number and Tonnage of Vessels resorting to CALCUTTA, MADRAS, and BOMBAY, and also Value of the Imports into, and Exports from, the three Presidencies; for the Years 1833–4, and 1843–4.

ARRIVALS	CALCUTTA.				MADRAS.				BOMBAY.			
	1833-34		1843-44		1833-34		1843-44		1833-34		1843-44	
	SHIPS	TONS	SHIPS	TONS	SHIPS	TONS	SHIPS	TONS	SHIPS	TONS	SHIPS	TONS
UNDER British Colors	330	122,952	494	208,055	3,561	189,909	397	127,281	144	62,520	360	164,984
" French	31	10,771	47	13,673	21	6,571	28	6,710	9	1,852	3	645
" Dutch	2	352	5	1,868	8	917	2	208	1	424	"	"
" Portuguese	1	350	5	1,101	129	4,064	13	1,747	11	3,520	3	529
" American	22	7,342	15	6,893	3	958	4	1,686	1	211	5	1,760
" Arab	10	4,386	10	4,845	130	21,123	195	26,799	4	1,276	6	824
" Native	432	36,616	196	17,584	1,179	95,785	4,941	210,944	"	"	"	"
" Burmese	1	400	2	500	"	"	"	"	"	"	"	"
" Austrian	"	"	"	"	"	"	"	"	"	"	1	305
" Swedish	1	302	"	"	"	"	"	"	"	"	1	190
Total of Arrivals	830	183,471	772	254,519	5,031	318,417	5,580	375,375	170	69,803	378	169,187
TOTAL VALUE of IMPORTS.	Sicca Rupees		Company's Rupees		Company's Rupees		Company's Rupees		Company's Rupees		Company's Rupees	
Of the same Periods	195,81,986		493,25,807		1,03,09,999		98,47,007		266,74,031		176,06,865	
At 2s. pr. Company's Rupee.	£2,088,745		£4,932,580		£1,030,999		£984,700		£2,667,403		£1,760,686	
DEPARTURES	SHIPS	TONS	SHIPS	TONS	SHIPS	TONS	SHIPS	TONS	SHIPS	TONS	SHIPS	TONS
UNDER British Colors	333	122,845	532	224,318	4,225	218,159	610	189,395	173	78,864	386	178,906
" French	29	10,416	45	13,085	23	5,666	45	10,950	10	3,066	4	922
" Dutch	2	352	4	1,580	10	1,185	2	208	1	424	"	"
" Portuguese	1	350	3	1,207	146	4,557	9	1,429	7	1,956	3	529
" American	19	6,765	18	8,372	3	958	3	1,307	3	876	5	1,860
" Arab	12	5,221	9	4,223	183	24,736	296	38,347	5	1,844	7	2,013
" Native	432	36,616	197	18,045	970	87,336	5,825	237,410	"	"	"	"
" Austrian	"	"	"	"	"	"	"	"	"	"	2	610
" Swedish	1	315	"	"	"	"	"	"	"	"	"	"
" Spanish	"	"	3	580	"	"	"	"	"	"	"	"
" Burmese	"	"	2	344	"	"	"	"	"	"	"	"
Total of Departures	829	182,880	813	271,754	5,560	342,597	6,790	479,046	199	87,030	407	184,840
VALUE of EXPORTS.	Sicca Rupees		Company's Rupees		Company's Rupees		Company's Rupees		Company's Rupees		Company's Rupees	
Of the same Periods	3,79,12,649		9,78,66,356		1,38,46,794		2,22,96,369		4,05,881,135		6,84,30,869	
At 2s pr. Company's Rupee.	£4,044,015		£9,786,635		£1,384,679		£2,229,637		£4,058,813		£6,843,087	

NOTE.—The small country craft carrying the coasting trade, which are separately returned in the Bombay Official statements and have not been included in the above abstract, are apparently entered in the Madras returns, which will account for the disproportionately large tonnage of that Presidency.

In estimating the gross trade of Calcuttà—the amount of its imports and exports together, an allowance of about 7 per cent. in 1833–4, and above 3 per cent. in 1843–4, should be made for imports re-exported.

To face p. 174.]

APPENDIX TO THIRD EDITION.

STATEMENT OF THE TRAFFIC BETWEEN CALCUTTA AND DELHI, FROM OFFICIALLY AUTHENTICATED GOVERNMENT RETURNS.*

Goods Traffic between Calcutta and Mirzapore.

Ganges Traffic (Goods).

In the year 1844-5, it appears, from the official statement of the Collector of tolls at Jungypore, on the Bhaugerruttee River, that boats passed through that branch of the river, containing 21,497,750 maunds; or, taking 27 maunds to the ton, the tonnage of the laden cargo boats was	796,213 tons.
To catch the vessels coming through the rivers of the Sunderbunds, a toll is imposed on the vessels navigating Tolly's Nullah, and the circular Canal at Calcutta. The toll is half a rupee for every hundred maunds of tonnage (boats of less than a hundred maunds not being counted), and in 1844-5 it yielded 177,791 rupees; showing that 35,558,200 maunds of tonnage had passed through it, which, at the rate of twenty-seven maunds to the ton, gives—per annum	1,316,970 „
Traffic in native boats is therefore	2,113,183 tons.

---

* Vide 1st Report of Directors East India Railway Company.

Brought forward	2,113,183 tons.
In 1844-5, seven steamers made thirty-nine trips upwards, and carried 112,765 measurement feet, and 1,156,909 lbs. weight of cargo. Reckoning a cubic foot to weigh 30 lbs., we have, carried UPWARDS by steamers	2,027 „
The number of DOWNWARD trips, and goods carried, cannot be precisely ascertained; but the number of downward trips must have been about the same as the number of upward trips; and, from the return of *several* downward trips which *are* ascertained, the proportion of goods carried downwards would appear to be about one third of the goods carried upwards. We therefore have, carried downwards, of measurement goods, 37,588 feet, and 385,636 lbs. weight of cargo, or ...	675 „
Total of goods carried on the Ganges	2,115,885 tons.

Traffic on the Mirzapore Road and Damooda River.

Between Calcutta and Burdwan 2,000,000 maunds of coals are carried, say	74,074 tons.
On the road leading through Burdwan, the yearly traffic is 7,360 hackeries, and 3,650 laden bullocks. A hackery load is twelve maunds; but as the whole number of hackeries would not probably be fully laden, we may take the load at ten maunds each, which gives 73,600 maunds as the weight carried, say..	2,726 „
Twelve bullocks will carry about a ton; there are, therefore, annually carried by bullocks...	304 „
Carried over	77,104 tons.

Brought forward			77,104 tons.
Besides this, we have carried along the road—			
Of Sugar and Goor	maunds	500,000	
Salt	. . . . .	350,000	
Cotton	. . . . .	1,000	
Rice	. . . . .	50,000	
		901,000, or	33,370 „
Making a total of goods carried along Mirzapore Road and Damooda River	. . .		110,474 tons.

RECAPITULATION.

Traffic by native boats	2,113,183 tons.
Ditto in steamers	2,702 „
Ditto along the road	110,474 „
Total tonnage	2,226,359 tons.

Passenger Traffic between Calcutta and Mirzapore.

By native boats . .	about	60,000	passengers	per annum.
„ Steamers . . .		2,000	„	„
„ Passengers passing over the Annabad Bridge in various conveyances, and on foot .	about	508,000	„	„
Total . .		570,000	„	„

Goods Traffic between Mirzapore and Delhi.

In the returns obtained, the goods traffic is variously stated, at 1,051,881 tons; 1,017,500 tons; and 900,000 tons, consisting of salt, sugar, cotton, and general merchandize.

Passenger Traffic between Mirzapore and Delhi.

By Carriages . .	about	56,804	passengers	per annum.
,, Palkees . . .		1,959	,,	,,
,, Dhoolies . . .		1,437	,,	,,
,, Elephants . .		1,323	,,	,,
,, Camels . . .		668	,,	,,
,, Horses . . .		38,916	,,	,,
On foot . . .		334,744	,,	,,
Total .		446,851	,,	,,

[The average speed and cost of conveyance is given in the ol lowing page.]

NOTE.—The value and tonnage of imports and exports of Calcutta by sea for 1844-5—£18,024,420—and	531,262 tons.
(Vide *Calcutta Review*, No. 14).	
Showing an increase in imports and exports over the previous year—in value—£3,305,205—in tonnage . . .	4,989 ,,
(Vide p. 176).	

AVERAGE SPEED AND COST OF THE PRESENT MODES OF CONVEYING PASSENGERS AND GOODS IN BENGAL AND N. W. PROVINCES.

(One person).	Time.	Distance.	Fare. s. d.
By Dâk (post)	in 24 hours. —	60 miles	1 0 per mile.
,, Palkee	(Vide p. 159).	15 ,,	0 8 ,,
,, Gharry*	(native carriage)	12 ,,	0 5 ,,
,, Steamer	,,	50 ,,	1 6 ,,
,, Budgerow†	,,	20 ,,	2s. to 0 6 ,,
,, River boats‡	,,	25 ,,	0 0½ ,,
,, Horse	,,	15 ,,	0 1⅛ ,,
,, Hackery with goods	,,	10 ,,	0 1¾ ,,

Goods per ton per mile.

By steamers 2½d.|| By river boats 1¾d. to ½d. § By land .4d.¶

---

* Can accommodate three or four travellers.

† Is hired for the trip—and if large—can accommodate a family of five persons.

‡ If there are eight passengers, the charge for each will be as above—only natives, whose means are very moderate, travel in this way, the wealthy native trader pays a much higher fare.

|| A higher rate is charged for short distances.

§ The speed of the cargo boats is much less than that of those which convey passengers.

¶ This is by the common cart of the country—by pack-bullocks, camels, and ponies it is more expensive.

Travelling by land in Madras and Bombay is much the same as in Bengal—they have no navigable rivers.

The Madras rate for Government stores by cart, is 5½d. per ton per mile.

In Bombay the rate is very fluctuating, but the average may be taken at 5d. per ton per mile for the conveyance of cotton from the interior to the port of Bombay—pack-bullocks are generally used from the want of roads in this presidency.

Vide *paras.* 77, 78, *&* 79 *of the Report of the Government Commission on the cultivation of cotton in India.*

TABLE OF THE QUANTITY AND VALUE OF TROPICAL PRODUCTIONS IMPORTED INTO ENGLAND.

"*Statement made by Mr. Montgomery Martin, in the Court of the East India Proprietors, as to the Quantity and Value of Articles Imported into England, the whole of which may be obtained from British India.*"

1.	Sugar, 4,500,000 cwts. at 20s. per cwt.	£4,500,000
2.	Molasses, 500,000 cwts. at 10s. per cwt.	250,000
3.	Rum, 5,000,000 gallons, at 1s. per gallon	250,000
4.	Coffee, 40,000,000 lbs. at 6d. per lb.	1,000,000
5.	Tea, 40,000,000 lbs. at 1s. per lb.	2,000,000
6.	Cocoa, 3,000,000 lbs. at 6d. per lb.	75,000
7.	Tobacco, 50,000,000 lbs. at 6d. per lb.	1,250,000
8.	Cotton, 400,000,000 lbs. at 6d. per lb.	10,000,000
9.	Indigo, 7,000,000 lbs. at 3s. 6d. per lb.	1,225,000
10.	Saltpetre, 300,000 cwts. at 20s. per cwt	300,000
11.	Rice, 300,000 cwts. at 10s. per cwt.	150,000
12.	Pepper, 7,000,000 lbs. at 4d. per lb.	125,000
13.	Cinnamon and Cassia, 1,500,000 lbs. at 6s. per lb.	450,000
14.	Ginger, 25,000 cwts. at 20s. per cwt.	25,000
15.	Spices (general), official value	250,000
16.	Cochineal, 600,000 lbs. at 5s. per lb.	150,000
17.	Wool, 60,000,000 lbs. at 1s. per lb.	3,000,000
18.	Hemp and Flax, 2,000,000 cwts. at 20s. per cwt.	2,000,000
	Carried over	£27,000,000

	Brought forward	£27,000,000
19.	Vegetable Oils, 6,000,000 gallons, at 1s. per gallon	300,000
20.	Hides, 400,000 cwts. at 36s. per cwt. . .	720,000
21.	Skins untanned or dressed, number, 4,000,000, at 6d. each	1,000,000
22.	Linseed, 3,500,000 bushels, at 30s. per quarter	600,000
23.	Tallow, 1,000,000 cwts. at 20s. per cwt. .	1,000,000
24.	Dye Woods, &c. official value . . .	500,000
25.	Drugs and Gums, ditto	500,000
26.	Sundries	1,000,000
	Total	£31,720,000

"There is scarcely one important article of tropical produce, which is consumed in this country, either as the raw material of our manufactures, or as an article of daily use for the production of which India is not as well, or better adapted than any other country; while its dense and industrious population would seem to offer an illimitable demand for our manufactures. Nor are there opposed to these natural and flattering elements of commerce any fiscal restrictions to counteract their beneficial results."

The Economist, August 28, 1847.

APPENDIX TO FOURTH EDITION.

RETURN TO AN ORDER OF THE HONOURABLE THE HOUSE OF COMMONS. *Dated* 28*th July*, 1846.

EAST INDIA HOUSE, *3rd August*, 1856. } JAS. C. MELVILL.

(PERFECT RETURN).

REPORT UPON THE PRACTICABILITY OF INTRODUCING RAILWAYS INTO INDIA, AND UPON AN ELIGIBLE LINE TO CONNECT CALCUTTA WITH MIRZAPORE AND THE NORTH-WEST PROVINCES.

From *F. W. Simms, Esq.*, Consulting Engineer to the Government of India, and Director of the Railway Department; *A. H. C. Boileau*, Captain Bengal Engineers; and *J. R. Western*, Captain Bengal Engineers; March 13, 1846.

1.—We have the honour to submit our Report upon the practicability of introducing a system of railways into India, and of their application to the peculiarities and circumstances of the country and climate; to answer the questions relative thereto, as proposed in the Minutes of the Honourable the Court of Directors of the 7th May, 1845; and likewise to make our report, from a personal examination of the country, upon the direction of a line to be recommended for a railroad from Calcutta to Mirzapore and the North-West Provinces.

2.—We would commence by stating our opinion that railroads are not inapplicable to the peculiarities and circumstances of India, but, on the contrary, are not only a great desideratum, but, with proper attention, can be constructed and maintained as perfectly as in any part of Europe. The great extent of its vast plains, which may, in some directions, be traversed for hundreds of miles without encountering any serious undulations, the small outlay required for parliamentary or legislative purposes, the low value of land, cheapness of labour, and the general facilities for procuring building materials, may all be quoted as reasons why the introduction of a system of railroads is applicable to India.

3.—In the Minute of the Honourable Court of Directors of the 7th May, 1845, the following occurs in the third paragraph: "Independently of the difficulties common to railroads in all countries, there are others peculiar to the climate and circumstances of India, which may render it advisable that the first attempt should be made on a limited scale. These peculiar difficulties may be classed under the following heads, viz. 1st. Periodical rains and inundations. 2nd. The continued action of violent winds, and the influence of a vertical sun. 3rd. The ravages of insects and vermin upon timber and earthwork. 4th. The destructive effects of the spontaneous vegetation of underwood upon earth and brickwork. 5th. The unenclosed and unprotected tracts of country through which railroads would pass. 6th. The difficulty and expense of securing the services of competent and trustworthy engineers.

4.—To these difficulties we beg to reply as follows:—

I. As to the periodical rains and inundations, we do not expect that, with a judiciously-selected and well-constructed line, any serious mischief to the works may be anticipated from this cause; nothing but what a moderate annual outlay will set to rights. The practicability of keeping a railway in order is shown by the existence of bunds and roads, both metalled and unmetalled, in various parts of the country, which are kept in order at a trifling outlay. It must, however, be borne in mind, that although this opinion is based upon what we have ourselves witnessed as the effects of a season when the floods were unusually high, both in Bengal and the Upper Provinces, yet, in after years, unprecedented inundations may occur, causing serious damage to works which shall have been constructed with a view to resisting only the highest floods hitherto known.

II. The continued action of violent winds and influence of a vertical sun. Suitable arrangements in the construction of the works will overcome any difficulty arising from these causes as to the line itself. These effects will be more felt in working the trains, especially the wind at high velocities, but no fears need be entertained upon this subject as to the ultimate result, though, during the prevalence of the hot winds, more than usual attention will be requisite in watching and guarding against the effects of friction of such parts of the engines or carriages that may be exposed to the most intense heat.

III. The ravages of insects and vermin upon timber and earthwork. If the information we have received be correct, that the destructive action of insects upon the teak and ironwood of Arracan amounts to nothing, or next to nothing, that question is at once disposed of; but should further investigation show that such is not the fact, recourse must be had either to the use of stone or to the employment of one or more of the various preparations for timber now in use in England, which, it is probable, may also be found desirable on the score of economy, to render the timber more durable. This, however, at present, is by no means certain; Captain Western, who has been in Arracan, states that he would not guarantee teak as resisting damp and insects, but iron-wood he knows, from practical experience, to resist both, and has seen a post taken up, after having been in the ground fifteen years, as sound as the day it was put in. To the earthwork no serious mischief is to be apprehended from this cause, if the overseers and labourers on the line discharge their duties in a proper manner. It is true that earthworks in the Upper Provinces, constructed in a loose soil, have occasionally been damaged by the undermining of rats, crabs, otters, or other burrowing animals, but it appears that constant vigilance would provide an effectual remedy for this, as well as for the next following difficulty.

IV. The destructive effects of the spontaneous vegetation of underwood upon earth and brickwork. To obviate this evil, nothing more is required than a faithful discharge of the duties of the overseers and labourers in rooting up every germ of such vegetation as soon as it appears. Captain Boileau suggests that the attention of the persons in charge of those portions of the line passing through Young Saul Forests must be particularly directed to this point, as trees of this kind, after having been cut down to clear ways for trigonometrical operations, have been known to spring up again to an altitude of about fifteen feet in two years, and, in various parts of the country the rapid growth of Palma Christi (the Castor-oil plant), the gigantic reed called Surkunda and Nurrul, and many other such wild productions, may give considerable trouble, though the strong roots of the latter are admirably adapted for giving stability to an earthen bank. The roots of the Peepul tree are particularly injurious to brickwork, but are tolerably easy of extraction.

V. The unenclosed and unprotected tracts of country. A fence similar to our quick fences in England will answer through the open and cultivated parts of the country, which may or may not be employed through the districts covered with jungle, as circumstances may require. Such fence may be formed of the plant called the Berandu, or the Mysore Thorn, or the Prickly Pear, all of which, and perhaps many others, if kept well trimmed, would make a suitable fence. In several localities where stone is obtainable in abundance, this material might, and in certain cases where the soil is too barren for the growth of hedges, must be used for boundary walls, and in the vicinity of Saul Forests, the exceeding straightness of this wood renders it particularly valuable for the construction of posts and railing.

VI. The difficulty and expense of securing competent and trustworthy engineers. This difficulty, we make no doubt, will be overcome by a suitable arrangement by the Railway Companies, at an early period. Such, we should think, would be the sending of a few native or East Indian young men to England, to be trained, until some engines are ready to be sent to India; upon their return in charge of such engines, and under the superintendence of one or two English engineers, there would be laid the foundation for the training of as many native engine drivers as might be required. Such native youths, while in England, should not only be instructed to drive an engine, but to repair them when out of order.

5.—In the second paragraph of the Minute of the Honourable Court of Directors, allusion is made to the probable returns of merchandize and passengers; this appears to be one of the bearings to be investigated and reported upon by us, but, from an entire want of statistical information, we are at present unable to give any opinion.

6.—With the above view of the case we should not deem it inexpedient or unwise to attempt the introduction of railways into India to any extent that private enterprize might be found willing to embark capital upon; subject, however, to whatever equitable conditions and regulations the Government might think proper to require for the promotion of their own and the general interests of the country at large; at the same time having due regard to that of the parties engaged in the enterprize.

7.—As, however, the Honourable Court of Directors have, in the fourth paragraph of their Minute, dated 7th May, 1845, noted, for the instruction of this committee, that one of its objects will be "to suggest some feasible line, of moderate length, as an experiment for Railroad Communication in India," we beg to suggest that there is a line in the North-West Provinces which would answer admirably as an experimental line, viz., from Allahabad to Cawnpore; but if this line be thought too extensive as an experimental one, we believe that a line from Calcutta to Barrackpore would find no lack of British capitalists, both able and willing to undertake its immediate construction.

8.—Having thus expressed our opinion, in general, upon the subject of introducing railways into India, we will proceed to describe the route we would recommend, from personal examination of the country for a line of railway, connecting Calcutta with Mirzapore, and from thence to Delhi and the North-West Frontier.

9.—On the line from Calcutta to the North-West Provinces, first impressions would lead to the supposition that the proper direction for a line of railway, connecting Calcutta with the North-West Provinces, passing through Mirzapore, would be to cross the river Hoogly at Calcutta, and proceed in the direction of Bankoora; this course would take the railway across a district of country not only subject to periodical inundations that are among the greatest in the lower provinces of Bengal, but, in the event of the breaching of the bunds of the Damooda and other rivers that it would have to cross (as was the case during the last rainy season), would be subject to the action of powerful torrents acting injuriously, if not destructively, upon the works of any railway. These considerations led to an examination of the country further to the northward, which, commencing at Calcutta, was extended along the left or east bank of the Hoogly, past Barrackpore, and crossing the river a little below Chandernagore, at right angles to its stream. The line would then leave Chinsura and Hoogly on the right, and cross the trunk-road to Benares, near to Mucklumpore, and from thence, nearly in a straight line, to Burdwan; at this place it would cross the Banka Nullah, and be continued nearly parallel to the trunk-road, and enter upon the land that rises above the general level of the periodical inundation.

10.—The object in making this apparent detour is, that by flanking the Damooda we should in part escape the water that flows towards the sea in the direction of that large river, but not be wholly free from its effects; and whenever an occurrence should hereafter take place similar to what took place during the late inundations (viz., the breaching of the bunds of the river), a considerable amount of damage would arise to the works of the railway.

11.—So long as the water is confined within the river banks, no material injury would arise to the works of the railway simply from the submersion of the country during the rains; but upon the accident before named the body and rush of water was so great as entirely to undermine and destroy a bridge near Dullah Bazar, and to threaten destruction to the bridge over the Banka Nullah at Burdwan, by which Nullah the surplus waters, in a great degree, found their vent towards the river Hoogly.

12.—In addition to the foregoing considerations, it is possible that hereafter it may be considered advisable to abandon the preservation of the river bunds, and to allow the waters during the rainy season to overflow the surrounding country, in the expectation that the sedimentary matter that is now raising the bed of the river may overspread the country, and tend to raise the general level: (this has been hinted to us as a suggestion that has been made, but upon which we must be understood to give no opinion): such a procedure would have an effect upon the railway works that is difficult to foresee or provide for, except in all probability by the construction of a larger quantity of viaduct for the free passage of the waters than would otherwise be necessary, and thus increase the cost and maintenance of the works.

13.—The above considerations and information obtained from Lieutenant-Colonel Forbes, Captain Anderson, &c., led to an examination of the country still further to the northward, from which it appears that a very advantageous line of country for a railway exists on the left bank of the Hoogly, and crosses that river at a short distance below where it is first formed (or takes that name) by the junction of the Bhaugerruttee and Jellinghee at Nuddea, from which crossing it would proceed due west, and pass about ten miles to the north of Burdwan, near to a place called Balkishun.

14.—This line would quit Calcutta at its northern extremity, skirt the gun-foundry at Cossipore, and take a direct line northwards nearly parallel to the Barrackpore road, which it would cross at the bend near Barrackpore. Hereabouts a station for the accommodation of that district might be advantageously established. From thence it might follow the general direction of the river, to accommodate Chinsura and Hoogly, &c., and onward by a straight course to Goonpulla, on the road between Barrasut and Ranaghat.

15.—As regards simply the construction of a railway, it might, with equal advantage to the works, be constructed in a straight line from Calcutta to Goonpulla, and thus, by avoiding Barrackpore, &c., would be a little shorter in distance than by that route; but it appears preferable to adopt the former line for the accommodation of that and the neighbouring localities of Serampore, Chandernagore, Chinsura, Hoogly, &c., which would then more than ever become the favourite resort of the citizens of Calcutta, and be a source of remuneration to the railway itself.

16.—From Goonpulla the line would take nearly a straight line towards Ranaghat, near which it would cross the Matabhanga river, and from thence proceed almost parallel to the road leading to Kishnagur, but gradually trending to the north-west, and cross the road from Kishnagur to Santipore, near to a place called Dignagur. It would then continue to curve until it crossed the Hoogly, near to an indigo factory, called Punchilla, which is south of the junction of the Jellinghee and Bhaugerruttee, as before described.

17.—After crossing the river, the railway would be carried in nearly a straight line past Singalee, Baljoree and Balkishurn, which is the place before alluded to as ten miles north of Burdwan.

18.—The railway, if constructed by Ranaghat and Nuddea, would be about thirty miles longer than by taking it in the direction of Hoogly and the trunk-road to Burdwan, which extra distance, although it would tell largely upon a short line of railway, becomes of less importance when it forms part of a railway of so great an extent as the one under discussion (namely, to the North-West Provinces about 900 miles in length); besides which, it will pass through and accommodate a rich district of country, in addition to affording the same amount of accommodation to the Burdwan district, and in all probability would hereafter form a trunk from which branch railways will be made to those parts of India north and north-east of Calcutta.

19.—In furtherance of this object, we extended our examination in November last to the country north of Kishnagur, through Berhampore and Moorshedabad to Bhagwangola, with a view to a branch railway from Kishnagur to those places; and although the country is highly favourable for such a project, yet the great mart at Bhagwangola is of so unfixed a character, from the extensive and continued changing of the bed of the Ganges, that unless its continuation northward and eastward be considered desirable, it would appear that a branch to Bhagwangola, simply to accommodate the trade that now passes along the Ganges to Calcutta by the Sunderbunds route, will not be found to answer as a commercial speculation; a permanent point, however, on the banks of the Ganges, exists at or near Rajmahl, which might be suitable to receive the great traffic of the river, and be connected with the trunk line a little northward of Burdwan, and be found advantageous to the general trade of the country, in like manner as the proposed canal of Lieutenant-Colonel Forbes would certainly have done, if that important work had been carried into execution. Such a branch railway would in no point be removed very far to the westward of the projected line of the canal in question.

20.—Also, as regards the comparative cost of the works on the above lines, we consider it would be less, mile for mile, on the Ranaghat Line than on either of the others, that is independent of the great bridge that must cross the Hoogly in either case, the cost of which would be less the higher up the stream it is constructed.

21.—The chief objection that appears to the above line is the fact that it involves the crossing of the Matabhanga river, near Ranaghat, in addition to that of the river Hoogly, which river must be crossed, at any rate, in order to bring the railway into Calcutta, unless it be resolved to terminate it at Howra, on the opposite side of the river to Calcutta, which would, at least, be very inconvenient for business, even supposing the country between that and Burdwan was as suitable for the construction of a railway, and offered as much general accommodation to the country, as the line further to the northward. Besides, the expense of constructing a bridge over the

Hoogly, at Calcutta, would be greater than a similar crossing sixty miles higher up the stream.

22.—With a view to the saving, if possible, of the extra bridge over the Matabhanga, which is a considerable river, we examined another line that would leave the last-described line nearly opposite to Chinsura, and take a more direct course to the river Hoogly, which it would cross near the villages of Collipore, on the east side thereof, and Damooda on the west, thence onward to Inchura, where it would cross a nullah, and, leaving Culna on the right, would curve to the north and west by Sacheroy, and, crossing the Bauha and Kurree nullahs, join the Nuddea Line, near to the before-named Balkishun, about ten miles northward of Burdwan.

23.—The latter route would be about fifteen miles shorter than by the Nuddea Line, but (pro rata) it would be more costly in its construction, and miss accommodating a very valuable district of country, which, in all probability, would pay for the extra length of railway. The crossing of the Matabhanga at Ranaghat, therefore, appears to be the chief consideration against the adoption of the more northern line, as compared with the line by Culna.

24.—Upon an inspection of the most eligible place for crossing the Hoogly on the Culna Line, near the village of Damooda, it also appeared that, in addition to the simple crossing of the stream, there was, on the left or east bank, a considerable extent of flat country between the wooded elevated land and the water, which is doubtless submerged during the rainy season, and seems to be the ground through which the river has wandered in former times and left dry, from the continued change in its bed. If this be correct, it will be necessary to construct a viaduct of great extent to carry the railway over this recent alluvial deposit, in addition to the actual bridge over the river; and the uncertain expense in founding and erecting such a work in that situation is so well known that the fact need only be named to ensure a dissent from its adoption.

25.—Such was our opinion formed upon the spot; but before a final decision be given upon the subject it might be advisable for the Railway Company who may undertake the work, to make a detailed survey and section of each line, and submit them for estimate and comparisons, as in a work of such magnitude the utmost saving of expense is desirable; but so impressed are we in respect to the public advantages to be derived from the more circuitous route, that we consider a comparatively small saving should not be allowed to weigh in favour of the Culna Line.

26.—From Balkishun, as a common point on the two northerly lines, the railway would proceed nearly direct to and cross the trunk-road at about Kagsa, where the Southern or Chinsura Line, after passing through Burdwan, and nearly following the course of the high road from that city, would be united with them; from thence it would take the left bank of the river Damooda, pass through the Raneegunge collieries, and onward to near where the river Barrakur joins the Damooda.

27.—The line will next take up the valley of the Barrakur, and follow, approximately, the course of that river, nearly for its whole extent, to the summit of the country at or near the Dhunwa Pass, where a very rapid descent occurs from the westernmost range of hills in Bengal to the plains of Behar. Up to near this place the gradients of the line will be very easy, and although steeper gradients will have to be here introduced to overcome this natural barrier, we do not expect, from the levels we have taken, they need be greater than can be worked by assistant power when the trains are heavy, and it is the only place upon the whole line where favourable gradients cannot be obtained at a small cost as regards the earthworks.

28.—After entering upon the plains of Behar, the line will proceed nearly direct by Shuhurghotee and Nowrungabad to the Soane River.

29.—The river Soane is a formidable obstacle to the cheap construction of a railway, being two miles and three furlongs in breadth, and the foundation, or natural substratum below (at present) an unknown depth of sand. The erection of a viaduct across this great river is, however, a matter of expense only, there appearing no difficulty in the case that perseverance and ingenuity will not overcome. The most suitable point for crossing the river seems to be about three miles higher up than where the trunk road now crosses it, at the foot of the range of sand-stone hills, from which much valuable material for the structure might be obtained, and for this purpose, also, granite of excellent quality may be quarried about two miles south-west of Nowrungabad, and about twelve miles south-east from the proposed site of the bridge. Lime also is obtainable on or near the spot.

30.—In the construction of this bridge, and of all others of great magnitude, as the crossing of the Hoogly and the Jumna, hereafter to be referred to, we would recommend that they be made of ample width, not only for the railway, but also for a common highway, which may be separated from the railway by a screen of masonry. The additional cost of such extra width at the time of construction will be but little, in comparison with the cost of a separate structure for the public highway, and compensation might be given to the Railway Company for the extra outlay, either by Government supplying an equivalent portion of the cost, or granting them the right of levying a toll for a given number of years.

31.—On the other hand, we would advise that all bridges of great magnitude erected by Government, for the purpose of any public highway, in any part of India, should be constructed of ample width to accommodate a railway also, if there should appear any moderate probability that such a work would become desirable for, or likely to be executed in, that direction within any reasonable period of time.

32—From the river Soane, the railway will skirt the foot of the hills to the town of Saseram, two miles north-west of the proposed bridge, and then in like manner for about seventy-four miles, west by north, to the town and fortress of Chunar, on the right bank of the river Ganges, leaving the trunk-road and the city of Benares considerably to the right. This is done in order to obtain better ground for the construction of the line, and a branch to Raj Ghât, opposite to Benares, seventeen miles in length (leaving the main line nine miles before reaching Chunar) would answer all the purposes of that great city and the district of country to the northward thereof.

33.—The railway will pass between the sand-stone

hills on the south side of Chunar, which will all along furnish valuable building materials for the very numerous masonry works along the line.

34.—From Chunar to Mirzapore, a distance of eighteen miles in the same direction, west by north, the line will still keep along the foot of the hills, although a little circuitous, as it will be desirable to avoid the bad ground in the more direct course.

35.—Having now explained our view as to a suitable line for a railway between Calcutta and Mirzapore, we will, before proceeding further, describe the branches we should propose to diverge therefrom, to give the most extensive accommodation to the country at large, and to relieve the traffic of the Ganges proceeding to Calcutta from its great drawback during at least eight months of the year; namely, the circuitous route by the Sunderbunds, when the waters of the Bhaugerruttee are too low to admit of the more direct route from the Ganges to the capital of India.

36.—The first branch should be from a point near Burdwan to Rajmahl, along the district of country selected many years ago by Lieutenant-Colonel Forbes, for the Rajmahl Canal: such a railway will, in future, supersede the necessity for the canal, which, however, would have conferred great benefit on the trade of the country, if carried into execution when he first proposed it; the fact that such a canal has been for many years a desideratum, proves the same thing in favour of the more modern mode of intercommunication.

37.—Besides the accommodation of the trade of the Ganges, it will give accommodation to Purneah, Malda, Dinagepore, Rungpore, and the country in that direction, through which it may possibly hereafter be found desirable to extend this refined mode of transit.

38.—After all that has been stated from time to time in favour of Lieutenant-Colonel Forbes's important work, nothing more need be added in favour of a branch railway in that direction. This branch would be about 120 miles in length.

39.—The second branch we would propose would leave the main line about five miles eastward of Shuhurghotee, and pass northward through Gaya to Patna and Dinapore, thus accommodating a very important district of country, as well as the military and civil stations above named, and, on the opposite side of the Ganges, the valuable districts of Tirhoot and Sarun, &c. This branch will be about eighty miles in length.

40.—Another branch might probably be advantageously made from the main line, up the valley of the Soane, to the coal-fields westward of Rotasgurh, but we do not lay much stress upon its immediate formation as a branch until it be ascertained whether or not the main line from Bombay will take that course, as it appeared some time ago probable that such might be the case. Such a branch may be found desirable, if not indispensable, to the interests of the Railway Company, as they might thereby obtain coal for their own purposes as well as to supply the public in that and the still higher parts of India.

41.—The last branch we should propose for immediate construction on this portion of the Great Trunk Line from Calcutta to the North-West Provinces, should be, as stated in Para. 32, from about nine miles before reaching Chunar to Raj Ghât opposite Benares, a distance of about seventeen miles.

42.—We have described our view of the most suitable direction for a line of railway from Calcutta towards the North-West Provinces; but it may be argued that the line passes through a comparatively barren portion of the country, as compared with the valley of the great river Ganges, which has been suggested by other parties as the most eligible route for a line of railway, and which is stated to have in its favour a great probability of becoming more lucrative than the line we have recommended.

43.—First impressions might be favourable to this view of the question; such a result might be expected if either line was dependent only for its support upon the agricultural produce and population of the district through which it passes; but, upon further consideration, it appears to us that the ultimate result will be favourable to the direct line; for, by means of its branches to Patna and Rajmahl, it will take all, or nearly all, the trade likely to be transposed from the river to the railway, in either case, and give nearly as good accommodation to the country around, and to the district northward of the Ganges, as Tirhoot, Purneah, Dinagepore, &c. through which it will probably hereafter be found advantageous to extend the railway system, by starting from the opposite respective termini at Patna and Rajmahl, and, in addition to accommodating the trade of the river and surrounding district, it will bring forward a country now much neglected in consequence of its imperfect communication, a district which contains mineral wealth, and possesses great capabilities, as is evident from the proofs of recent improvement, to a great extent contiguous to the line of the trunk-road, within the last few years, a greater part of which until then was abandoned to the beasts of the forest: this great benefit will therefore be in addition to nearly the same amount of accommodation being given to the whole country as could be given by the river line alone; and, lastly, a direct line between the extreme termini, where attainable, is always most desirable, especially in a political point of view, and in a country circumstanced as India is. Thus much for the traffic considerations of the subject; and it only remains to be stated that we cannot give a decided opinion upon the engineering question without a personal examination of the river line.

44.—On the extension of the line from Mirzapore to Delhi: but little need be said respecting this portion of the proposed works. In length it will be about the same as that of the line we have already described, Mirzapore being about midway between Calcutta and Delhi. The direction of the line will be nearly as follows: between Mirzapore and Allahabad it will trend a little to the south of a direct line, to secure better ground for a foundation to the works. Upon this portion of the line the railway will cross the river Tounse, and, in order to extend it into the Doab, the river Jumna must also be crossed at or near to Allahabad: a suitable spot for crossing exists near the present Bridge of Boats: thus the military magazine at Allahabad would be connected by railway with Calcutta, and, by the extension to Agra and Delhi, with the magazines at those places respectively.

45.—Leaving Allahabad the railway would keep on the south-west side of the trunk-road to Futtehpore and Cawnpore; from thence it might take a direct line to Mynpooree, which would be its proper course if continued direct to Delhi; but if it be finally resolved that the line shall pass through Agra, and thence to Delhi, along the right bank of the river Jumna, it would be more desirable that the railway should proceed from Cawnpore by Shekoabad to Agra, as that line would not only be shorter, but would avoid the crossing of one or more nullahs that it would have to do if taken by Mynpooree.

46.—Supposing that its route would be through Agra, it would again cross the river Jumna at the latter city, a suitable site for which purpose would be a little northward of the present Bridge of Boats; and, passing the civil lines to the north of the Government offices, and Ackbar's Tomb at Secundra, take a tolerably direct course through Muttra to Delhi.

47.—A suitable place for a station at Agra exists where the rails continued from the bridge would become level with the present surface of the ground, about midway between the river and the civil lines; and, if necessary, such station could be connected with the banks of the river at a much lower level than the railway, by a branch descending to the water's edge.

48.—Before, however, determining that the main line should pass through Agra to Delhi, it is a subject for consideration, whether or not it would be more desirable to take the line direct through Allyghur, and cross the river Jumna, at Delhi; for this purpose a suitable place for crossing the river is immediately to the northward of the palace, from whence it could be continued along the bank of the river to a station on the vacant ground at the back of the magazine; and, if necessary, can at any time be prolonged northward, past cantonments towards Kurnal.

49.—The advantages of the direct line to Delhi over that by Agra, would be, 1st. The shortening of the distance between Calcutta and the frontier. 2nd. Passing through probably a richer agricultural district than would be done on the route between Delhi and Agra; and, 3rd. In case of invasion from the westward, a possible, although not probable occurrence, the railway would be protected by the river Jumna. On the other hand, the city of Agra, at present the capital of the North-West Provinces, with its magazine, would be less directly connected with the frontier and the Magazine at Delhi, if situated at the extremity of a branch, than if placed upon the main line. The country also to the west of the river Jumna, although perhaps not so productive to the agriculturist as that in the Doab, yet is admitted to possess a very considerable trade.

50.—As respects the two routes, in an engineering point of view, there appears to be no great difference; for although on the direct line there would be the additional cost of crossing the river Hinden (no trifling matter certainly, unless, as suggested by his Honor the Lieutenant-Governor of the Upper Provinces, the crossing be effected below the junction of the Hinden with the Jumna, if the Jumna itself be as manageable there as at Agra or Delhi). The route by way of Agra would be about twenty miles longer, and consequently, from that cause, increase the cost of construction to probably within a trifle of that of the direct route.

51.—If Agra be accommodated with a branch line only, and that branch be terminated on the opposite side of the river to the city, it would be highly inconvenient and undesirable; but if a bridge is to be constructed at

Agra, at all events, to carry the railway into the city, which it should by all means do, then the consideration would be greatly in favour of taking the main line by the Agra route, for the more perfect accommodation of that great capital of Upper India.

52.—Whichever of the two directions for the main line between Cawnpore and Delhi be finally fixed upon by Government as most desirable, the line can, at any future time, be extended to Kurnal, and to the frontier, where a terminus might be established on the highest navigable part of the Sutlej, and thus connect the great rivers, the Indus and the Ganges.

53.—The branches to be recommended for construction on this upper portion of the main line from Calcutta to the north-west would be one to Furruckabad, a second to Allyghur, a third to Meerut, and, upon the future extension of the line to Kurnal, a branch could be advantageously constructed from thence north-eastward towards the hills on which the sanitary stations of Simla and Mussooree are situated, or wherever else it may be found desirable.

54.—The first branch, or that to Furruckabad, would leave the main line about sixty miles north-westward of Cawnpore, and proceed direct, the length being about forty-five miles from the line, through Shekoabad to Agra, and thirty-two miles if taken from the direct line to Delhi through Mynpooree.

55.—The second branch, or that to Allyghur, would lead direct from Agra, and would be about forty-eight miles long; but if the direct line to Delhi be adopted, this branch would not be required, as the line itself would pass through Allyghur.

56.—The third branch would be from Delhi to Meerut, about thirty-six miles long, and which, if the main line takes the right bank of the river, we propose should terminate opposite to the city of Delhi, as it appears to us the traffic would not be sufficient to warrant the expense of constructing a costly bridge over the river Jumna for the purpose.

57.—The fourth branch, namely, from Kurnal towards the hills, requires no further remark at the present time than we have already bestowed upon it.

58.—If, however, it should ultimately be resolved that the direct line to Delhi through Allyghur be adopted, the branch to Agra would leave such main line near to Sikundra, a distance of about forty miles.

59.—We have given, as we consider, the leading facts on both sides of the question, necessary for the final choice of the direction for the main line; these appear to us so nicely balanced that we would refrain from making a positive recommendation upon the subject; but if called upon to state which of the two we would prefer, we should be disposed to recommend the route by Agra.

60.—The general character of the works, &c.—The heavy works upon the whole line from Calcutta to Delhi, will, for the most part, be of masonry, consisting of bridges to cross the very numerous rivers and nullahs in its course, many of which are of great magnitude, and all very considerable. The earthworks will be light, except at the summit of the country described in Para. 27, at which place it may be found necessary to undertake works of a heavier kind: but, upon the whole, it is not to be expected that there exist in the world many lines of equal length requiring so small an amount of earthwork to be performed.

61.—The great bridges comprise those over the rivers Hoogly and Soane upon the lower portion of the line, and the crossings of the Jumna, at Allahabad, and Agra, or Delhi, upon the upper portion; and although these structures will be very costly, yet there is nothing in their character that can cause them to be considered as insurmountable difficulties; the chief difficulty will be in their cost.

62.—With a view to enable contracting parties to open the whole line at the earliest period with the least possible outlay, it might be advisable to permit of the laying down, in the first instance, of a single line of railway, with all necessary passing places; but this should distinctly apply to the permanent way only, as the earthworks and masonry (but more especially the masonry works) should be constructed for the reception of a double line: this latter observation regarding the masonry should apply also to the branches, so that at any future time a second line could thereon also be applied without difficulty. The earthworks upon the branches might with safety refer to a single line only, as they will, in the branches already named, amount altogether to a trifle.

63.—It is highly probable that a double line of rails will be absolutely necessary upon the main trunk-line at no distant period, if not required in the first instance, and therefore we would recommend, that in consenting to a single line to begin with, it should be understood to imply that such single line is only admissible until the whole length is opened to the public, when a second line should be added forthwith, if the Railway Company be called upon by the Government to do so.

64.—We cannot but view the whole distance from

Calcutta to Delhi as one line, for we are of opinion that as such it would be better worked and conducted under the management of one company than if it were divided and in the hands of more numerous bodies; besides which, we consider that it would also be advantageous as well as fair, that the whole should be granted to one company, if a sufficiently sound party will come forward to undertake it, because they would then have a great length of line for a reasonable average outlay. The lower half, from Calcutta to Mirzapore, costing considerably above that average, and the upper half, from Mirzapore to Delhi, as much below it.

65.—We conclude by adding, that, in addition to the line from Bombay joining the main trunk-line between Allahabad and Calcutta, as before alluded to, it has been suggested to us by his Honor the Lieutenant-Governor of the North-West Provinces, that a suitable line of country may hereafter be found for the construction of a railway from Agra to Bombay; by these two lines, the North-Western Provinces would be effectually supplied with communication, not only with the seat of the Supreme Government at Calcutta, but with the great seaports on the two opposite coasts of the continent of India.

(Signed) F. W. SIMMS, C. E.
A. H. C. BOILEAU, CAPTAIN ENGINEERS.
J. R. WESTERN, CAPTAIN ENGINEERS.

Camp Sersoul,
13th March, 1846.

(True copy.)
T. L. PEACOCK,
Examiner of India Correspondence.

East India House,
3rd August, 1846.

REPORT ON THE INTRODUCTION OF RAILWAYS IN BENGAL, ADDRESSED TO SIR ARCHIBALD GALLOWAY, K.C.B., CHAIRMAN OF THE EAST INDIA COMPANY, 1849. By *W. P. Andrew*, with Introductory Remarks, by the Editor, reprinted from the *Artizan*, of June, 1859.*

"THOSE who recollect our former articles upon railways in India, (says the Editor of the Artizan) will remember, that in the district of Bengal two distinct projects presented themselves before the public for favourable acceptation. The first of these proposed to connect Calcutta with the great central mart of Mirzapore, by means of a line four hundred and fifty miles long, carried by the most direct route between the two termini, and running for the greatest part of its length nearly parallel with the great trunk road which connects Calcutta and Benares. The other project proposed to accomplish the same objects by connecting Calcutta with Rajmahl, a town lying on the main stream of the Ganges, at the head of the Delta, one hundred and eighty miles from Calcutta, and below which the chief difficulties in the navigation of the river are found to exist; and, as that part of the Ganges lying between Mirzapore and Rajmahl and Calcutta, and in which the water is split up into many streams, would be superseded by the proposed railway, an efficient

* The line seems to have been adopted which was originally recommended by Mr. W. P. Andrew.—*Times*, 19*th Nov.* 1851.

system of communication with the interior would, it was contended, be obtained by the proposed railway at a comparatively small expense. The line between Calcutta and Mirzapore was the line proposed by the East India Railway Company, of which Mr. Macdonald Stephenson was the originator, and Sir George Larpent, and subsequently Mr. Aglionby, was chairman, and was also the line recommended by Mr. Simms and the Indian Railway Commission. The line between Calcutta and Rajmahl was the line advocated by the Great Western of Bengal Railway Company, of which General Macleod was chairman, but which was first brought prominently into notice by the 'Old Indian Postmaster,' Mr. W. P. Andrew, who obtained for it, by his writings, the recognition of the authorities. The advocates of the East India Railway maintained that the speed of the existing Ganges steamers, which did not exceed fifty miles a day, was quite inadequate to warrant such an expedient of communication to be accepted as part of the main line connecting the interior with the coast. It was also contended that the transhipment of merchandise at Rajmahl would be attended with loss and inconvenience. Mr. Andrew contended, on the contrary, that a railway four hundred and fifty miles long was too gigantic a work for the commencement of railways in India; that some parts of the line, especially the bridge over the Hoogly at Sooksauger, and that over the Soane (the absurdity of the former is now acknowledged, while the latter is upwards of two miles long, with only quicksand for a foundation, and with a rise of water in the river of thirty or forty feet during the rains,) would be liable to be carried away by the floods; and that as the rivers in Bengal have not in general defined channels but deviate over the plains, the bridges, even if they stood, might be deserted by the rivers, and new bridges be made necessary elsewhere. At Rajmahl, however, the river happens to run in a rocky bed, and there are no great rivers lying between that point and Calcutta; so that it was contended this particular line would be free from physical impediments of a weighty character. With regard to the deficient speed of the steam vessels navigating the Ganges, it was maintained that vessels of an improved class might be introduced, by which in all probability a superior speed would be obtained; but that a high speed was not the great *desideratum* in India, as much as cheapness with a moderate speed, and safety and regularity in the arrivals.

"We have never been among the advocates of the Rajmahl line, and the opinions we have on former occasions expressed respecting it we still entertain. But when the East India Railway Company, finding their undertaking too gigantic, proposed to make a fragment of the line leading from Calcutta into the jungle, and which never could possibly acquire a remunerative traffic, it became very obvious to us that the alternative lay between making the Rajmahl line, and having no railway at all in Bengal. Accordingly we find the East India Railway Company at length abandoning its fragments, and proposing to itself the formation of the Great Western of Bengal line, which for years it has sought to discredit. But it succumbs, as all human powers must do, to the gravitation of fact. It has tried all issues, and now finds, at the eleventh hour, that it must adopt the very counsels which years ago it rejected. Years ago we saw that to undertake a fragment of the line was an unsound and untenable measure. It has well nigh proved fatal to the project, and, after all, has to be abandoned in favour of another measure, formerly the object of reprobation. Surely the reflection is not irrelevant, that infinite mortification would have been avoided—much waste of effort and much waste of time—if a little less obstinacy had been exhibited and a little more docility.

"But enough of these reflections, which cannot recal the past, though with this past before them our readers may, perhaps, acquire more confidence in any prognostications of the future which we may hereafter put forth. On the present occasion, however, we shall content ourselves with laying before our readers a valuable report, by Mr. Andrew, the consistent advocate of the Rajmahl line, giving a condensed view of his published opinions, illustrative of the advantages of that undertaking. This report, of which we have been fortunate enough to obtain a copy, was, we understand, submitted to the late Sir A. Galloway, at his own request, when Chairman of the East India Company in 1849; and, at the present moment, when the intimation reaches us from India, that the railway to which this report refers is one which is actually proposed to be constructed, the document will have peculiar interest for our readers."

"But at the outset of the career of improvement, the rivers should, we consider, be availed of as much as possible; and when, by their aid, a district has been nursed into importance, and cultivation and irrigation have been largely extended, then a railway may be carried into that district with the certainty of a remunerative result, and a remunerative result is quite indispensable to the wide introduction of the railway system. And as in the earlier career of the railway system, the rivers may lend, in many cases, important aid by acting as feeders, and may gradually so develope the resources of remote districts, as to enable railways to be carried into them with advantage; so, on the other hand, the railways thus carried into the country will be available for the transmission of its productions, when the rivers are dried up from their waters being employed for irrigation, and this we are persuaded is their ultimate destiny. The railway and the river navigation systems, therefore, must go hand in hand. Without the aid of the rivers, the railways can never acquire any large extension during the present generation; but with that aid they may be expected to grow with all the rapidity due to success, and in the proportion in which any district flourishes, and its irrigation is extended, so will the importance of the rivers for all purposes of communication gradually decline, leaving to the railways the inheritance of the traffic and prosperity they have created. With these cursory remarks we introduce Mr. Andrew to our readers, omitting such portions of his report as we deem less essential on the present occasion."

REPORT.

To Major General Sir Archibald Galloway, K.C B., &c. &c. &c.

London, May, 1849.

The East India Railway Company having been exclusively identified in the public mind with a direct line from Calcutta to Mirzapore, a gigantic, difficult, and costly undertaking, mainly for political purposes, was necessarily, in a great measure, dependent for success upon the amount of liberality accorded to it by the authorities.

The character of the undertaking itself, viewed as a commercial speculation, irrespective of the 5 per cent. guaranteed by the Honourable East India Company, holding out to the adventurer little inducement to embark his capital therein; the line not being in any way adapted for an experimental or preliminary line from its vast extent (450 miles in length), and from the unprecedented, and now admitted, fact, that no beneficial result could be obtained, either by the Government or the commercial public, until the entire undertaking should have been completed, bringing Calcutta into railway connexion with the Ganges at Mirzapore*—the extent and formidable nature of the physical obstacles to be surmounted—the want of population in 250 miles of the regions to be traversed by the proposed railway—the difficulty (in seed time and harvest, the impossibility) of

* This commercial entrepot stands some fifty miles below the confluence of the Ganges and Jumna, and by following the downward course of the former we are brought to the Bhaugerruttee, which flows into the Hoogly, on the left bank of which stands Calcutta: this is the track of commerce; a continuous water communication, in the form of a bow or arc, connecting Calcutta with Mirzapore. Look now at the course of the proposed railway to Mirzapore, and you will see that it is the string to the bow or arc, and the irresistible conclusion is at once arrived at, that no traffic can accrue till the cord of that arc is completed, or until the railway from Calcutta touches the Ganges at Mirzapore. (1849).

there collecting, housing, and feeding labourers and artisans, as well as of preserving the health and lives of such, and of their European or other superintendents when collected from a distance, and of inducing them to remain in the pestilential jungle-covered hills of a great portion of the line *—the expense, delay and labour in the conveyance of materials to localities remote from river transit; and, finally, the utter impracticability of affording any sufficient protection to the line when finished, against the depredations and mischievous attempts of adjacent and uncertain hill tribes to destroy the railway, or against wild animals.

Many other reasons might further be adduced to show that the completion of the Mirzapore direct line must necessarily be a work of great delay, expense, and difficulty, requiring, at the most moderate computation, from fifteen to twenty years for its completion, and involving an expenditure of ten millions sterling before it could make any return on capital, or answer any purpose, political or commercial. Even when finished, it could prove useful to Government but in a very limited degree, as three-fourths of the Bengal army are cantoned above Mirzapore, and all emergent movements of troops and stores take place more to the north-west, or in advance of Mirzapore. But in a commercial point of view it is physically and geographically impossible that it could ever

* As was painfully exemplified when the attempt was made of making the grand trunk road (by means of convicts collected from surrounding districts) from Calcutta to Benare, in 1836-7, the lives of more than half of those sent from their respective Zillahs were sacrificed. (1849).

meet the wants of the country; for it would facilitate but in a very limited degree the transit of the valuable products of the opposite side of the Ganges to their ocean outlet, and it was ascertained in evidence before the Wet Dock Committee at Calcutta, that the great bulk of the traffic arriving at Calcutta comes from points on the Ganges below Mirzapore.

The proposed railroad eschews the ancient and beaten track of commerce, turning away from the rich and populous valley of the Lower Ganges,—the grand arena of production, and, consequently, of trade, and which must ever continue to be so till the great river forgets to overflow its banks, and ceases to be navigable,—choosing rather to scale or tunnel the desolate and impenetrable mountain-ranges running parallel to its course.

The export trade being mostly of heavy goods, could not be expected to ascend the river to the terminus at Mirzapore against the stream, or ascend to the railway by branches, contending the whole way (the one proposed to Patna, for instance, being eighty miles in length) against the natural inclination of the country. It is evident, therefore, that a line of railway having Calcutta for its lower terminus, and a point on the Ganges for its upper terminus, that the traffic, of necessity, must be in an inverse ratio to the length of the line, that is to say, the further you extend your railway before debouching on that great commercial artery, the less must be the traffic.

Objections so formidable and incontrovertible, have doubtless been long apparent to the Honourable Court, as they have assuredly been to all those acquainted with the country who have taken an interest in a question of such moment; and it is under this impression, and being aware that the best mode of granting relief to the vast and impeded traffic of Lower India, has long been the subject of anxious solicitude to the Honourable Court, that I venture to recall your attention to another project, essentially different,—not liable, when thoroughly explained and understood, to fluctuate in public estimation according to the exact ratio of prestige or credit attachable to the names of those connected with it, or founding its entire and only claim to the support of the capitalist of England on the extent of liberality accorded to it by the authorities; but one comparatively moderate in extent, yet having a great and defined object, simple and easy of execution; adapted to the requirements of commerce, co-operating with, not suddenly, but gradually, superseding where most defective the existing means of transit, and susceptible of making a large return, from the cheapness of construction and the extent of the traffic.

On former occasions, in conjunction with General M'Leod and others, I had the honour to lay before the Honourable Court the unambitious but important results obtainable by a line of railway connecting Calcutta with the Ganges, at or near Rajmahl, from which point the river is continuously navigable at all seasons of the year for steamers upwards, or in a north-westerly direction, for a distance of five hundred miles; but it was intimated to us that it would be more agreeable to the Honourable Court, as well as more convenient, and tend to facilitate the adjustment of a great national question, to waive pressing at that time this more limited, and therefore more practicable project. This suggestion was at once acceded to from deference to the authorities, although contrary to settled opinions derived from personal knowledge of the country.

I beg now, however, again to state, that I am still convinced that this project, strictly in accordance with the views originally entertained by the Honourable Court, in sanctioning Colonel Forbes's projected canal for establishing a direct permanent water communication between the Ganges at Rajmahl and the Hoogly at Mirzapore,* is a scheme well worthy of the early attention of the Honourable Court, and of the Indian Government.

I have received from Mr. Greaves, the engineer employed in surveying the Rajmahl line, and who is now in London, plans and sections in detail of the line from Howrah, opposite to Calcutta, to Rajmahl, all of which have been submitted to the inspection of Colonel Forbes; and I am now in a position to prove, from surveys made during the rains, by boat and otherwise, everything which I have advanced, and feel assured that there is not in India, or in any other country, a line possessing such peculiar facilities for construction and working, combined with an existing traffic so large and so susceptible of being augmented;† and I would re-

---

* *Vide*—accompanying Extracts of Report of Canal Committee.

† It is apparent, from the statistical tables attached to the first report of the East India Railway Company, that the traffic which they claim for the Mirzapore line belongs in reality to the Rajmahl line, for it will be seen that nearly all the traffic which is appropriated to the former, is taken at two points, namely, Calcutta and the Bhaugerruttee River, the principal portion of which, coming either from the opposite bank of the Ganges, or from points below Mirzapore, would of necessity be obliged to

spectfully beg leave to refer the Honourable Court to that high authority in engineering projects, Colonel Forbes, in confirmation of these views.

The upper terminus of the proposed railway at Rajmahl would necessarily become the steam port of Calcutta, and the grand depot of all the valuable commodities constituting the inland trade; while the lower terminus at Howrah, meeting contiguously in the same focal area, with wet docks, and communicating with Calcutta by means of a steam ferry or suspension bridge, would economise and expedite in an extraordinary degree the transactions of the external commerce of India.

By connecting in this manner the two great channels of commerce, the Hoogly and Ganges, five hundred and twenty-eight miles of a circuitous route, large por-

---

pass over the Rajmahl, or some such line, to reach the Calcutta and Mirzapore direct line. The river traffic is estimated at more than two million tons, while that by the road is only 33,370 tons; both evidently exaggerated, many boats and carts being empty, or nearly so.

There has been always one great omission in the traffic returns, from taking only the traffic at Jungypore on the Bhaugerruttee. The tolls on the other two rivers, tributaries to the Hoogly, are very great; that for the Jellinghee is collected at Kishnagur, and though not equal to Jungypore, is large, owing to its having more water all the year: that for the Matabanga and Ishamuttee, is collected either at Ranaghat, Sibnibas, or Hanskhalee, and should be entered in traffic returns in preference to the gross collections of the eastern canals, which includes all the traffic of Dacca and Sylhet, to which neither the project of the East India Railway Company, nor the line which I advocate can lay claim. (1849).

tions of which are extremely dangerous and intricate, through the labyrinth of the Soonderbunds, would be saved for eight months in the year, and the "rapid and ever tortuous Bhaugerruttee," always dangerous to commerce, and annually occasioning numerous wrecks, attended with the total loss of large amounts of property, would be avoided for the remaining four months. The railway train would, with certainty, perform in ten or twelve hours what now takes the steam vessel, on the average, as many days, and what is only precariously accomplished by the heavily-ladened country boat in a month.

After having thus endeavoured to supply what has long been considered by the Honourable Court and the Government of India the grand *desideratum* for the commerce of the country,* and having thereby not only solved the problem of the practicability of railroads in India, but from having selected the line of all others likely to yield a large immediate return, demonstrated that a railway in India is a highly remunerative undertaking, we should then have no difficulty in making another line or section, recommencing where the navigation again becomes defective, for instance, from Benares to Allahabad, or from Allahabad to Cawnpore, the river intervals between these sections being provided for (until united) by a sufficient number of powerful iron steamboats. We should thus gradually, easily, and profitably for the government, the public, and proprietary body, establish an extensive and available railway development, every part of which might eventually become an integral

* *Vide*—Extracts from Reports accompanying this letter.

portion of a complete trunk line of railway communication between Calcutta and the north-western frontier: pursuing along the entire route the beaten track of commerce through the most populous and productive regions in India; connecting the great towns and military and civil stations; and having every facility for construction by means of river transit and a dense population; the comparative salubrity of the climate, the perfect security to the works during their progress, the peaceable and industrious habits of the people, so entirely under control; together with the abundant supply of food, and all other requisites.*

---

* Another reason, according to papers recently received from India, for the construction of this line (Calcutta to Rajmahl), is, that the largest river connecting the Ganges with the Hoogly is yearly closed up; and they add that:—

"There are many local circumstances which may render the construction and working of this line (Calcutta to Rajmahl) the cheapest, as it would be the most valuable. Coals, for instance, may be brought down the Adjie River and laid down under twenty-five rupees per hundred maunds (27 maunds = 1 ton). Lime may be taken from the bed of the same river and laid down burnt ready for use, for less than the above sum. Bricks may be burnt by the people of the country all along the line, at two rupees eight annas per thousand. Granite for sleepers, or wooden ones, if preferred, are easily obtained. Timber of large size can be brought down the Ganges from Gurruckpore at low rates, and landed at Rajmahl, or it may be obtained in the district itself.

"The country through which the line would pass is populous, and the people *au fait* at bunding, levelling, making watercourses, none but mere Coolie labour would be needed beyond that supplied along most part of the line itself. This line is neither

The comparative merits of the two modes of connecting Calcutta with Delhi and the north-west frontier, may be stated in a few words. A line from Calcutta by Burdwan, Hazareebaugh, Shergotty, and Mirzapore to Delhi, or, a line from Howrah, opposite to Calcutta, by Rajmahl, Bhagulpore, Monghir, Patna, Benares, and Mirzapore, to Delhi. By the latter, the actual or lineal distance would not be increased more than eighty miles, and the time occupied in traversing the entire distance would scarcely be affected, as it would be essentially a level throughout; while the former would have on several portions stiff gradients, requiring assistant power, so that the question resolves itself into one of time—not distance, for *pro rata* to the power required, so is the distance—while to many intermediate points (Patna, for instance) the lineal distance by the Gangetic Valley would be actually less, and the necessity would no longer exist for a number of branches to supply the railway with traffic; the main trunk itself meeting the requirements of both the through and local traffic of the country, and thereby saving the cost of construction of upwards of one hundred miles of railway. Every few miles of such a railway, when opened, would be available for traffic, and yield some return on the capital expended, while scarcely any beneficial result could be expected from the Mirzapore direct line until the whole was completed.

---

subject to inundation, nor to being flooded by the bursting of Damoodah bunds, the embankment therefore may be low; and for nearly fifty miles scarcely any is wanted. The construction of this railway may thus be easily effected with economy and prudence." (1849.)

It may, however, be deserving of the Honourable Court's deliberate consideration, whether the East India Company can withdraw from the pledge which was given to the commercial community, when its Government in Bengal engaged to devote all surplus collections from the tolls established on the Nuddea Rivers, to the great object of securing to the commerce of that country a secure and permanent communication with the Ganges at a point free from circuitous navigation.

In the spirit of that pledge the survey of the projected canal between Rajmahl on the Ganges, and Mirzapore on the Hooghly, was undertaken by one of the Honourable Court's most zealous and able engineer officers, Lieutenant Colonel Forbes. And it is only necessary to refer the Honourable Court to its dispatch of the 23rd December, 1844, finally disposing of Lieutenant Colonel Forbes's elaborate surveys and estimates of the projected navigable canal, to remove the slightest doubt that that project was merely postponed with the view of ascertaining whether the more expeditious mode of internal transit by means of a railroad, might not be substituted for that by water.

This, however, still remains to be done. It is true, as is explained in a note attached to this paper,* that the Rajmahl line has been incidentally considered by Mr. Simms, the advising civil engineer in Bengal; but there is no evidence to show that Mr. Simms was required to report upon this great work as a primary object, embrac-

* Vide Extracts from Railway Reports from India, ordered by the House of Commons to be printed, 15th February, 1847, p. 241.

ing the ready transit of commodities between the port of Calcutta and the interior of India, by the ancient channels of the internal and external commerce of that country.

It is, therefore, this defined and comparatively practicable project, that I would again earnestly press upon your consideration: trusting that the direct communication being once established between Rajmahl and Calcutta, the improvement of the steam navigation from that point to the north-westward would rapidly follow, and ultimately tend to the formation of railroads in the upper provinces, which are admitted to be free from those obstructions which render the scheme of the East India Railway Company (from Calcutta to Mirzapore), exceedingly problematical as a financial undertaking. I would also recal to the recollection of the Honourable Court, that the paramount importance of commencing the railroad system in Bengal was strongly and emphatically urged by the Chairman of the Honourable Court, at the Court of Proprietors, in June, 1847, in the following words:—" As to cotton, in Bengal, it was more important to have railways for that article than in any other part of India; because the cotton produced in the Nerbudda lost twelve months from the time it was gathered until it was exported. It was liable during that period to great deterioration, to charge for warehousing and transport." " But it should be in the recollection of the Court, that they had other objects of paramount importance in view; a connection between the western provinces and the seat of government was pre-eminently necessary, and this they proposed commencing as soon as they could."

It cannot be doubted that the social position and

general prosperity of the inhabitants of the British Empire in the East, as well as the maintenance of the commercial and manufacturing pre-eminence of England, must be most powerfully influenced by the success or failure of the first railway in India. The momentous results involved in the solution of this question must plead my apology for having ventured to extend this letter to such an unusual length.

I am, &c.,

W. P. ANDREW.

London, July, 1853.

In further confirmation of the views expressed in the foregoing communication, addressed by the writer to Sir A. Galloway, in 1849, reference is now made to the accompanying extract from the speech of Sir Chas. Wood, as reported in the *Times* of the 4th June, 1853:—

"I cannot here avoid expressing an opinion, that the Indian railroads were commenced without sufficient consideration, and the consequence has been that in both cases, it has been found necessary to change the line originally laid out. In the first instance, it was intended that the line from Calcutta should run along the old turnpike road; but after it had been carried to a certain point, it was wisely determined that it should run along the line of the river, and through the most populous parts of the country."

"Statistical Papers," printed for the Court of Directors of the East India Company in 1853, are still more explicit as to the partial adoption of my views:—

"The railroad from Calcutta to the north-western provinces was projected in 1844. The contract for its construction, between the East India Company and the Railway Company, was signed in August, 1849. The expenditure of £1,000,000 was sanctioned for the first section, *viz. from Howrah, opposite Calcutta, to Raneegunge, viâ Pandooah and Burdwan.*

"*The line is to be continued from Burdwan, in a northerly direction, to Rajmahl, and thence probably along the right bank of the Ganges to Patna, Mirzapore and Allahabad.* A further sum of £1,000,000 has been sanctioned for the purpose of continuing the extended line to Rajmahl, the whole expense not having yet been estimated. The East India Company guaranteed interest on the capital advanced for this purpose, at the rate of five per cent. per annum for the first million, and four and a-half per cent. for the second."*

And Lord Dalhousie is understood to have recommended in a recent despatch, that *the Rajmahl line should be carried up the valley of the Ganges to Allahabad.*

In surveying the vast extent of territory embraced by the British dominions in India, with a view to the introduction of railroads into that country, it would appear obvious, that the local demarcations which have been found convenient in the administration of the Indian government, should be kept in view. Some such limitation, the official paper just quoted from, appears to

---

* Vide Minute by the Governor General, 20th April, 1853. p. 255.

indicate, while the "Friend of India," and other leading journals, adduce weighty and practical reasons for confining the operations of each company within reasonable bounds; and the report recently received from the Governor-General of India affirms in express terms the principle of restricting the operations of companies within certain limits.

It was evident from the beginning, that *little* railways in Bengal and Bombay, especially when competing with water carriage, must of necessity, from the nature of the country and the traffic, prove *great* failures. Yet in 1850, we were told authoritatively in parliament, that the mighty problem of the applicability of railroads in India would be solved, if it could be proved that in that country sleepers could be laid, and water would boil! That although the adaptability of the railway to the traffic of the country could not be ascertained, unless a much larger sum were guaranteed than £1,000,000, the experiment might be regarded as perfectly successful, even if the railway should only be able to carry its own fuel, and have just vitality enough now and then to startle a tiger from his lair; the great point being, to ascertain the adaptability of the railroad and its appliances *to the country and climate, and not to the people and traffic.* This is simply absurd. *Were it merely necessary to ascertain the adaptability of a railroad to the country and climate of India, an experiment of one mile would have sufficed as well as one hundred.*

The completion of the Calcutta and Rajmahl line (or of any other properly selected line, terminating somewhere, instead of nowhere), would have solved the adaptability of railroads to India to some purpose, by showing not only that railroads could be made in that country, *but that they would pay.*

I had, in various publications, frequently and earnestly pointed out, that making a portion of the Rajmahl line must inevitably result in disappointment. In the first edition of my work on "Indian Railways," the following passage occurs:—"On the whole, then, it is our conviction that the Great Western of Bengal (from Calcutta to Rajmahl), and the line from Allahabad to Delhi, co-operating with fleets of river steamers, from Rajmahl to Allahabad, would at once be the most judicious, the easiest, the least costly, the soonest constructed, and in every other point of view, the most advantageous mode of *introducing* the railway system into India." Two years afterwards, in the preface to the third edition of "Indian Railways," I return to the subject in these words:—

"The above suggestions are again respectfully recommended to the consideration of the authorities with the following explanation:—

"In June, 1846, when the writer advocated as above, that a line should be made in Upper India simultaneously with one in Lower India, it was under the impression that a minimum rate of interest on £5,000,000 would have been guaranteed, which would have sufficed for completing the line from Calcutta to Rajmahl, and a large section in Upper India; but as £3,000,000, the sum actually guaranteed, is declared inadequate for these purposes, the impolicy is apparent of burthening the, certain to be productive upper section with a fragment of a section in Lower India leading, comparatively speaking, to nothing. *No assistance could be given to the Government, or general commerce of India by opening a portion of the Rajmahl line, unless that portion from Rajmahl to Mirzapore on the Hooghly,* 120 *miles in length, and which is the exact line of Colonel Forbes's celebrated canal. But if the railway is to commence at Calcutta, or rather, as the writer wishes, at Howrah, on the opposite side (where wet docks could also be made), and connected with Calcutta by a steam bridge, then in that case no great purpose could be answered until the railway debouches on the main Ganges,* and thus supersede the present tedious, uncertain and dangerous channels of commerce, the Nuddea rivers and Sunderbunds, which convey to and from Calcutta and the main Ganges upwards of 2,000,000 tons annually. When the railway from Calcutta to Rajmahl relieved the inland trade from these various impediments, the necessity would no longer exist, for the steamers having their machinery in one vessel, and their passengers and goods in another, and the native cargo-boats would no longer, for nine months in the year, be confined to the alternative of either subdividing their freights amongst a number of small frail craft to pass the Nuddea rivers, or to go by the Sunderbunds an extra distance of 320 miles. Rajmahl would thus become the head-quarters of the inland trade, and a railway from it to Calcutta would, by bringing the vast descending trade of the Ganges into contact with the ships of all nations anchored off Calcutta, supply in the most effectual manner the only link wanting in the chain between the internal and external commerce of the country. *By making a portion of the Rajmahl line nothing would be achieved—*

by connecting Calcutta with Rajmahl by means of a railway—a new impetus would be given to the commercial prosperity of India.'"*

To the Editor of the Artizan.

LONDON, 20*th June*, 1851.

[EXTRACT.]

SIR,

IN your last number I have perused with much interest and satisfaction the observations which you prefix to my letter, submitted some years ago to the late Sir Archibald Galloway, on the Introduction of Railways into Bengal.

Entertaining, as you have all along, views but little in accordance with those which I have advocated, so far, at least, as the Rajmahl line is concerned, I cannot but appreciate the candid spirit which pervades your remarks, and the courtesy which assigned to my paper so prominent a place in your publication. In addressing you, on this occasion, for the first time, it is less with the view of calling in question the accuracy of any of your

---

* "It is gratifying to the writer to find that his views are corroborated by the authority of the deputy-governor of Bengal."

"'A railroad from Calcutta to Bagwangala or Rajmahl, *will not answer the purpose for which it is undertaken, till it is complete, so as to connect the termini with one another;* for both these projects contemplate as their main objects the conveyance of merchandize from the river Ganges, at the points of their northern termini, to Calcutta."' *Vide Minute, by the Hon. Sir T. Herbert Maddock, ordered by the House of Commons to be printed*, 15*th February*, 1847.

opinions and statements, than with the object of bringing out and placing more prominently before the public the great question of Railways in connexion with River Navigation in Bengal.

I have ever contemplated the one in relation to the other, thinking it reasonable and desirable to aid the river navigation, where it was defective, by the removal of natural obstacles, or by surmounting them by means of steam vessels of improved construction, and co-operating with this improved river navigation by means of a railway, where the traffic was great and the rivers cease to be navigable, and where the absence of physical and other obstacles would render the construction of a railway comparatively of easy attainment.

This gradual mode of introducing the railway system of transit was peculiarly adapted, in my opinion, to the Bengal Presidency, where the traffic, however vast in extent, being mostly of a bulky nature, was more adapted to water conveyance than to transit by railway, unless some great advantage had to be gained, and that more affecting safety than speed. The Rajmahl line, for instance, would give 180 miles of railway, instead of, for eight months in the year, 528 miles of dangerous navigation by the Sunderbunds, and for the remaining four months in the year supersede the tortuous and uncertain Nuddea rivers, which flow from the Ganges to the Hoogly.

I also considered that it was of the utmost consequence, in introducing so great an innovation as the railway mode of transit must of necessity be in such a country as India, to select, in the first instance, some line of moderate extent, yet having "a great and defined object," that would yield a good return on capital spent on its construction, that would disturb the existing interests and order of things as little as possible; for in the words of an eminent writer on India—" It has been observed in every age, that when any branch of commerce has got into a certain channel, although it may be neither the most proper nor the most commodious one, it requires long time, and considerable efforts, to give it a different direction."

In addition to the above reasons for introducing the railway system into India in a gradual manner, I adduced others that would ensue, and amongst them, that the want of skilled labour in that country would be best obviated by making the first railway constructed a school for teaching skilled labourers for subsequent operations, and that by relieving in this gradual manner the river steamers from the most difficult, dangerous, and circuitous portions of the navigation, many improvements might be expected to result in the superior adaptation of vessels navigating the waters of the main Ganges.

I feel so strongly impressed with the truthfulness of what I propounded so far back as 1846, that I cannot forbear quoting a short passage from my work on Indian Railways :—

" We have already stated our decided preference for that plan of commencing improved transit, which would only supersede the river navigation where it was most defective, and co-operate with it where it was always available, *i.e.*, a railroad from Calcutta to deep water in the Ganges at Rajmahl; from this point, river steamers to Allahabad, at the confluence of the Jumna and Ganges, where deep water ceases, and a railroad from Allahabad to Delhi and the Sutlej. This would be nearly one thousand miles of railroad, exclusive of branches, traversing the easiest, the richest, and most densely peopled portions of our dominions, where the river transit is either dangerous or tedious, as by the Nuddea rivers and Sunderbunds, or only applicable to the smaller country craft, and closed entirely to steamers, as the great rivers are beyond Allahabad. Above this point it is impossible by land or by water to move military stores or merchandize, in any quantity beyond the average of twelve miles per diem. No Utopian ideas of a railroad system starting at once into complete perfectibility should divert enterprise and capital from so fair and inviting a field, with such feeble rivals, as the carts and boats of the country* to compete with the river steamers which accomplish fifty miles per diem, and which will soon nearly double that rate, when a railroad relieves them from the Nuddea rivers and Sunderbunds. If such a rail be established, the steamers, instead of starting from Calcutta, will start from its northern terminus, which will thus become, in fact, the steam port of Calcutta. The narrow and often angular streams in the Sunderbunds, and lower Bengal will thus be avoided, the necessity of a double vessel will cease, single vessels of larger dimensions, and engines of greater power, may then be employed, by which a large saving of time and money will be effected."†

---

* The charge by the former is 4*d.* per ton per mile—by pack bullocks, camels, and ponies, it is more expensive—native boats are cheap, but slow and precarious.

† See 2nd edit. *Indian Railways.* By an Old Indian Postmaster. p. 116.

The government have for years given an example to private enterprise by keeping up a fleet of steamers, which, although the first that were floated on the Ganges, and evidently capable of being greatly improved upon, have yielded a return of 10 per cent. on the capital invested, and leave their rivals far behind in regularity of dispatch and safety. But even by the government boats, a Calcutta merchant desirous of visiting Benares, distant by land 428 miles, by water for four months in the year 620—and for the remaining eight months about 1000 miles,—incurs an expenditure of £40, and loses more than a month on the journey there and back.

The great *desideratum* that is required in India is, increased facilities for transporting large bodies of passengers; for instance, entire regiments and their baggage,—besides the bulky commodities constituting the inland trade. I mention these circumstances, as it appears to me, from an observation that you make, you do not render that justice to the Rajmahl line, in connexion with improved river transit, which the perfect fairness with which you had in your preceding remarks, recited the chief arguments I had been in the habit of adducing, as well as those of my former opponents, yourself amongst the number, might have led me to expect.

You say,—"Unless the river communication between Rajmahl and the north-west be materially accelerated, the journey from Calcutta to Mirzapore and Benares, by way of Rajmahl, will be longer in point of time, even after the railway is opened, than the present dawk journey by the road."

At present the journey from Calcutta to Benares is performed by the steamers during four months in the year, in ten days, and for the remaining eight months, in about twenty days, which is much more rapid than by any other conveyance, with the exception of travelling post in a palanquin, which is only available for one or two persons at a time; and the Rajmahl line, by relieving the existing steamers of the Sunderbunds and Nuddea rivers, would certainly reduce the time occupied between Calcutta and Benares to about seven days all the year round, which is about the time occupied in travelling post, inclusive of halts, sixty miles being the average performance in twenty-four hours in a long journey, and I think you will admit that the Rajmahl line, aided by steam boats of an improved construction, would readily forward the passenger in five days from Calcutta to Benares, the entire distance, making allowance for the bends in the river, being six hundred miles by this route, and for an expenditure of from £6 to £10. On the other hand, an European, or a wealthy native, going by *dâk* (post) from Calcutta to Benares, a distance of four hundred and twenty-eight miles, will incur an expense of one shilling per mile, besides buckshees (presents) to the bearers, about one shilling per stage, making in all about £25 for the journey, which he will be five days in accomplishing (exclusive of halts). If by palkee with eight bearers, going fifteen miles per diem, he will have to pay £12 10s., besides £2 10s. for a banghy, (a bhangy wallah, or bearer of two light boxes), and will consume nearly a month on the road. This mode of travelling, besides the loss of time, is attended with danger from robbers. The journey is accomplished in sixteen days on horseback.

But the question ought not to be narrowed as to the comparative delay and expense incurred in conveying a single individual from one point to another, and I am confident you did not intend so to deal with it when you instanced the time occupied in *dâk* travelling: but from my experience I know that this is a source only capable of meeting the requirements of one or two individuals at a time. This was strikingly demonstrated at the commencement of the first campaign against the Sikhs; and as what I published soon after on that subject was thought of sufficient importance to be quoted by a gallant proprietor (General Briggs) well acquainted with India at a Court of Proprietors of India stock, and as it illustrates the point in question better than anything else which occurs to me at this moment, I hope you will pardon my again bringing a part of it forward.

"In the annual relief, infantry regiments are often moved from one end of India to the other, at an average of ten miles and a-half per day, halting six days in the month, so that it takes about six weeks to move from Calcutta to Benares: hence arises the necessity of the concentration at all times of a large force in the neighbourhood of an enemy. There are not the means existing (in India) of concentrating troops on a sudden emergency. This was strikingly exemplified in various ways, on occasion of the recent war on the north-west frontier. When it broke out, all officers whose regiments were in the field were ordered to join the army. About one hundred, we believe, in the different services, engineers, artillery, infantry and medical, required to go from Calcutta. They were sent at the public expense, and with the greatest dispatch. How many do our readers suppose the Postmaster-general was enabled to send daily? Three!—and as the journey took sixteen days, travelling night and day, few arrived before the war was over.* Even this could not have been accomplished at any other period of the year.

"Under the order, now countermanded, for the establishment of depôts, the regiments stationed in the Presidency division, were ordered to supply about six hundred men to the depôt intended to be formed at Benares. The utmost dispatch was desired by government; bullock hackeries, the only kind of carriage ever available here, were put in requisition in the usual manner, but the *garriwans* (drivers) had taken alarm at the rumour, industriously, and perhaps maliciously, circulated, that they were to go to the seat of war. They were consequently obtained with difficulty. Many ran away, and from these causes several days were lost before the march could commence, and a halt of some days more became necessary at the end of the first day's journey. Is this a predicament proper for the government to be placed in, within a few miles of a great political and commercial capital? Is it just to the great interests involved in the stability of British power, that the movement of troops should depend on native opinion, or on the caprice of the drivers or owners of bullock hackeries? I shall only add to this, that when European troops are sent by the country boats, two months are occupied in the journey from Calcutta to Benares, and a charge incurred of £3 per man for conveyance alone, without taking into consideration boats for sick, row boats, store boats, and extra establishments proceeding with a regiment or detachment, to say nothing of the privations

---

* About 1400 men were required to carry each officer, at a charge of £120 for the entire journey.

of the men, the loss of time, and the risk of loss of life and property.

I do not think that the above extract meets the question of transit in India, as you, and all others, who have paid attention to the subject would wish to see it met, for of course any means of transit, to be useful in that country, either to the Government or the community, and beneficial to the shareholders, must have, as an essential ingredient, the power of conveying, at an improved speed, large numbers of persons with safety and certainty, and at a moderate rate of charge; and this the Rajmahal line, coupled with steamers of greater power and lighter draught of water, would easily accomplish.

After having advocated the Rajmahal line for so many years, it is certainly gratifying to me to find that it is at length recommended for adoption by Mr. Turnbull, the engineer of the railway company, and Major Pitt Kennedy, the consulting engineer to the Government of India, so that the views I so long ago put forth are now apparently about to prevail.

I am, Sir,

Your obedient Servant,

W. P. Andrew.

EXTRACT.

Administration Report of Railways in India, 1882–3, by Colonel F. S. Stanton, R.E.

Gauge 5′ 6″.

State Line worked by Company.

	Length of line sanctioned.	Length of line completed.
East Indian	1,513	1,506½

Guaranteed Companies.

Great Indian Peninsula	1,288	1,288
Scinde, Punjab, and Delhi . .	688	663½
Madras	861¼	861¼
Bombay, Baroda, and Central Indian	438½	438½
Oudh and Rohilcund	686½	546¾
Eastern Bengal	160	160

State Imperial.

	Length of line sanctioned.	Length of line completed.
Indus Valley and Khandahar . .	653	652
Punjab Northern	355¼	352¼
Sindia	74¾	74¾
Dhond-Manmad	145¾	145¾
Wardha Coal	46½	46½
Patri	22½	22½

State Provincial.

Calcutta and South Eastern . .	56½	43
Patna-Gya	57	57
Amritsur Pathankot	65	—
Poradaha-Damukdia	13	13
Dildarnagar-Ghazipur . . .	12	12

Native State.

Nizam	121	121
Bhopal	62	11½
Khamgaon	8	8
Amraoti	6	6

Assisted Companies.

Bengal Central	125½	20
Serafuli-Tarkessur	22	—
	7,554¾	7,123¼

Gauge 3′ 3⅜″.

	Length of line sanctioned.	Length of line completed.
Guaranteed Company.		
South India	653½	653½
State Imperial.		
Rajputana-Mulwa	1,419¼	1,205¼
Punjab Salt Branch	73¾	73¾
State Provincial.		
Northern Bengal	252½	232½
Tirhoot	243	158¾
Cawnpore-Farukhabad	197	86
Rangoon to Toungoo	163½	—
„ Prome	161	161
Prome to Allamyo	42	—
Nagpur to Chhattisgarh	149	149
Dacca-Mymensingh	85	—
Hathras-Muttra-Achnera	53	52
Bareilly-Pilibhit	33	—
Native State.		
Bhavnagar-Gondal	192½	192½
Mysore	129	86
Jodhpore	18½	18½

Assisted Companies.

	Length of line sanctioned.	Length of line completed
Southern Maharatta	435	—
Bengal and North Western . .	455	—
West of India Portuguese . .	49½	—
Assam Light Railway . . .	75	15
Rohilkhund-Kumaon	62	—
Pondicherry	7¾	7¾
Baidynath-Deogarh	6	4
	4,955¾	3,095½

GAUGE 4′.

State Provincial.

Nalhati	27¼	27¼

GAUGE 2′ 6″.

State Provincial.

Kaunia-Mogul Hât Tramway . .	13½	13½
Kaunia-Dhurla Tramway . . .	21	21

Native State.

Gaekwar of Baroda's . . .	60¼	60¼

Assisted Company.

Burdwan-Kutwah	40	—
	134¾	94¾

Gauge 2′.

State Provincial.

	Length of line sanctioned.	Length of line completed.
Kokilamukh	6½	—

Assisted Company.

Darjeeling-Himalayan . . .	50	50

Summary.

East India and Guaranteed Lines .	6,288¾	6,118
Assisted Lines	1,327¾	96¾
State Imperial	2,790¾	2,572¾
State Provincial	1,650¾	1,026
Native States	597¼	503¾
	12,655¼	10,317¼

FEEDER ROADS FOR RAILWAYS.

A Suggestion.

I HAVE repeatedly drawn the attention of Government to the urgent importance of feeders to Railways in general, and to the great deficiency that exists in this respect on the Railways under my control in particular. I have no doubt that the Government is ready to admit the necessity of the case, but would reply that the question is one entirely for the Local Governments, and is with them simply a question of funds.

2. I wish to point out, however, that the question is one in which the Railways themselves are far more interested than the Local Governments, and this for the simple reason that, to the former, the construction of good feeder roads means an immediate increase of revenue, while to the latter it means a loss of revenue, owing to the annual cost of mantenance, as well as the first cost of construction, without any tangible receipts whatever. The practical result is that the Railways are perpetually calling on the Local Governments to make feeder roads, which it is utterly out of their power to construct and maintain with their present resources, and the uses of the Railway are greatly restricted for want of them, being practically confined to a narrow breadth of country on each side of the line.

3. Take the case of the best section of the Sindh, Punjab and Delhi Railway, that from Lahore to Gházi-abad, a length of 335 miles. This is fed by metalled roads

only at the Stations of Amritsar, Jullunder, Ludhiána, Rájpura, Umballa, Saháranpur, Muzaffarnagar and Meerut, *i.e.* at intervals of 32, 49, 35, 53, 13,[1] 55, 36, 35 and 27 miles; while the other stations, 36 in number, are practically unapproachable by cart traffic for three months in the year, and during the remaining nine months only at a heavy cost in carts and bullocks, which have to make their way over the village tracks which do duty for roads. To anyone who sees the actual state of the case, the wonder is that a large portion of the traffic ever gets to the line at all. I have shown, indeed, in more than one of my Inspection Reports, from cases that have actually come under my notice, that the cost of cartage to the line even in fair weather is from 10 to 40 times the cost of carriage over the same length on the Railway; though even this is a mild statement of the case, for such is the state of the cross country roads that, in the rainy season, they are practically impassable by carts, and traffic is more or less suspended all over the country.

4. Let it be borne in mind that the above line passes through a richly cultivated and populous country for the whole of its length, and is very much better provided with roads than other lines in the north. The Punjab Northern, the Indus Valley and the Mooltan and Sindh Sections of the Sindh, Punjab and Delhi Railway may be said to have no metalled feeders whatever, and on the Indus valley line traffic is practically suspended during the flood season, *i.e.* from June to October. It is not very wonderful, therefore, that these lines do not pay.

5. I know very well it is often said that kacha roads

do well enough for the country traffic; that the bullocks are employed in drawing carts when not required for ploughing, and if not so employed would be idle; and that the difference in draught over a metalled and unmetalled road is often exaggerated. I can only repeat that the practical effects of the present state of things are to restrict the traffic very seriously all the year round, and during part of the year to suspend it altogether, and in any case to make a very heavy difference in point of cost. And that these assertions may easily be tested by anyone who doubts them.

6. Seeing, then, how largely interested Railways are in the construction of proper feeder roads to their various stations, by which the produce of the country may reach the line at a moderate cost, I venture to make what I think is a very obvious suggestion, *viz.* that the railways should themselves devote a certain portion of their revenues towards the construction of these indispensable adjuncts to them, in the assurance that the amount so expended will be almost immediately recovered in the shape of extra traffic.

7. The net revenue of the Sindh, Punjab and Delhi Railway (for example) now amounts to about 35 lakhs per annum. I would take (say) one per cent. of this, and with it raise a loan to be expended entirely on feeder roads. If the money is raised at four per cent., this will give a sum of Rs. 8,75,000; enough, probably, to construct 175 miles of good metalled cross roads, at Rs. 5,000 per mile. The Railway will continue to pay the interest on the cost of construction; and as the additional traffic brought to the line will very soon cover

that small charge, the Railway will be able to make a further grant from its revenue for additional loans from time to time as the traffic continues to develop.

8. I feel confident that it would be well worth while for any line thus to spend a portion of its revenue in order to open up the districts through which it runs, and draw to itself the adjacent traffic, which is now often unable to move to it. And by waiting until the interest on the first loan had been entirely recovered in the shape of increased traffic, the amount of money risked by the Railway would be very small.

9. To show what is approximately required in the case of the line mentioned above—from Lahore to Gháziabad—the Railway may be said to serve a strip of country, approximately eighty miles wide, or forty miles on each side of the line; by which I mean that there is no present likelihood of any parallel line of railway being made at a less distance from the main line than that. In order to develop its traffic properly, it may therefore be fairly reckoned that that length of cross road would be required, at least at twenty miles intervals, or 1,360 miles of road altogether, in addition to the few miles already made.

10. Of course I do not propose to rule the country with parallel lines of road at fixed intervals independent of existing towns and villages. I am only giving an idea of the total length that will be required at the most moderate computation. If, for instance, we had a road only twenty miles long on each side of the line from the thirty-six stations still without any, this would give us 1,440 miles, while, from some stations, it might be preferable to make three or four diverging roads of ten

miles each. The calculation in any case will show that some 1,400 miles of road are needed.

11. It will be seen, therefore, that something like 70 lakhs of rupees would eventually be required to meet the wants of this particular line, in the shape of feeder roads—a large sum, but still only about two years' purchase of its present net revenue, and which I am convinced would be more than fully repaid to it, if expended gradually and judiciously as above proposed.

12. A difficulty will, of course, present itself as to the cost of maintaining these roads. It would seem fair that if the whole cost of construction is defrayed by the Railway, the Local and District Funds should be charged with the cost of maintaining them, the amount being assessed on the land to the value of which their construction will obviously add very largely. Whether this is practicable or not, I cannot say. The construction of these feeder roads is of such vital importance to the Railway, that, rather than be without them, it would, I am sure, be worth while, if necessary, to maintain as well as make them out of its own revenues.

13. But a preferable course would doubtless be to do what has often been suggested, *viz.* after raising and bridging the roads to substitute a light steel tramway for the metalling, on which goods could be carried in trucks or wagons at a rate sufficient to cover the working expenses and repairs, if not a fair interest on the Capital. Even if no interest were obtained, we should still be better off than with metalled roads, which cost a considerable yearly sum to maintain without any tolls being received.

14. It may easily be shown that such tramways can, at the present price of steel, be laid down at the same cost as road metal; and if bullock draught were at first employed until the increased traffic demanded steam power, we should avoid committing ourselves to a heavy expenditure and secure economical results.

15. For such a roadway I should advocate a 2 ft. gauge and a rail weighing 19 lbs. per yard, which would do either for cattle or steam draught. Specimens of such rails were shown in the Calcutta Exhibition, and full particulars as to prices, &c., can easily be obtained.

16. If the traffic on any particular road developed sufficiently to warrant the construction of a regular Railway, on the metre or broad gauge, the tramway could be easily removed and laid down elsewhere. It may be said, generally, that such short branches would not pay to work with steam power if they involved a break of gauge. With long branches the case is different, and the break of gauge, though a nuisance in the case of a heavy traffic, at any rate is an improvement on a break between a cart track and the railway, as at present.

17. The question as to who is to work such cattle tramways is one merely of detail. The new Local Boards or Road Fund Committees should be able to arrange for this, and might be permitted to do so under supervision of the Railway or the Provincial Government; I will not anticipate any friction between these two authorities. My object has been to insist on the heavy stake that the Railways have in the matter and the propriety of applying a portion of their revenues to make the roads in question rather than wait for the action of the Local

Governments who are not specially interested in the matter at all. The particular machinery by which the roads should be made and maintained is a matter to be settled by competent authority when the principle has been accepted. To postpone their construction until the resources of the Local Governments are adequate for the purpose, under existing rules, is virtually to prevent the railways from earning a fair return on their capital, and so to retard the construction of other lines.

J. G. MEDLEY, COLONEL. R.E.,

Consulting Engineer.

Lahore, 27th February 1884.

MEMO. BY MR. J. LIGHTFOOT, AUDITOR, SIND, PUNJAB AND DELHI RAILWAY, LAHORE, ON THE SUBJECT OF THE IMPROVEMENT OF TRADE IN INDIA.

As it has been thought expedient to make a special Parliamentary enquiry into the question of increased Railway facilities in India, it may be useful to bring forward a few points which, in the interest of trade, require Capital expenditure and consideration as much as the construction of new Railways; indeed, some existing Railways can scarcely hope to be thoroughly productive until these points have been settled:—

I.—Improve Harbours and other natural outlets of traffic.

II.—Reduce to a minimum Cartage, handling, and intermediate Agencies at the seaboard by the erection of Landing Wharves and "along shore" Warehouses.

III.—Increase available Shipping at the sea-board by establishing regular lines of steamers from England for Government Stores, Troops, and Mails to all Depôts and Stations connected with Railways, and thereby seriously reduce sea freights from such ports.

IV.—Build Warehouses up-country in which traders can store and clean country produce until the state of the markets permit of its despatch to the sea-board.

V.—In connection with such cleaning Depôts provide Bonded Warehouses connected with the Railway stations at all large centres of trade, where imports and exports may remain free from Octroi and other Imposts until actually required for consumption or export.

VI.—Bridge, or otherwise arrange for a cheap transit over large rivers and torrents.

VII.—Empower Railways to establish a system of through-booking between India and Europe.

VIII.—Construct feeder-roads to connect all agricultural centres with existing Railway stations.

IX.—Place through systems of railway, from the grain-producing centres to the sea-board, as far as possible under one management.

X.—Remove impediments and afford additional conveniences rather than unduly reduce Railway rates.

The remarks herein contained are confined to such points as more particularly concern the trade of the Punjab, but no doubt some of the questions will be equally applicable to other parts of India.

One of the most serious impediments to the development of the Punjab trade is the want of accommodation, and the cost of Cartage, handling, and intermediate Agency at the Port of Kurrachee, which, being under the control of the Bombay Government, cannot in any way be assisted by the Government of the Province of which it is the natural outlet, even if that Government had funds available.

The extracts hereto annexed from a Punjab Government Resolution, dated November 28th, 1882, will show the importance attributed by the Administrators of that Province to the Port.

Indeed, no stronger arguments can be adduced for the necessity of considering the whole of the questions now raised than those contained in this resolution, and the extracts from other correspondence which are also attached to this memo., viz. :—

Extracts from Acting Agent, Sind, Punjab and Delhi Railway's letter to Sir William Andrew, dated August 31st, 1882.

Extracts from a memo. by the Auditor, Sind, Punjab and Delhi Railway, on the subject of Ferozpur and Sukkur Ferry charges, dated March 12th, 1884.

Extracts from the "Civil and Military Gazette," dated March 14th, 1884.

It will, therefore, be inadvisable to repeat such arguments, and separate attention will only be called in the present paper to points not already made clear in the various extracts, which are briefly as follows :—

Kurrachee Harbour Improvements.

The Sind, Punjab and Delhi Railway, since the date of the Acting Agent's letter above referred to, have taken the initiative in the matter of improvements at Kiamari, and have erected a limited quantity of shedding and wharfage accommodation upon their own immediate property, but nothing has yet been done towards the carrying out of any comprehensive scheme by the Harbour Board, the delay being mainly attributable to the difficulties attending the formation of a Port Trust, and the want of the necessary funds. It would appear desirable to transfer the custody of this Harbour to the Punjab Government, and empower that Province to raise a special Loan chargeable upon the Harbour Revenues for the purpose of executing all the necessary improvements; after the completion of which, a Port Trust might probably be much more readily established.*

The importance of sending all up-country Mail viâ Kurrachee.

The whole of the Punjab and Sind, embracing an area of more than 200,000 square miles, including the "hot weather" seat of Government at Simla, as well as all the

---

* Note.—Since writing the above, sanction has been accorded to raise a loan of Rs. 10,00,000; of which, however, only Rs. 3,00,000 will be expended at Kiamari upon the Merewether Pier, the remainder being devoted to the improvement of the inner part of the Harbour about five miles from the anchorage ground for large vessels. This work will, therefore, not make much reduction on the present heavy cost of lighterage, Cartage, and intermediate Agency, and will indefinitely postpone the execution of the most important works required for the removal of Deep Water Point and the establishment of Long Shore Wharves, and Landing Arrangements near the anchorage.

Frontier out-posts, would receive their letters during the north-west monsoon in most cases three days earlier, and in some a week earlier, than by the Bombay route. Troops and Government stores, if sent *viâ* Kurrachee, would save a considerable distance in the Railway journey, and a consequent reduction in Railway fares and time, while officers proceeding on leave to and from England would largely benefit by the regularity in running of a recognized Mail Steamer. Men with limited leave dare not now venture to use the Kurrachee route, owing to the irregularity of the service, although, if it were otherwise, they would save largely in Railway fares to the seaboard.

The Kurrachee and Sind Mails from England are now carried to Bombay, and there transferred into British India Steamers for conveyance to Kurrachee. It would seem a far better and simpler arrangement if this transfer was effected at Aden; not only for the Kurrachee and Sind Mails, but for the Mails and Passengers of all Northern India. Moreover, such an arrangement would give an additional impetus to Punjab trade by the increase of available shipping.

Transit Charges over large Rivers and Torrents.

The cost of ferrying rivers, and the delay attendant upon crossing torrents, reduces materially the exporting power of the Punjab by increasing the cost of its exports.

The cost of the Ferry at Ferozpur at its best period is equal to a Railway charge of over 150 miles, while the torrents in the river Chukki between Pathankot and Nurpur, at certain seasons, will completely stop the export of tea from the Kangra Valley. These two are only cited as examples, there being many other crossings of great importance, notably the Jhelum at Pind Dadan Khan, the Indus at Dera Ismael Khan, and the Chenab and Indus at Deri Ghazi Khan, &c. &c., at all of which the crossing charges and cartage are almost prohibitive to the export trade.

Bonded Warehouses.

In most Indian cities the Municipal revenues are derived from octroi, and nearly all agricultural produce brought within such limits is taxed. But if the produce be re-exported within a certain prescribed limit of time, a refund is obtainable. The delay and trouble attendant upon such refunds, however, frequently results in no application for it being submitted, and the export trade suffers thereby. Again, the produce may be brought in, in small quantities by agriculturists who pay the duty, while it is exported in large bulk by traders who purchase the aforesaid small quantities, and who, from want of sufficient detail or lapse of the specified period, are not able to claim the refunds.

Through Booking to Europe.

Sir William Andrew, the talented and enterprising Chairman of the Sind, Punjab and Delhi Railway, has for a long time advocated this measure, and offered to give it a trial from Kurrachee, but owing to the peculiar constitution of the contracts between the Guaranteed Railways and the Secretary of State, the system cannot be legally adopted.

Amalgamation of the S. P. and D. Railway and I. V. S. Railway Systems.

So much has been said and written on this subject, and its advisability is so generally admitted, that it would be useless to occupy any of the space in this paper beyond stating that it would result in a great saving of State expenditure, and afford much greater facilities for the development of trade.

Removal of Impediments rather than Undue Reduction in Railway Rates.

Upon this subject it would be well to remember that, the working expenses of Railways in the north of India are necessarily very heavy.

Coal has to be imported at very high prices, supervision is expensive, and English stores have to be conveyed at great expense from the seaboard to the workshops, and up-country stations. Moreover, the lines are subject to frequent damage from floods and inundations.

Notwithstanding these heavy charges, grain is carried at $\frac{1}{6}$ pie per maund per mile, or at an exchange of 1·7½ per rupee, at a rate of ·46 of a penny per ton per mile, and in some cases it is carried at ·39 of a penny per ton per mile.

If the produce had only to bear the Railway charges, it might possibly be exported on very favourable terms, but unfortunately natural impediments beyond Railway control occasion such a large addition to the cost of transit, that, no amount of reduction on Railway rates within the limits of absolute loss would suffice to nullify their effect.

The same remarks apply to imports, as may be readily seen by a perusal of the following figures :—

Transit charges on small iron imported by way of Kurrachee to Ferozpur—

	s.	d.	£	s.	d.
Through Railway rate at ·46 pence per ton for 830 miles - - - per ton			1	11	8
Further charges owing to natural impediments and want of conveniences—					
Cartage, &c. in Kurrachee, per ton	2	8			
Intermediate Agency in Kurrachee, per ton	4	1			
Ferry charge at Sukkur ,,	2	9			
Do., and Cartage at Ferozpur, per ton	6	10			
			0	16	4
Total cost - -			£2	8	0

In addition to this, the iron will probably be carted some ten or twelve miles over unmetalled roads to native villages for the manufacture of ploughs or other implements, at an additional cost of 3s. 4d. per ton, bringing the total cost of transit up to £2 11s. 4d. per ton. It may also by lapse of time occasionally become liable to Octroi at both Kurrachee and Ferozpur.

To reduce Railway rates to an extent necessary to nullify these natural impediments, the Railway would have to carry the traffic at twelve shillings per ton for the 830 miles, which would be equal to a rate of only $\frac{1}{6}$ of a penny per ton per mile, which would not pay working expenses. Probably existing Railway rates might still bear reduction with a larger traffic: but this can scarcely be looked for until the heavy charges beyond Railway control are reduced to a minimum.

Concluding Remarks.

Provincial Governments have no funds available for improvement other than savings of revenue, which are totally inadequate for the purpose; the amount available in the Punjab for new public works, as mentioned in the extract from the "Civil and Military Gazette" hereto annexed, being only about £65,000 per annum, and to increase taxation sufficiently to make adequate provision for roads, bridges, ferries, and harbours out of revenue would be manifestly unjust to the existing population, if, indeed, their incomes would bear such heavy taxation.

State assistance is wanted for such improvements as much as for "directly productive," railways and canals, and until such assistance is given, the trade of the country must remain undeveloped, and its people continue to exist in a state of semi-barbarism. The State, moreover, would receive a return for its outlay in the shape of increased land, and Railway, Revenues occasioned by the more thorough development of the country; indeed, such expenditure might fairly be classified as "indirectly productive" works.

Nothing in this paper is intended to demonstrate that more Railways are unnecessary; on the contrary, the trade can only be fully developed by Railway extension, but State assistance for metalled roads, ferries, harbours, and other works offering facilities to commerce should be looked upon as an essential portion of every Railway system in India.

Should further information be desirable upon the points raised herein, it may be well to mention that Sir William Andrew, Chairman of the Sind, Punjab, and Delhi Railway, has been for years past endeavouring to initiate reforms and improvements in Kurrachee, and other places along his line of Railway, and his valuable advice might consequently be of great assistance to a Parliamentary Committee in the present emergency. Sir Douglas Forsyth, Chairman of the Southern Mahratta Railway, and one of the Directors of the Sind, Punjab, and Delhi Railway, has also very recently visited the Punjab, and made himself personally acquainted with the subject.

(Sd.) JABEZ LIGHTFOOT,

Auditor, S. P. & D. Railway.

Lahore, 22nd March, 1884.

Extracts from Punjab Government Resolution No. 6,436, of November 28th, 1882.

Relating to Kurrachee Harbour.

For the larger portion of the Province the natural outlet for its surplus produce may be said to be Kurrachee.

This port is situated at the extreme northern end of the Indus delta, and is connected with the entire river system of the Punjab. It possesses a harbour safe and easy of approach, with fairly regular soundings and few formidable currents. It has the additional advantage of being northward of the limit of cyclones. It is less affected by the south-west monsoon than most parts of Western India. Being nearer by 200 miles to Aden, and bringing as it does a great part of the frontier 1,000 miles nearer to England than the route *viâ* Bombay, the importance of the port of Kurrachee as an outlet to this Province can hardly be exaggerated.

There are certain disadvantages at Kurrachee that require to be remedied in order to make a popular and successful port. These are principally—1st, the heavy cartage and agency charges; 2nd, the inadequacy of existing harbour accommodation and conveniences; and, 3rd, the scarcity of shipping, due in great part to a preponderance of the tonnage of exports over imports and consequent high ruling rates of export freight.

The cartage, shipping, and agency charges are reported to be such that even wheat purchasable in Kurrachee at almost the same rate as that ruling in Calcutta cannot be exported on such favourable conditions. Excluding agency, these amount to about R.1-11-0 per ton shipped from the native jetty, and R.2-12-0 shipped from the pier on Kiamari island. There is little inducement, therefore, for traders to use the latter. In so far as the charge for cartage is attributable to the fact that much of the grain sent down for export requires cleaning, and has therefore to be unloaded, carried to the merchants' godowns in the town, and again to either jetty or pier, the real remedy rests with the cultivators or those who purchase from them direct. The cleaning process only requires to be done once, and it ought to be arranged for at depôts up country. If the grain were sent down ready for shipment, there would be a saving in the carriage of refuse to Kurrachee, and nearly the whole of the cartage charges at Kurrachee, amounting in the case of the pier to R.2 a ton, or over 2 per cent. in the value of the wheat, would be saved, as the grain would be run straight out to the shipping.

Relating to the Encouragement of Additional Shipping in Kurrachee Harbour.

The export trade is at present heavily handicapped by the want of return traffic from Kurrachee, and the wheat has to bear the cost of its own haulage and of the return of the empty wagons in which it has been carried.

Therefore, to obtain cheap transit charges downward, an up traffic must be sought for and fostered as far as possible. The best way to accomplish this is undoubtedly to encourage import trade to the port of Kurrachee.

This will be further noticed below in connection with that port; but it may here be said that a good deal may be done by judiciously offering special advantages for up country traffic. His Honour is of opinion that liberal concessions might be made in this direction with much advantage.

The scarcity of shipping available for outward freight is due in great measure to the fact that ships have generally to be specially chartered, and to come in ballast from other ports.

They seldom come into the harbour to look for freight; even those consigned from England with railway stores and material are often pre-engaged to take return cargoes from other ports and go away in ballast. Home freights consequently run high, and it is a question worth considering whether it might not be the interest of both the Railway Company and the Government to give special encouragement for a limited period to a line of steamers to and from this port in return for some concessions to be given on freight from England, and on condition of ships so employed giving the Kurrachee trade a preference when freight from the port is available.

Relating to Improvement of Communication by Metalled Roads and Ferries.

Among the most important of the measures for the development of the export and import trade of the Province must be placed the improvement of communications in the shape of feeder lines, either rail, tramway, or metalled roads. Although river carriage can undoubtedly compete with the Railway in respect of rates of carriage, the trader has by the latter the advantage as regards speed, certainty of delivery, and safety—all of which are material advantages for a large trade in grain. The competition between river and rail, however, tends to secure low rates of freight. The river traffic should not be destroyed, but rather fostered, and used as a feeder to Railway depôts.

Fazilka is a town on the Sutlej already doing a good trade with Kurrachee in corn, seeds, and wool. A metalled road, or, better still, a steam tramway, from the right bank of the river to Okara, is another much needed feeder, the great drawback to extension of this traffic being the excessive cost of carriage.

At both Ferozpur and Fazilka improved ferries are needed, and these will be still more necessary when the railway lines from Ludhiana and from Hissar-Rewari are completed, so as to enable a system of through booking to be carried out.

At other points much may be done by improvements of existing roads, important lines communicating with the railway systems being as far as possible metalled.

Relating to Cleaning and Storage Warehouses up country.

Among the minor miscellaneous improvements desirable to facilitate trade, is the erection of warehouses or godowns as near as possible to Railway Stations, where, on payment of a small rental, traders could store and clean their grain until such time as the markets were favourable for its despatch by rail. These will no doubt in time be constructed by the private agency of merchants and others who, in a few cases, have already shown a willingness to do so. But where large quantities of grain are brought to the line, it might be to the interest of the Railway itself to provide them. Such depôts would also afford a means of gauging probable requirements in carriage.

The cleaning and bagging of wheat (and it may be noted that, both for rail and sea, bags afford the most convenient means of carriage) at such depôts, and its despatch to Kurrachee ready for shipment, has been already alluded to as a matter to be desired, saving both the cost of unloading and cartage at Kurrachee, and the carriage of extraneous matter. It would also to a great extent obviate the necessity for the intermediate agency which falls heavily on the smaller traders. Many small consignments are at present despatched to native merchants at the port who deal with large English firms, and anything tending to break up this system and transfer the agency from Kurrachee to the grain-producing districts would be a saving. Were the grain thus finally bagged for shipment, it is probable some understanding might be come to between the Railway Company and the shipowners to enable wheat to be consigned direct to foreign ports without the intervention of brokers at Kurrachee.

Resolution of Punjab Government.

Under the circumstances above explained, His Honour the Lieutenant-Governor considers that while every effort consistent with the resources of the Province should be made for the improvement of communications, whether in the form of feeder lines of railway, the provision of improved ferries, and the extension of metalled roads or steam tramways, the attention of the Government of India should be drawn to the desirability of liberal concessions for the encouragement of up-country traffic and to the possibility of arranging with the Store Department to consign additional stores to the Kurrachee port, and of giving encouragement to steam vessels trading there.

It is also greatly to be desired that existing disadvantages at Kurrachee, should as far as possible be removed, in order to give to the natural outlet for Punjab trade those facilities which its importance demands."

Extract from Acting Agent, Sind, Punjab and Delhi Railway Company's Letter to Sir William Andrew, dated August 31st, 1882.

On the subject of Kurrachee Harbour.

Although more than twenty years have elapsed since their first commencement, the Harbour works are not yet completed.

The principal anchorage is at the extreme end of the Harbour, near Manora point, *about two miles from the nearest available Landing Stage at Kiamari, and four or five miles from the Native Jetty near the town,* moreover at neither of the Landing Stages is the slightest sign of effort to afford merchandise convenience apparent; with the exception of the recently-erected Merewether Pier, which is scarcely completed, and of a very limited capacity.

Looking at Kiamari as a Landing-place, we find that its whole face available for landing is scarcely 1,600 feet in extent; that it is entirely occupied by the new ship pier and a few small private Jetties, only one of which, the Railway Jetty, has facilities for landing goods.

The shore space available moreover is very scanty; there are no sorting or storing arrangements whatever, and all traffic has to find its way by cart along the Mole, a distance of over three miles to the Merchants' Godowns, at a cost of about one rupee eight annas per ton; there it has to be unloaded and stored for a short time until required up country, when another eight annas per ton are expended in carting it to the Railway Station.

These cartage charges are virtually an increase to the Harbour dues and prevent the development of the trade of the port.

Turning to the Native Jetty as a landing-stage, we find that the goods are brought by boat from the ships to this point, a distance of about five miles, at a cost of five annas per ton, and carted from thence to the Merchants' Godowns at a cost of eight annas per ton, to be again carted to the Railway Station at a cost of eight annas per ton when proceeding up country.

There is, moreover, no space available on the Native Jetty for large warehouses, as it is simply a double-sided wharf.

Do what he may, therefore, a trader cannot possibly get his goods from ship to land, and from thence to the Railway Station, at a less cost than one rupee five annas per ton, which amounts to far more than the Harbour dues, and is equivalent to a Railway transit of over fifty miles.

Ship Captains moreover complain that the port is badly appointed, that there are no head and stern moorings, no facilities for refitting and repair, and that the water-supply is unsatisfactory.

To make Kurrachee a popular and successful trading port, something must be done to remedy existing disadvantages. And I would venture to suggest that full consideration may be given to my proposals to provide increased Sea frontage and Warehouse accommodation at Kiamari.

By such a system twenty or thirty ships at a time might, if necessary, be simultaneously loaded and unloaded with ease by lighters, &c., at a point almost opposite the anchorage. Goods could be warehoused by merchants until required for Railway or shipment, and the expensive cartage charges would be abolished, and the cost of shipment reduced to a minimum. The present pier could be utilized for all heavy articles, and for mails, passengers, troopships, and Railway stores, which would in all probability keep it almost fully employed.

It may be said there are no Funds available for such purposes; the simple business answer to which is *borrow them* or *get them somehow.*

The rental of the sheds and grounds would repay the interest on the whole of the Capital outlay, and the reduction in cartage and boat-charges should largely increase the revenue of the port by bringing additional trade and shipping.

A system of doing Harbour work *piecemeal, as annual grants can be spared from dues,* is financially unsound, detrimental to trade, and unjust to merchants.

The amount of Harbour dues devoted annually to Capital works, if devoted to the payment of interest on Harbour works loans, would permit of twenty times the accommodation being provided for existing shipping, and the completion of the works twenty years earlier. It is manifestly unjust to charge the merchants of a young port with the cost of providing a good harbour to benefit a future generation, who will enjoy its advantages without having contributed to its cost; such a policy, moreover, postpones the development of trade in proportion to the delay in the provision of conveniences.

Kurrachee has now shown itself of such vast importance as the outlet of the Punjab Trade, that no expenditure should be spared in perfecting its arrangements.

I fear, however, until it has been annexed to the Province of which it may justly be considered the Trade Estuary, it will scarcely meet with the consideration its Geographical situation and natural advantages demand.

(Sd.) JABEZ LIGHTFOOT,

Acting Agent, S. P. & D. Ry.

Lahore, August 31st, 1882.

EXTRACTS FROM MEMO. DATED MARCH 12TH, 1884, ON THE SUBJECT OF FEROZPUR AND SUKKUR FERRY CHARGES.

Cartage and Ferry Charges over the River Sutlej at Ferozpur.

The Ferry charge at Ferozpur for a two-bullock cart is 4 annas, which, assuming a load of about sixteen maunds, is 3 pies per maund; equal to a Railway distance of eighteen miles.

This rate in itself is not excessive, but, owing to the rudeness of the Ferry arrangements, the Cartage charges from Ferozpur to Gunda Singh range from 2 annas in the cold season, to 4 annas in the floods; the contract rate for Ordnance Stores being 4 annas per maund all the year round, inclusive of Ferry tolls. A charge of 4 annas at the rate of $\frac{1}{6}$ pie per maund per mile, is equal to a railway distance of 288 miles; so that if a Railway were laid from Ferozpur to Ludhiana, a distance of seventy miles, *the rates from Ferozpur to Ludhiana and thence to Raewind viâ Lahore, would be less than the rates viâ Gunda Singh to Raewind, although the distance is 175 miles more.*

Even the cold season rate of 2 annas Cartage and 3 pie Ferry charge, is equal to a distance of 162 miles by

Railway; and as the greater part of the trade is carried on after the April harvests, the bulk of the traffic must be taxed to a much higher rate, owing to the floods.

The present grain rates by Sind, Punjab and Delhi Railway, and the future rates to Bombay by Rewari-Ferozpur Line, may roundly be stated as follows:—

	Distance.	Rate per maund. As.	p.
Ludhiana to Kurrachee - - -	937	12	6
Ferozpur to Bombay *viâ* Rewari (about)	1,066	13	4
Ferozpur to Kurrachee *viâ* Gunda Singh, plus cold weather rate of 2 annas and 3 pies for Cartage and Ferry charge - - -	830	14	0
Through Railway rates at $\frac{1}{6}$ pie from Ferozpur to Kurrachee, provided the line ran into Ferozpur - -	*830*	*11*	*9*

From these figures, it will be seen that grain may be despatched from Ludhiana to Kurrachee for 12 annas and 6 pie per maund, or 18 pies less than it can be despatched from Ferozpur, although the distance is 107 miles greater.

Again, the rate to Bombay *viâ* the Rewari-Ferozpur Line, although the distance is 236 miles more, will be 8 pies less than the cost from Ferozpur to Kurrachee with the present imposts.

But if the town of Ferozpur were connected with the Railway, and the river were bridged, the actual cost of despatch at Railway rates for the entire distance would be only 11 annas 9 pie, or considerably less than the rate by either of the other Railway routes; and taking into consideration the additional safety and speed, would compare favourably with the combined cost of river transport to Adamwahan, and Railway freight from thence to Kurrachee, which ranges from 10½ to 11 annas.

The distance from Ferozpur to Kurrachee being 236 miles less than the distance from Ferozpur to Bombay, it follows that all stations on the Rewari Line within a radius of less than 118 miles from Ferozpur would be able to make advantageous use of the Kurrachee route, provided the existing difficulties in the way of transit charges were removed; but so long as the trade is taxed to the extent of an average Railway freight charge of nearly 200 miles, the use of this most important feeder line will be nullified, and communication blocked, not only with the sea-board at Kurrachee, but with all the important districts lying north of Raewind including Lahore, Amritsar, Jhelum, Rawalpindi, and Peshawur.

Ferry Charges over the River Indus at Sukkur.

The quantity of goods of all classes, except Railway material for Sind, Punjab and Delhi Railway imported to the Punjab *viâ* Kurrachee during the past three half-years, and the Ferry charges thereon, were as follows :—

	Maunds.	*Ferry charge at one anna per maund.* Rupees.
December 1882 - -	4,26,037 -	26,628
June 1883 - - -	4,67,343 -	29,209
December 1883 - -	4,21,475 -	26,342

If a bridge had been in existence, the Railway freight charge upon this traffic for the distance would not have exceeded Rs. 1,000 in either of the half-years under reference; the difference between the Railway freight and Ferry charge is a tax placed upon imports, and unless it is removed, trade cannot be expected to increase.

In reality, Ferry charges ought not to be borne by either the traders or the Railway gross Revenues. They are fairly chargeable against the net Revenue as interest on Capital, for which they are merely a temporary substitution.

(Sd.) JABEZ LIGHTFOOT,
Auditor, S. P. & D. Ry.

Lahore, 12th March, 1884.

EXTRACTS FROM THE "CIVIL AND MILITARY GAZETTE," DATED MARCH 14TH, 1884, THE ACCURACY OF WHICH HAS BEEN TESTED.

On the subject Feeder Roads and Provincial Loans.

And—most pressing of all in a great agricultural Province—more means of communication are urgently needed. The Province has an area under direct British administration of 105,000 square miles, and as yet it has only some 1,000 miles of metalled roads, or about one mile per 100 square miles of country; considerably less in fact than the length of open line of Railway. This is supplemented by 16,000 miles of unmetalled roads, but a *kutcha* road can hardly be called an efficient means of communication; and owing to this, many districts are said to be "notoriously only partially developed." A Railway station without efficient feeder-roads is in the rainy season practically cut off from traffic for some months of the year; and, even during the remaining months of dry season, is very heavily handicapped by the cost of cartage, which, under favourable circumstances, is often twenty to forty times as costly as the same distance by Railway. Even the best sections of the existing lines of Railway are very badly provided in this respect, while the more northern lines may be said to have no metalled feeders at all; and if the Punjab is to compete successfully with other grain-exporting countries, not only more Railways, but a very large increase in the number of metalled feeder-roads must be constructed and maintained for the lines already made.

There is seldom more than 7 to 8 lakhs available for new Provincial works of all kinds, spread over the thirty-two districts of the Province. From this has to be provided funds for all the administrative buildings, for Law, Justice, Jails, Police; to build the Chief Court of the Province; to keep out the Indus at Dera Ghazi Khan; provide Lahore with pure water, and Amritsar with a system of drainage; construct approach roads to the Indus Bridge at Attock; improve the roads through the Pezu pass; and conserve the historical buildings, "from the Topes at Manikyala to the plains of Kurukshetra."

When a commercial Company finds that to develop its business profitably, more capital is absolutely required, the natural procedure is either to increase that capital or issue debentures; and why should not the provincial Government, seeing that to develop its agricultural resources and insure an export trade increased facility of communication is a necessity, endeavour to meet the difficulty by a similar process, and construct its feeder-roads, and branch lines or tramways, by a loan. Supposing the calculation is sound, and the value of these in the development of trade assured, they would seem to have as good a claim upon the Imperial loan funds as either navigable canals or railways themselves. It might be more difficult to show the net result of a feeder-road in actual percentages, but might it not be accepted as an integral part of the Railway system?

PUBLICATIONS,

BY

SIR WILLIAM ANDREW, C.I.E.

F.R.G.S., ETC.

(1846.)

INDIAN RAILWAYS.

BY AN OLD INDIAN POSTMASTER.

3rd Edition, 1848. *8vo. Maps*, 10*s.* 6*d.*

NEWBY: PELHAM RICHARDSON.

"The third edition of a work on railways is a fact in literature almost unprecedented, and one which speaks trumpet-tongued for the value of the publication. . . . In fact there has not been such a valuable contribution to the civilisation of India, as this work on Indian Railways."—*Observer*, February 13, 1848.

"It is not a little remarkable, on reviewing the past and present position of the Indian railways, to perceive that the views of a private individual have prevailed against, and finally overthrown, the plans of the Indian Railway Commission (composed of a civil engineer, sent at a great expense from this country, aided by two talented officers of the Hon. East India Company's engineers), approved of by the Governor-General, the India House, and Cannon Row authorities, and applauded by the press. . . . Indeed, the Railway Companies in Bengal and Bombay that have obtained concessions are carrying out the views of 'the Old Indian Postmaster' to the letter, so far as the limited capital at their disposal will allow them; and it may be predicted that whenever a concession is given for a railway in Madras, it will be for the line that writer so strongly advocated, viz. to Arcot, the only short line in India which, in his opinion, would prove commercially remunerative. . . . The Government and people of India are therefore indebted to the 'Old Indian Postmaster.'"—*Observer*, November 23rd, 1851.

"By which public and official notice was mainly, if not first, directed to the great object of railway communication in India."—*Morning Herald*, September 14th, 1852.

"Had the authorities acted (more promptly) upon Mr. Andrew's views, a large and useless expenditure of time and money would have been saved."—*Britannia*, December 13, 1851.

"The best testimony of the soundness of the 'Old Postmaster's' views is, that, in the settlement of Indian railways, as far as it has recently taken place, not a few of his opinions have been followed by those in authority." —*Indian News*, February 22nd, 1848.

"The line (in Bengal) seems to have been adopted, which was originally recommended by Mr. W. P. Andrew."—*Times*, 19th November 1851.

(1847.)

Second Edition of

LETTER TO THE SHAREHOLDERS OF THE EAST INDIAN AND GREAT WESTERN OF BENGAL RAILWAYS.

BY ONE OF THEMSELVES.

SMITH, ELDER, & CO.

(1848.)

IS INDIA TO HAVE RAILWAYS?

W. H. ALLEN & CO., 13, Waterloo Place.

"The writer is a man evidently well-versed in his subject, which he treats in a manner that exhausts the whole question, and leaves nothing to be desired."—*Observer*, November 17th, 1848.

(1853.)

RAILWAYS IN BENGAL.

W. H. ALLEN & CO.

(Being the Substance of a Report addressed to the Chairman of the East India Company in 1849, by his own desire.) With Map and Appendix.

"The following paper (Railways in Bengal) giving, in a condensed form, the published opinions of the writer, was at the request of the late Sir A. Galloway, K.C.B., submitted to him when chairman of the East India Company in 1849, and forwarded by him to the Board of Control, who considered it sufficiently important to retain possession of the original. The East India Railway Company being about to apply for additional capital, to enable it to carry out the views contained in this report, in place of those propounded by its own promoters and founders, and recommended by the Indian Railway

Commissioners, the document comes before the public at this moment invested with additional interest and authority."—*Colonial and Asiatic Review*, July 1852.

(1856.)

THE SCINDE RAILWAY,

In relation to the Euphrates Valley and other Routes to India, with Illustrative Maps, Statistical Tables, &c., from Official Sources.

8vo., 10*s.* 6*d.*

W. H. ALLEN & CO.

"In reference to the Punjaub, the capacity of moving troops to a given point was of immense importance. In a military point of view the advantage would be this, that if the Khyber pass should be closed to our forces, they could be moved with rapidity to the Bolan pass, and in either case the enemy would be taken in flank or in the rear. The Euphrates Valley railway would give them the command of the sea-board of the Persian gulf; the completion of that railway would practically make Chatham nearer to any point of action in the Persian territory, than any military force which could be brought to bear upon it from Central Asia. If the triumphs of Great Britain are to be permanent, they must be rendered so by a mutuality of interests, by the material and civilising influences of expanding commerce. The great battle of the country for the tranquillity of Central Asia must be fought at Manchester and Liverpool. (Hear, hear.) If we would command Central Asia, that dominion must be established by opening up a ready market for their raw produce, and subjecting them by the force of their own material interests."—*Extract from Speech of the Right Hon. Sir Bartle Frere, Bart., G.C.B, G.C.S.I., at a Meeting of the Scinde Railway, February* 1857.

LETTER TO VISCOUNT PALMERSTON, K.G., ON THE POLITICAL IMPORTANCE OF THE EUPHRATES VALLEY RAILWAY.

BY W. P. ANDREW.

W. H. ALLEN & CO.

With Reports by Major-General Chesney and Sir John Macneil, and Memorandum by Sir Justin Sheil, K.C.B.; also Minutes of Evidence before the House of Commons, on the establishment of Telegraphic Communication with India through Turkish Arabia by Sir W. B. O'Shaughnessy, T. K. Lynch, Esq., and W. Ainsworth, Esq., &c.; with coloured Map.

M. Lesseps, the great founder of the Suez Canal, has borne in eloquent words his testimony to the importance of the Euphrates Valley railway.

TELEGRAPHIC COMMUNICATION WITH INDIA.

LETTERS REPRINTED FROM THE "TIMES," ETC.

W. H. ALLEN & CO.

"The ever-active master mind to which India is indebted for that railway system of which others have obtained the credit, and the profit, cannot but at last compel that recognition of his services, which it ought to have been the pride of those who rule to have long since gratefully and publicly acknowledged. In projecting and in pledging himself, supported as he ever is, to carry out the European and Indian Junction Telegraph from Seleucia to the head of the Persian Gulf, Mr. Andrew is doing yeoman's service to the cause of civilisation. His little Scinde line was a good step in the right road. His projected, and we may now say his accepted, extensions of it, coupled with his Euphrates Valley line, and its electric telegraph, all lead in the same direction, and tend to the same important result—the solution of the time-honoured question—the shortest route from the far west to the fabled Cathai—the completion of almost daily intercourse between the most distant nations of the universe."—*Bell's Weekly Messenger*, August 2nd, 1856.

In 1856 Mr. Andrew concluded an arrangement with Her Majesty's Government for the establishment of telegraphic communication with India, and in the same year obtained the only act of Parliament ever granted for the purpose; Lord Stanley (now Lord Derby) being the Chairman of Committee of the House of commons on the Bill.

(1857.)

MEMOIR ON THE EUPHRATES VALLEY ROUTE TO INDIA,

WITH OFFICIAL CORRESPONDENCE AND MAPS, AND APPENDIX.

DEDICATED TO THE EARL OF CLARENDON, K.G.

8vo., 10s. 6d.

W. H. ALLEN & CO.

"It is impossible to refer to the surveys and Reports of General Chesney and his colleagues on the Euphrates, published twenty years ago, without astonishment that even at that period the British Government and people failed to take immediate steps to avail themselves of its capabilities."—*The Times.*

"It is hardly possible to overrate the effects thus to be produced (by the Euphrates railway and telegraph) upon the commerce of the world."—*The Times.*

In "the words of the Austrian War Minister, Field-Marshal Baron Kuhn von Kuhnenfeld . . . 'Whatever the commercial value of the Suez Canal to Central Europe, there is no doubt that it is secondary in importance to the Euphrates Railway, which affords the only means of stemming Russian advances in Central Asia, and which directly covers the Suez Canal.' "—*The Edinburgh Quarterly Review.*

TRAMROADS IN NORTHERN INDIA,

In connection with the Iron Mines of Kuman and Gurhwal.

EFFINGHAM WILSON.

PORT OF KURRACHEE, DEPTH OF WATER, AND COMMERCE,

FOR THE OFFICIAL YEAR 1856–57.

With Map of Comparative Distances.

W. H. ALLEN & CO.

THE PUNJAUB RAILWAY,

Official Correspondence.

WITH MAP OF SCINDE AND THE PUNJAUB.

W. H. ALLEN & CO.

At the formal commencement of the Punjaub railway at Lahore in February 1859, Sir Richard Temple (then Commissioner of Lahore) said: "Mr. Andrew has by his enterprise and spirit as a public man, and by his talents as an author, largely contributed to the great undertaking of which we have this day celebrated the commencement. . . . Mr. Andrew showed with descriptive eloquence, with statistical accuracy, with local information, gathered from various sources, that Kurrachee and the Indus are to North-Western India what Calcutta and the Ganges are to Bengal; that Kurrachee can compete with Bombay; that all the traffic from the Jumna, westward, will find its natural outlet by the Indus. . . . Besides this, Mr. Andrew showed how this project is connected with the navigation of the Persian Gulf, the Euphrates Valley route, and the commercial lines in the mountainous regions of Central Asia."

Sir R. Temple, when Governor of Bombay, at a farewell dinner in Scinde, said, "there was no one the Province ought to be more proud of than the chairman of the S. P. and D. Railway."

(1858.)

COLONISATION IN INDIA AND AUSTRALIA COMPARED.

W. H. ALLEN & CO.

THE INDUS AND ITS PROVINCES; THEIR POLITICAL AND COMMERCIAL IMPORTANCE.

With Maps and Appendix, 10*s*. 6*d*.

W. H. ALLEN & CO.

"*The Indus and its Provinces* is really as interesting to the general reader as it is essential to the merchant, the trader, the politician, and the historian."—*Morning Chronicle*, May 27th, 1858.

"A magazine of information which may be most profitably consulted by the Statesman, the merchant, the manufacturer, and the student."—*Economist*

"Not contented to repose on his laurels as the early advocate for the construction of railways in India, Mr. Andrew has steadily persevered in developing his original idea, and now, after twelve years of incessant application, we find him concentrating his energies on the improvement of land and river communication in Scinde and the Punjaub, though with ulterior views extending far beyond the immediate benefit of those provinces."—*Allen's Indian Mail*, June 12, 1858.

"The union [says Mr. Andrew] of the Punjaub with the Meerut and Delhi territory, for political and military purposes, has been so plainly marked out by recent events, that their political connection under one distinct government appears inevitable, and the fortunes of these extensive and important regions are inseparably connected with that of Scinde. 'The two provinces (Scinde and Punjaub),' says a late writer, 'have been inseparably connected by the hand which made them. They have been connected also by the fortunes of the great empire to which both belong. They are *the provinces of the Indus*, as Bengal and Behar are *the provinces of the Ganges*.' . . . They constitute one section of the empire, and are separated from every other part of it by rivers, mountains, the sea, or broad belts of sandy desert. Their commercial interests are inseparably united. . . . Both depend for their communication with the external world upon one and the same port. . . . Again, the physical, political, and social characteristics of the two countries are identically the same. . . . It (the union) would strengthen, not root up, the system already successful; and on every other ground it is indispensable. . . . The Presidency of the Indus would be the second of the great divisions of British India."—*The Indus and its Provinces*.

LETTERS REPRINTED FROM THE "TIMES" ON TELEGRAPHIC COMMUNICATION WITH INDIA.

W. H. ALLEN & CO.

(1861.)

THE GOVERNMENT GUARANTEE ON INDIAN RAILWAYS,

As officially explained and recognised by the Railway Boards, the Government, and the Stock Exchange. Compiled by the Chairman of the Scinde Railway.

W. H. ALLEN & CO.

(1869.)

LETTER TO THE DUKE OF ARGYLL ON THE COMPLETION OF THE RAILWAY SYSTEM OF THE VALLEY OF THE INDUS.

With Maps.

W. H. ALLEN & CO.

(1870.)

LETTERS TO SECRETARIES OF STATE FOR FOREIGN AFFAIRS AND INDIA ON EUPHRATES VALLEY RAILWAY.

With Map.

W. H. ALLEN & CO.

LECTURE BEFORE SOCIETY OF ARTS ON RAILWAYS IN INDIA BY GUARANTEED COMPANIES.

With Map.

(1871.)

LETTERS TO THE GRAND VIZIER OF TURKEY AND THE BRITISH AMBASSADOR AT CONSTANTINOPLE, ETC., ON THE EUPHRATES ROUTE TO INDIA.

With Map.

W. H. ALLEN & CO.

LETTERS ON THE EUPHRATES VALLEY ROUTE TO INDIA.

REPRINTED FROM THE "TIMES," ETC.

W. H. ALLEN & CO.

(1872.)

PAPER READ BEFORE BRITISH ASSOCIATION AT BRIGHTON ON EUPHRATES VALLEY ROUTE TO INDIA.

With Map.

W. H. ALLEN & CO.

(1873.)

LECTURE DELIVERED AT THE ROYAL UNITED SERVICE INSTITUTION ON THE EUPHRATES ROUTE TO INDIA,

IN CONNECTION WITH THE CENTRAL ASIAN QUESTION.

With Map.

THE BREAK OF GAUGE IN INDIAN RAILWAYS.

With Reports by Messrs. Fowler, Bidder, Hawkshaw, and Molesworth.

Two editions.

W. H. ALLEN & CO.

"If there be any line in the world that requires to be placed in perfect communication with all the railways which are made in that country [India], it is the line of the Indus Valley; if there be any railway in existence which requires to be efficient and strong, and ready to carry great numbers of people, and a heavy description of traffic—such, for instance, as warlike stores and heavy ordnance—that is the railway; and yet that is a railway that some people would put on a different gauge from other lines in India. . . . Instead of having the enormous rolling stock of India available on any great emergency, they will have nothing but trumpery waggons and weakly little locomotives; and before they could have reinforcements sent, they would ascertain what a mistake they had made, and that a common road, if they would only bridge it, would be a better means of conveyance than the narrow gauge light and inefficient railway."—*Speech of Sir William Andrew, 23rd December* 1870, *at Meeting of S. P. and D. Railway.*

Sir William Andrew led the DISCUSSION ON THE GAUGE OF INDIAN RAILWAYS AT THE INSTITUTION OF CIVIL ENGINEERS, WESTMINSTER, IN FEBRUARY AND MARCH, 1873, and

Mr. Hawkshaw remarked: The narrow gauge proposal might be one of the greatest calamities that could be brought on the country.

Mr. Bidder said: The alleged saving was altogether illusory.

Captain Tyler: The question was a very serious one: serious to the Indian Government, serious to the maintenance of the British rule in India.

Mr. Harrison: The mixed gauge proposed on these lines would be a great evil, and would entail a large additional cost for maintenance.

Sir G. B. Airy was surprised to find that the introduction of such an evil had ever been seriously entertained.

Captain Douglas Galton said: From much acquaintance with the question in official positions, he considered it undesirable to introduce a second extensive network of railways upon a different gauge [in India].

Mr. Allport having had much experience of break of gauge, pronounced it so great an evil, that on low-priced articles it was destructive to the traffic. The Canadian Grand Trunk railway had decided to expend a very large sum in abolishing it. He thought if there was a curse on a railway system in any country it was having different gauges; and it was the duty of the Government of any country to insist on uniformity of gauge. He described some experiments made on the transfer of troops, which proved that to tranship an army of even only 20,000 or 30,000 men, with horses and equipments, would be so prejudicial, and would cause such a vast loss of time, that it would be better, in his judgment, to march by the road rather than undergo such an operation.

Mr. J. Grierson gave a copy of a memorial from 269 firms of manufacturers, merchants, and traders, praying for the abolition of the break in the South Wales district, and stating its disadvantages in the strongest terms. In consequence of this the Company had expended about £600,000 in altering a portion of their line; and to one firm alone the abolition of the break had made a difference in their business of fully £20,000 a year. In India, according to the plan shown, there would not only be twenty-one points of break, but there would be eleven separate systems having no through communication with each other; and these would be as badly off as if they were made on eleven different gauges. There was no parallel to such a thing in this country. . . . If there was one reason more than another which should weigh powerfully against any break of gauge on trunk lines, it was that they might be required for strategic purposes. There should be certainty, rapidity, and the power to use every available means of transport.

General Sir L. Simmons, as a soldier, protested in the strongest possible way against the low estimate of inconvenience caused by a break of gauge in what would become the great strategical lines of communication in India.

Condensed from the Abstract of the Discussion.

(1874.)

THE STRATEGIC AND COMMERCIAL EVILS OF A BREAK OF GAUGE IN INDIA.

With Map and Appendices.

W. H. ALLEN & CO.

"Mr. Andrew had the foresight to perceive and the boldness to lay before his countrymen the great importance and practicability of connecting those points [the sea, the capital of the Punjaub and Delhi] by railway. . . . He must now, I think, look back with satisfaction to the relations which then existed between him and the merchant princes who ruled India, and those of Her Majesty's Government who controlled the rulers of India. . . . One great cause of congratulation seems to me to be the success of your efforts to have a continuous unbroken gauge. Those who have concurred with your chairman and myself in from the first deprecating any such break in the great lines in the valley of the Ganges and the Indus will appreciate what an enormous advantage this unbroken gauge is. I can look at it in no other light, occurring in such an enormous length of trunk line as your railway, than that with the break of gauge you could get no more than half the advantages your railway would otherwise offer. . . . You will not reap half the advantages you ought to have unless you have uniformity of management. I do not suppose there is a gentleman present who has any kind of mercantile experience who will not endorse this truth. . . . Complete the work, and, once completed, I cannot imagine a railway shareholder who would fail to see that without uniformity of management your work is but half complete; the advantages you are entitled to reap from it and the advantages the country are entitled to reap from it are but half realised. I trust, therefore, that the arguments which your chairman has so well put before the authorities in this matter will lead to a speedy concession of a uniform management throughout the whole of your great line."—*Extract from Speech of the Right Hon. Sir Bartle Frere, Bart., G.C.B., G.C.S.I., at a Meeting of the S. P. and D. Railway on 23rd December* 1880.

(1878.)

INDIA AND HER NEIGHBOURS.

With Maps. 15s.

W. H. ALLEN & CO.

"Fortune has favoured Mr. Andrew in the opportune appearance of his book on India. . . . If we are to oppose effectual barriers to Russian encroachments, we must tighten the bonds and consolidate the communications that unite us to our fellow subjects in Hindostan. . . . While M. Lesseps was agitating his great project, Mr. Andrew had always been the consistent advocate of a railway down the Valley of the Euphrates, which should connect the Mediterranean with the Persian Gulf. . . .

"It ought to prove as useful as it is certainly extremely interesting. In the chapters on 'British Rule in India,' and 'Governors-General,' he has given a succinct and lucid history of the growth of the trading-posts that were established on sufferance in the mighty Empire that has been casting its shadows over Constantinople and the deliberations of the Congress at Berlin. Mr. Andrew, in a series of rapid sketches, depicts what the people of Hindostan had to suffer in the old, unruly times. . . . Mr. Andrew relates acts of heroism and chivalry that may vie with anything in the chronicles of Monstrelet or Froissart."—*Times*.

"A work which we should be glad to find have an effect in removing that blank feeling of utter ignorance about India which is so general even among cultivated Englishmen who have no direct relations in or with that vast empire."—*The Edinburgh Quarterly Review*.

"Among the many services rendered to India by Mr. Andrew the present must be regarded as both opportune and acceptable. It presents all the salient points of Indian history in a picturesque and graphic form, and gives a very complete view both of the past and present of that great country and its people. The leading facts are well marshalled, and the chief actors brought out in bold relief. . . . Several chapters of great brilliancy, devoted to the 'remarkable women of India.' . . . The characters of our several Governors-General, from Clive down to Viceroy Lord Lytton, are dashed off in a chapter of their own."—*Morning Post*.

"M. Andrew, dans l'intéressant ouvrage qu'il vient de publier sous ce titre, *l'Inde et les pays voisins*, nous retrace à grands traits l'histoire du développement primitif de l'empire indien sous la domination brittanique."—*Revue des Deux Mondes*.

"He has the historian's faculty of gathering up and sorting his materials, and he tells the history of India and describes its physical features and characteristics with the pen of knowledge and experience."—*Times of New York.*

"The book is one which was much required, is admirably drawn up, and, so far as we have tested the statements, may be relied upon throughout. We must dismiss it with praise for its general accuracy, its completeness, precision, and, not unfrequently, also for its eloquence."—*Examiner.*

"He foresees that Russia will certainly possess herself of Merv, and will gain over all the neighbouring tribes to her own interests.

"In order to put a stop to this Russian expansion in Central Asia, and to protect the Suez Canal, and with a view to giving timely succour to Turkey and Persia, the author is of opinion that the Euphrates Valley Railway should be constructed, which will connect the Mediterranean with the Persian Gulf." —*The St. Petersburg Vedomosti.*

"It is now upwards of a quarter of a century since the chairman of the Scinde Railway commenced to broach the idea of connecting the Kyber and the Bolan passes with the railway system of India. For more than a quarter of a century he has unsparingly advocated these views, not only in weighty official communications to the Indian Government, in repeated letters in our columns, but in books replete with valuable information concerning the trade and history of India. Last year we reviewed a work by Mr. W. P. Andrew, in which he energetically insisted on the immediate completion of a railway to our scientific frontier. Only a few days ago we published a letter from him adverting to the same subject. Had the views so persistently advocated by Mr. Andrew and so repeatedly brought forward by us been adopted at the commencement of the struggle last October, as we then ventured to insist upon, vast sums would have been spared in the hire of transport, and we should have been spared the ignominy of feeling that a British army, nominally on active service, has occupied five weeks in covering less than seventy miles."—*Times*, October 13th, 1879.

(1879.)

ASIA MINOR AND EUPHRATES VALLEY RAILWAY.

W. H. ALLEN & CO.

(1880.)

THE BOLAN AND KHYBER RAILWAYS.

W. H. ALLEN & CO.

"The first scheme for such a line (the Kandahar Railway) was publicly mooted about the time of the Indian mutinies by Mr. W. P. Andrew."—*The*

First Section of the Kandahar Railway. By James Richard Bell, M. Inst. C.E.

Excerpt Minutes of Proceedings of the Institution of Civil Engineers, vol. lxi. Session 1879–80.

PAPER READ BEFORE THE SOCIETY OF ARTS ON THE EUPHRATES ROUTE TO INDIA.

With Map by Stanford.

FIELD-MARSHAL THE LORD STRATHNEARN, G.C.B., G.C.S.I., IN THE CHAIR.

OUR SCIENTIFIC FRONTIER.

With Sketch Map.

W. H. ALLEN & CO.

"For more than twenty years he (Mr. Andrew) has had opportunities of discussing frontier questions with the distinguished officers who have served in the border-lands, and his own interest in the subject is shown by the numerous works he has written. He is emphatically an apostle of railways; and though under existing conditions he can hardly hope to see launched his great scheme of the Euphrates Valley line, he can yet affirm with pardonable pride that disastrous experience has compelled the Government of India to give effect to the views which a quarter of a century ago he enunciated as to the necessity of extending the Indian railway system to the frontier."—*St. James's Gazette*, October 20th, 1880.

"The advantages of the railway communication we now enjoy in Scinde and Northern India are entirely due to the enterprise and untiring perseverance of one man, Mr. Andrew, the indefatigable Chairman of the Scinde, Punjaub and Delhi Railway, who so ably withstood official opposition for so many years, and in spite of all rebuffs carried out his ideas to the immense benefit of India as well as England. Nay, we ask, if it had not been for Mr. Andrew, how would the army lately engaged in the Afghan campaign have been conveyed, with horses, war material, and all the impedimenta pertaining to such an immense host? and if not exactly landed at the mouths of the Khyber and the Bolan, it was not for the want of reiterated representation by the Chairman of the Scinde, Punjaub and Delhi Company as to the necessity for railway extension to Peshawur and also towards Quettah. . . . In honouring such a man, the pioneer of railway enterprise in India, the Government would only be honouring themselves."—*Lahore Paper*, Feb. 1881.

"As early as 1857, Mr. Andrew, as mouth-piece of a deputation to Lord Palmerston, took occasion to express his views as to scientifically strengthening this frontier. He pointed out the importance of railways to the Bolan and Khyber passes, the two gates of India. What he then spoke of as of importance has since been painfully demonstrated to be a necessity. After some three-and-twenty years of apathy the necessity has been realised, and now these railways are being constructed. . . . Sir Bartle Frere, then Commissioner of Scinde, in the same year said, 'In reference to the Punjaub the capacity of moving troops to a given point was of immense importance." . . . In a military point of view the advantage would be this—that if the Khyber pass should be closed to our forces they could be moved with rapidity to the Bolan, and in either case the enemy would be taken in flank or in rear.' . . . General Hamley, in an excellent lecture delivered at the United Service Institution in December 1878, advocates views much in harmony with our author's. . . . Mr. Andrew's views, stated throughout with remarkable fairness and honesty, reduce these requisites (for defence) to a minimum, for his aim is not aggression, but defence."—*The Morning Post*, March 27, 1880.

"While listening to the lecture [General Hamley's at the United Service Institution] and hearing the arguments upon it, it occurred to him (Mr. Thornton) that he was hearing that which had been urged in that room for many years past, and advocated by their chairman more than twenty years ago in the book he then published, entitled *The Indus and its Provinces*; . . . in that book he found all the conclusions arrived at were in remarkable concurrence with those which were come to by the military men who discussed the lecture to which he had referred. He (Mr. Thornton) regarded this as so remarkable an instance of the fore-sight and prescience of their chairman that he thought it a circumstance which was worthy of being mentioned on the present occasion."—*Extract from the speech of Mr. E. Thornton, C.B., at a meeting of the S. P. and D. Railway, in December* 1878.

"Identified during many years with the history of progress in India, from his earliest work, published under the *nom de plume* of 'The Old Indian Postmaster,' the advocate and apostle of the Euphrates Valley route, with which enlightened scheme his name and that of the late gallant General Chesney are indissolubly connected, the father of Indian railways, and the undaunted champion whose energy carried him victoriously through the 'battle of the Gauges,' to win for the public the boon of an unbroken gauge upon our frontier line."—*Edinburgh Courant.*

"He has for years been known as the most prominent advocate of the Euphrates Valley railway, and the chief object he has had in view in writing the present work has been to show the necessity of constructing a railway to the Bolan pass, and retiring from all our posts in Afghanistan except Candahar, which should be 'made the Kars of our north-west frontier.'"—*Scotsman*, April 16th, 1880.

"On matters connected with our Indian policy, Mr. W. P. Andrew has the right to be heard which attaches to extensive knowledge of a subject."—*Daily News*, July 12th, 1880.

Our Scientific Frontier was referred to in both Houses of Parliament when discussing Central Asian politics in January 1881.

"The dignity of knighthood, and that of the Companionship of the Indian Empire, that have recently been conferred on the able and patriotic Chairman of the Sind, Punjab, and Delhi Railway have been *omnium consensu* richly deserved; and will, we trust, prove only the forerunners of those hereditary honours which are the accustomed rewards of public services so important and so long-continued as those of Sir William Andrew, C.I.E."—*Allen's Indian Mail*, January 23, 1882.

"Sir W. P. Andrew has well deserved the honour of knighthood at length accorded him. No man has laboured more sedulously in these latter times to draw India nearer to Europe than the Chairman of the Scinde Railway Company, and the indefatigable advocate of the Euphrates Valley railway. If the latter project be realised by English enterprise the fact will be due as much to his untiring zeal as to General Chesney's labours in ascertaining and establishing its practicability."—*The Bombay Gazette Summary*, February 2, 1882.

"In these border-lands (Beloochistan and Afghanistan) to have a rival in prestige and power would be dangerous—to have a superior impossible."—*India and Her Neighbours*, p. 319.

JANUARY 1884.

BOOKS, &c.,

ISSUED BY

MESSRS. W. H. ALLEN & Co.,

Publishers & Literary Agents to the India Office,

COMPRISING

MISCELLANEOUS PUBLICATIONS IN GENERAL LITERATURE.

MILITARY WORKS, INCLUDING THOSE ISSUED BY THE GOVERNMENT.

INDIAN AND MILITARY LAW.

MAPS OF INDIA, &c.

13, WATERLOO PLACE, LONDON, S.W.

Works issued from the India Office, and Sold by W. H. ALLEN & Co.

Illustrations of Ancient Buildings in Kashmir.

Prepared at the Indian Museum under the authority of the Secretary of State for India in Council. From Photographs, Plans, and Drawings taken by Order of the Government of India. By HENRY HARDY COLE, LIEUT. R.E., Superintendent Archæological Survey of India, North-West Provinces. In One vol.; half-bound, Quarto. Fifty-eight plates. £3 10s.

The Illustrations in this work have been produced in Carbon from the original negatives, and are therefore permanent.

Pharmacopœia of India.

Prepared under the Authority of the Secretary of State for India. By EDWARD JOHN WARING, M.D. Assisted by a Committee appointed for the Purpose. 8vo. 6s.

The Stupa of Bharhut. A Buddhist Monument.

Ornamented with numerous Sculptures illustrative of Buddhist Legend and History in the Third Century B.C. By ALEXANDER CUNNINGHAM, C.S.I., C.I.E., Major-General, Royal Engineers (Bengal Retired); Director-General Archæological Survey of India. 4to. Fifty-seven Plates. Cloth gilt. £3 3s.

Archælogical Survey of Western India.

Report of the First Season's Operations in the Belgâm and Kaladgi Districts. January to May, 1874. Prepared at the India Museum and Published under the Authority of the Secretary of State for India in Council. By JAMES BURGESS, Author of the "Rock Temples of Elephanta," &c., &c., and Editor of "The Indian Antiquary." Half-bound. Quarto. 58 Plates and Woodcuts. £2 2s.

Archæological Survey of Western India. Vol. II.

Report on the Antiquities of Kâthiâwâd and Kachh, being the result of the Second Season's Operations of the Archæological Survey of Western India. 1874–75. By JAMES BURGESS, F.R.G.S., M.R.A.S., &c., Archæological Surveyor and Reporter to Government, Western India. 1876. Half-bound. Quarto Seventy-four Plates and Woodcuts. £3 3s.

Archæological Survey of Western India. Vol. III.

Report on the Antiquities in the Bidar and Aurungabad Districts in the Territory of H.H. the Nizam of Haidarabad, being the result of the Third Season's Operations of the Archæological Survey of Western India. 1875–1876. By JAMES BURGESS, F.R.G.S., M.R.A.S., Membre de la Societé Asiatique, &c., Archæological Surveyor and Reporter to Government, Western India. Half-bound. Quarto. Sixty-six Plates and Woodcuts. £2 2s.

Illustrations of Buildings near Muttra and Agra,

Showing the Mixed Hindu-Mahomedan Style of Upper India Prepared at the India Museum under the authority of the Secretary of State for India in Council, from Photographs, Plans, and Drawings taken by Order of the Government of India. By HENRY HARDY COLE, Lieut. R.E., late Superintendent Archæological Survey of India, North-West Provinces. 4to. With Photographs and Plates £3 10s.

The Cave Temples of India.

By JAMES FERGUSON, D.C.L., F.R.A.S., V.P.R.A.S., and JAMES BURGESS, F.R.G.S., M.R.A.S., &c. Printed and Published by Order of Her Majesty's Secretary of State, &c. Royal 8vo. With Photographs and Woodcuts. £2 2s.

Aberigh-Mackay (G.) Twenty-one Days in India.
Being the Tour of Sir Ali Baba, K.C.B. By George Aberigh-Mackay. Post 8vo. 4s.
An Illustrated Edition. 8vo. 10s. 6d.

Æsop, the Fables of, and other Eminent Mythologists.
With Morals and Reflections. By Sir Roger L'Estrange, kt. A facsimile reprint of the Edition of 1669. Folio, antique, sheep. 21s.

Akbar. An Eastern Romance.
By Dr. P. A. S. Van Limburg-Brouwer. Translated from the Dutch by M. M. With Notes and Introductory Life of the Emperor Akbar, by Clements R. Markham, C.B., F.R.S. Crown 8vo. 10s. 6d.

Alberg (A.) Snowdrops: Idylls for Children.
From the Swedish of Zach Topelius. By Albert Alberg, Author of "Whisperings in the Wood." 3s. 6d.

—— **Whisperings in the Wood**: Finland Idylls for Children. From the Swedish of Zach Topelius. By Albert Alberg, Author of "Fabled Stories from the Zoo," and Editor of "Chit-Chat by Puck," "Rose Leaves," and "Woodland Notes." 3s. 6d.

—— **Queer People.**
A Selection of Short Stories from the Swedish of "Leah." By Albert Alberg. 2 vols. Illus. Crown 8vo. 12s.

Alexander II. (Life of) Emperor of all the Russias. By the Author of "Science, Art, and Literature in Russia," "Life and Times of Alexander I.," &c. Crown 8vo. 10s. 6d.

Allen's Series.

1.—Ansted's World We Live In. 2s.
2.—Ansted's Earth's History. 2s.
3.—Ansted's 2000 Examination Questions in Physical Geography. 2s.
4.—Geography of India. (See page 13.) 2s.
5.—Ansted's Elements of Physiography. 1s. 4d.
6.—Hall's Trigonometry. (See page 14.) 2s.
7.—Wollaston's Elementary Indian Reader. 1s. (See p. 43.)

Ameer Ali. The Personal Law of the Mahommedans (according to all the Schools). Together with a Comparative Sketch of the Law of Inheritance among the Sunnis and Shiahs. By Syed Ameer Ali, Moulvi, M.A., LL.B., Barrister-at-Law, and Presidency Magistrate at Calcutta. 8vo. 15s.

Anderson (Ed. L.) How to Ride and School a Horse.
With a System of Horse Gymnastics. By EDWARD L. ANDERSON. Cr. 8vo. 2s. 6d.

——— **A System of School Training for Horses.**
By EDWARD L. ANDERSON, Author of "How to Ride and School a Horse." Crown 8vo. 2s. 6d.

Anderson (P.) The English in Western India. 8vo. 14s.

Anderson (T.) History of Shorthand.
With an analysis and review of its present condition and prospects in Europe and America. By THOMAS ANDERSON, Parliamentary Reporter, &c. With Portraits. Crown 8vo. 12s. 6d.

—— **Catechism of Shorthand**; being a Critical Examination of the various Styles, with special reference to the question, Which is the best English System of Shorthand? By THOMAS ANDERSON, Author of "Synopsis of a New System of Shorthand Writing," "History of Shorthand," &c. Fcap. 1s.

Andrew (W. P.) India and Her Neighbours.
By W. P. ANDREW, Author of "Our Scientific Frontier," "The Indus and Its Provinces," "Memoir of the Euphrates Route." With Two Maps. 8vo. 15s.

—— **Our Scientific Frontier.**
With Sketch-Map and Appendix. 8vo. 6s.

—— **Euphrates Valley Route,** in connection with the Central Asian and Egyptian Questions. Lecture delivered at the National Club, 16th June 1882. By SIR WILLIAM ANDREW, C.I.E., Author of "India and Her Neighbours," &c. 8vo., with 2 Maps. 5s.

—— **Through Booking of Goods between the Interior of** India and the United Kingdom. By SIR WILLIAM ANDREW, C.I.E., M.R.A.S., F.R.G.S., F.S.A., Author of "India and Her Neighbours," &c. 2s.

Ansted (D. T.) Physical Geography.
By Professor D. T. ANSTED, M.A., F.R.S., &c. Fifth Edition. Post 8vo., with Illustrative Maps. 7s.

CONTENTS:—PART I.—INTRODUCTION.—The Earth as a Planet. —Physical Forces.—The Succession of Rocks. PART II.—EARTH.—Land.—Mountains.—Hills and Valleys.—Plateaux and Low Plains. PART III.—WATER.—The Ocean.—Rivers. —Lakes and Waterfalls.—The Phenomena of Ice.—Springs PART IV.—AIR.—The Atmosphere. Winds and Storms.— Dew, Clouds, and Rain.—Climate and Weather. PART V.—

FIRE.—Volcanoes and Volcanic Phenomena.—Earthquakes. PART VI.—LIFE.—The Distribution of Plants in the different Countries of the Earth.—The Distribution of Animals on the Earth.—The Distribution of Plants and Animals in Time.—Effects of Human Agency on Inanimate Nature.

"The Book is both valuable and comprehensive, and deserves a wide circulation."—*Observer.*

Ansted (D. T.) Elements of Physiography.
For the use of Science Schools. Fcap. 8vo. 1s. 4d.

—— The World We Live In.
Or First Lessons in Physical Geography. For the use of Schools and Students. By D. T. ANSTED, M.A., F.R.S., &c. Fcap. 2s. 25th Thousand, with Illustrations.

—— The Earth's History.
Or, First Lessons in Geology. For the use of Schools and Students. By D. T. ANSTED. Third Thousand. Fcap. 2s.

—— Two Thousand Examination Questions in Physical Geography. pp. 180. Price 2s.

—— Water, and Water Supply.
Chiefly with reference to the British Islands. Part I.—Surface Waters. 8vo. With Maps. 18s.

—— and Latham (R. G.) Channel Islands. Jersey, Guernsey, Alderney, Sark, &c.

THE CHANNEL ISLANDS. Containing: PART I.—Physical Geography. PART II.—Natural History. PART III.—Civil History. PART IV.—Economics and Trade. By DAVID THOMAS ANSTED, M.A., F.R.S., and ROBERT GORDON LATHAM, M.A., M.D., F.R.S. New and Cheaper Edition in one handsome 8vo. Volume, with 72 Illustrations on Wood by Vizetelly, Loudon, Nicholls, and Hart; with Map. 8vo. 16s.

"This is a really valuable work. A book which will long remain the standard authority on the subject. No one who has been to the Channel Islands, or who purposes going there will be insensible of its value."—*Saturday Review.*

"It is the produce of many hands and every hand a good one."

Archer (Capt. J. H. Lawrence) Commentaries on the Punjaub Campaign—1848-49, including some additions to the History of the Second Sikh War, from original sources. By Capt. J. H LAWRENCE-ARCHER, Bengal H. P. Crown 8vo. 8s.

Armstrong (Annie E.) Ethel's Journey to Strange Lands in Search of Her Doll. By ANNIE E. ARMSTRONG. Cr. 8vo. With Illustrations by CHAS. WHYMPER. 2s. 6d.

Army and Navy Calendar for the Financial Year 1883–84.
Being a Compendium of General Information relating to the Army, Navy, Militia, and Volunteers, and containing Maps, Plans, Tabulated Statements, Abstracts, &c. Compiled from authentic sources 2s. 6d.

Army and Navy Magazine.
Vols. I. to V. are issued. 7s. 6d. each.

Aynsley (Mrs.) Our Visit to Hindustan, Kashmir, and Ladakh.
By Mrs. J. C. MURRAY AYNSLEY. 8vo. 14s.

Baildon (S.) The Tea Industry in India.
A Review of Finance and Labour, and a Guide for Capitalists and Assistants. By SAMUEL BAILDON, Author of "Tea in Assam." 8vo. 10s. 6d.

Belgium of the East (The).
By the Author of "Egypt under Ismail Pasha," "Egypt for the Egyptians," &c. Crown 8vo. 6s.

Bellew (Capt.) Memoirs of a Griffin; or, A Cadet's First Year in India. By Captain BELLEW. Illustrated from Designs by the Author. A New Edition. Cr. 8vo. 10s. 6d.

Berdmore (Sept.) (Nimshivich) A Scratch Team of Essays never before put together. Reprinted from the "Quarterly" and "Westminster Reviews." On the Kitchen and the Cellar—Thackeray—Russia—Carriages, Roads, and Coaches. By SEPT. BERDMORE (NIMSHIVICH). Crown 8vo. 7s. 6d.

Black (C. I.) The Proselytes of Ishmael.
Being a short Historical Survey of the Turanian Tribes in their Western Migrations. With Notes and Appendices. By CHARLES INGRAM BLACK, M.A., Vicar of Burley-in-Wharfedale, near Leeds. Second Edition. Crown 8vo. 6s.

Blanchard (S.) Yesterday and To-day in India.
By SIDNEY LAMAN BLANCHARD. Post 8vo. 6s.

CONTENTS.—Outward Bound.—The Old Times and the New.—Domestic Life.—Houses and Bungalows.—Indian Servants.—The Great Shoe Question.—The Garrison Hack.—The Long Bow in India.—Mrs. Dulcimer's Shipwreck.—A Traveller's Tale, told in a Dark Bungalow.—Punch in India.—Anglo-Indian Literature.—Christmas in India.—The Seasons in Calcutta.—Farmers in Muslin.—Homeward Bound.—India as it Is.

Blenkinsopp (Rev. E. L.) Doctrine of Development in the Bible and in the Church. By REV. E. L. BLENKINSOPP, M.A., Rector of Springthorp. 2nd edition. 12mo. 6s.

Boileau (Major-General J. T.)
A New and Complete Set of Traverse Tables, showing the Differences of Latitude and the Departures to every Minute of the Quadrant and to Five Places of Decimals. Together with a Table of the lengths of each Degree of Latitude and corresponding Degree of Longitude from the Equator to the Poles; with other Tables useful to the Surveyor and Engineer. Fourth Edition, thoroughly revised and corrected by the Author. Royal 8vo. 12s. London, 1876.

Boulger (D. C.) History of China. By DEMETRIUS CHARLES BOULGER, Author of "England and Russia in Central Asia," &c. 8vo. vol. I. With Portrait. 18s. Vol. II. 18s.

—— **England and Russia in Central Asia.** With Appendices and Two Maps, one being the latest Russian Official Map of Central Asia. 2 vols. 8vo. 36s.

—— **Central Asian Portraits**; or the Celebrities of the Khanates and the Neighbouring States. By DEMETRIUS CHARLES BOULGER, M.R.A.S. Crown 8vo. 7s. 6d.

—— **The Life of Yakoob Beg**, Athalik Ghazi and Badaulet, Ameer of Kashgar. By DEMETRIUS CHARLES BOULGER, M.R.A.S. 8vo. With Map and Appendix. 16s.

Bowles (Thomas Gibson) Flotsam and Jetsam. A Yachtman's Experiences at Sea and Ashore. By THOMAS GIBSON BOWLES, Master Mariner. Cr. 8vo. 7s. 6d.

Boyd (R. Nelson) Chili and the Chilians, during the War 1879–80. By R. NELSON BOYD, F.R.G.S., F.G.S., Author of Coal Mines Inspection. Cloth, Illustrated. Cr. 8vo. 10s. 6d.

—— **Coal Mines Inspection**; Its History and Results. 8vo. 14s.

Bradshaw (John) The Poetical Works of John Milton, with Notes, explanatory and philological. By JOHN BRADSHAW, LL.D., Inspector of Schools, Madras. 2 vols., post 8vo. 12s. 6d.

Brandis' Forest Flora of North-Western and Central India. By DR. BRANDIS, Inspector General of Forests to the Government of India. Text and Plates. £2 18s.

Brereton (W. H.) The Truth about Opium.
Being the Substance of Three Lectures delivered at St. James's Hall. By WILLIAM H. BRERETON, late of Hong Kong, Solicitor. 8vo. 7s. 6d. Cheap edition, sewed, 1s.

Bright (W.) Red Book for Sergeants.
Fifth and Revised Edition, 1880. By W. Bright, late Colour-Sergeant, 19th Middlesex R.V. Fcap. interleaved. 1s.

Buckland (C. T.) Whist for Beginners. Second Edition. 1s.

Buckle (the late Capt. E.) Bengal Artillery.
A Memoir of the Services of the Bengal Artillery from the formation of the Corps. By the late Capt. E. Buckle, Assist.-Adjut. Gen. Ben. Art. Edit. by Sir J. W. Kaye. 8vo. Lond, 1852. 10s.

Buckley (R. B.) The Irrigation Works of India, and their Financial Results. Being a brief History and Description of the Irrigation Works of India, and of the Profits and Losses they have caused to the State. By Robert B. Buckley, A.M.I.C.E., Executive Engineer of the Public Works Department of India. 8vo. With Map and Appendix. 9s.

Burke (P.) Celebrated Naval and Military Trials.
By Peter Burke, Serjeant-at-Law. Author of "Celebrated Trials connected with the Aristocracy." Post 8vo. 10s. 6d.

By the Tiber.
By the Author of "Signor Monaldini's Niece." 2 vols. 21s.

Carlyle (Thomas), Memoirs of the Life and Writings of,
With Personal Reminiscences and Selections from his Private Letters to numerous Correspondents. Edited by Richard Herne Shepherd, Assisted by Charles N. Williamson. 2 Vols. With Portrait and Illustrations. Crown 8vo. 21s.

Chaffers (William) Gilda Aurifabrorum.
A History of London Goldsmiths and Plateworkers, with their Marks stamped on Plate, copied in fac-simile from celebrated Examples and the Earliest Records preserved at Goldsmiths' Hall, London, with their Names, Addresses, and Dates of Entry. 2,500 Illustrations. By William Chaffers, Author of "Hall Marks on Plate." 8vo. 18s.

Challenge of Barletta (The).
By Massimo D'Azeglio. Rendered into English by Lady Louisa Magenis. 2 vols. Crown 8vo. 21s.

Collette (C. H.) The Roman Breviary.
A Critical and Historical Review, with Copious Classified Extracts. By Charles Hastings Collette. 2nd Edition. Revised and enlarged. 8vo. 5s.

Collette (C. H.) Henry VIII.
An Historical Sketch as affecting the Reformation in England. By Charles Hastings Collette. Post 8vo. 6s.

—— St. Augustine (Aurelius Augustinus Episcopus Hipponiensis), a Sketch of his Life and Writings as affecting the Controversy with Rome. By Charles Hastings Collette. Crown 8vo. 5s.

Collins (Mabel) The Story of Helena Modjeska (Madame Chlapowska). By Mabel Collins. Crown 8vo. 7s. 6d.

Colquhoun (Major J. A. S.) With the Kurrum Force in the Caubul Campaign of 1878–79. By Major J. A. S. Colquhoun, R.A. With Illustrations from the Author's Drawings, and two Maps. 8vo. 16s.

Cooper's Hill College. Calendar of the Royal Indian Engineering College, Cooper's Hill. Published by authority in January each year. 5s.

Contents.—Staff of the College; Prospectus for the Year; Table of Marks; Syllabus of Course of Study; Leave and Pension Rules of Indian Service; Class and Prize Lists; Past Students serving in India; Entrance Examination Papers, &c.

Corbet (M. E.) A Pleasure Trip to India, during the Visit of H.R.H. the Prince of Wales, and afterwards to Ceylon. By Mrs. Corbet. Illustrated with Photos. Crown 8vo. 7s. 6d.

Cowdery (Miss E.) Franz Liszt, Artist and Man.
By L. Ramann. Translated from the German by Miss E. Cowdery. 2 vols. Crown 8vo. 21s.

Crosland (Mrs. N.) Stories of the City of London; Retold for Youthful Readers. By Mrs. Newton Crosland. With ten Illustrations. Cr. 8vo. 6s.

These Stories range from the early days of Old London Bridge and the Settlement of the Knights Templars in England to the time of the Gordon Riots; with incidents in the Life of Brunel in relation to the Thames Tunnel; narrated from Personal recollections.

Cruise of H.M.S. "Galatea,"
Captain H.R.H. the Duke of Edinburgh, K.G., in 1867—1868. By the Rev. John Milner, B.A., Chaplain; and Oswald W. Brierly. Illustrated by a Photograph of H.R.H. the Duke of Edinburgh; and by Chromo-Lithographs and Graphotypes from Sketches taken on the spot by O. W. Brierly. 8vo. 16s.

Cunningham (H. S.) British India, and its Rulers. By H. S. CUNNINGHAM, M.A., one of the Judges of the High Court of Calcutta, and late Member of the Famine Commission. 10s. 6d.

Daumas (E.) Horses of the Sahara, and the Manners of the Desert. By E. DAUMAS, General of the Division Commanding at Bordeaux, Senator, &c., &c. With Commentaries by the Emir Abd-el-Kadir (Authorized Edition). 8vo. 6s.

"We have rarely read a work giving a more picturesque and, at the same time, practical account of the manners and customs of a people, than this book on the Arabs and their horses."—*Edinburgh Courant.*

Deighton (K.) Shakespeare's King Henry the Fifth. With Notes and an Introduction. By K. DEIGHTON, Principal of Agra College. Crown 8vo. 5s.

Destruction of Life by Snakes, Hydrophobia, &c., in Western India. By an EX-COMMISSIONER. Fcap. 2s. 6d.

Dickins, (F. V.) Chiushingura: or the Loyal League. A Japanese Romance. Translated by FREDERICK V. DICKINS, Sc.B., of the Middle Temple, Barrister-at-Law. With Notes and an Appendix containing a Metrical Version of the Ballad of Takasako, and a specimen of the Original Text in Japanese character. Illustrated by numerous Engravings on Wood, drawn and executed by Japanese artists and printed on Japanese paper. 8vo. 10s. 6d.

Diplomatic Study on the Crimean War, 1852 to 1856. (Russian Official Publication.) 2 vols. 8vo. 28s.

Doran (Dr. J.) "Their Majesties Servants": Annals of the English Stage. Actors, Authors, and Audiences, From Thomas Betterton to Edmund Kean. By Dr. DORAN, F.S.A., Author of "Table Traits," "Lives of the Queens of England of the House of Hanover." &c. Post 8vo. 6s.

"Every page of the work is barbed with wit, and will make its way point foremost. . . . . provides entertainment for the most diverse tastes."—*Daily News.*

Douglas (M.) Countess Violet; or, What Grandmamma saw in the Fire. A Book for Girls. By MINNIE DOUGLAS. Author of "Two Rose Trees." Illustrated. 5s.

Drury (Col. H.) The Useful Plants of India, With Notices of their chief value in Commerce, Medicine, and the Arts. By COLONEL HEBER DRURY. Second Edition, with Additions and Corrections. Royal 8vo. 16s.

Durand (H. M.) The Life of Major-General Sir Henry Marion Durand, K.C.S.I., C.B., of the Royal Engineers. By H. M. DURAND, C.S.I., of the Bengal Civil Service, Barrister-at-Law. 2 vols. 8vo., with Portrait. 42s.

Dutton (Major Hon. C.) Life in India. By Major the Hon. CHARLES DUTTON. Crown 8vo. 2s. 6d.

Duke (J.) Recollections of the Kabul Campaign 1879–1880. By JOSHUA DUKE, Ben. Med. Service, F.R.A.S. 8vo., with Illustrations and Map. 15s.

Dwight (H. O.) Turkish Life in War Time. By HENRY O. DWIGHT. Crown 8vo. 12s.

Écarte. By AQUARIUS. Sq. 16mo. 1s.

Edwards (G. Sutherland) A Female Nihilist. By ERNEST LAVIGNE. Translated from the French by G. SUTHERLAND EDWARDS. Crown 8vo. 9s.

Edwards (H. S.) The Lyrical Drama: Essays on Subjects, Composers, and Executants of Modern Opera. By H. SUTHERLAND EDWARDS, Author of "The Russians at Home and Abroad," &c. Two vols. Crown 8vo. 21s.

—— **The Russians At Home and the Russians Abroad.** Sketches, Unpolitical and Political, of Russian Life under Alexander II. By H. SUTHERLAND EDWARDS. 2 vols. Crown 8vo. 21s.

Ensor (F. Sydney) The Queen's Speeches in Parliament, from Her Accession to the present time. A Compendium of the History of Her Majesty's Reign told from the Throne. Edited and Compiled by F. SYDNEY ENSOR, Author of "Through Nubia to Darfoor." Crown 8vo. 7s. 6d.

—— **Incidents of a Journey through Nubia to Darfoor.** By F. SYDNEY ENSOR, C.E. 10s. 6d.

Eyre (Major-General Sir V.), K.C.S.I., C.B. The Kabul Insurrection of 1841–42. Revised and corrected from Lieut. Eyre's Original Manuscript. Edited by Colonel G. B. MALLESON, C.S.I. Crown 8vo., with Map and Illustrations. 9s.

Fearon (A.) Kenneth Trelawny. By ALEC FEARON. Author of "Touch not the Nettle." 2 vols. Crown 8vo. 21s.

Forbes (Capt. C. J. F. S.) Comparative Grammar of the Languages of Further India. A Fragment; and other Essays, the Literary Remains of Captain C. J. F. S. FORBES, of the British Burma Commission. Author of "British Burma and its People: Sketches of Native Manners, Customs, and Religion." 6s.

Foreign Office, Diplomatic and Consular Sketches. Reprinted from "Vanity Fair." Cr. 8vo. 6s.

Fraser (Lieut.-Col. G. T.) Records of Sport and Military Life in Western India. By the late Lieut.-Colonel G. T. Fraser, formerly of the 1st Bombay Fusiliers, and more recently attached to the Staff of H.M.'s Indian Army. With an Introduction by Colonel G. B. MALLESON, C.S.I. 7s. 6d.

Fry (Herbert) London in 188 Its Suburbs and Environs. Illustrated with 16 Bird's-eye Views of the Principal Streets, and a Map. By HERBERT FRY. Third year of publication. Revised and Enlarged. 2s.

Gazetteers of India.

Thornton, 4 vols., 8vo. £2 16s.

„ 8vo. 21s.

„ (N.W.P., &c.) 2 vols., 8vo. 25s.

Gazetteer of Southern India.

With the Tenasserim Provinces and Singapore. Compiled from original and authentic sources. Accompanied by an Atlas, including plans of all the principal towns and cantonments. Royal 8vo. with 4to. Atlas. £3 3s.

Geography of India.

Comprising an account of British India, and the various states enclosed and adjoining. Fcap. pp. 250. 2s.

Geological Papers on Western India.

Including Cutch, Scinde, and the south-east coast of Arabia. To which is added a Summary of the Geology of India generally. Edited for the Government by HENRY J. CARTER, Assistant Surgeon, Bombay Army. Royal 8vo. with folio Atlas of maps and plates; half-bound. £2 2s.

Gibney (Major R. D.) Earnest Madement; a Tale of Wiltshire. By MAJOR R. D. GIBNEY, late Adjutant 1st Wilts Rifle Volunteers. Cr. 8vo. 6s. (Dedicated by permission to Lieut.-Gen. Sir Garnet Wolseley, G.C.B.)

Gillmore (Parker) Encounters with Wild Beasts.

By PARKER GILLMORE, Author of "The Great Thirst Land," "A Ride Through Hostile Africa," &c. With Ten full-page Illustrations. Cr. 8vo. 7s. 6d.

—— **Prairie and Forest.** A description of the Game of North America, with Personal Adventures in its Pursuit. By PARKER GILLMORE (Ubique). With Thirty-Seven Illustrations. Crown 8vo. 7s. 6d.

Goldstucker (Prof. Theodore), The late. The Literary Remains of. With a Memoir. 2 vols. 8vo. 21s.

Graham (Alex.) Genealogical and Chronological Tables, illustrative of Indian History. 4to. 5s.

Grant (Jas.) Derval Hampton: A Story of the Sea. By James Grant, Author of the "Romance of War," &c. 2 vols. Crown 8vo. 21s.

Greene (F. V.) The Russian Army and its Campaigns in Turkey in 1877–1878. By F. V. Greene, First Lieutenant in the Corps of Engineers, U.S. Army, and lately Military Attaché to the United States Legation at St. Petersburg. 8vo. With Atlas. 32s. Second Edition.

—— **Sketches of Army Life in Russia.** Crown 8vo. 9s.

Griesinger (Theodor) The Jesuits; a Complete History of their Open and Secret Proceedings from the Foundation of the Order to the Present Time. Told to the German People. By Theodor Griesinger. Translated by A. J. Scott, M.D. 2 vols. 8vo. Illustrated. 24s.

Griffith (Ralph T. H.) Birth of the War God. A Poem. By Kalidasa. Translated from the Sanscrit into English Verse. By Ralph T. H. Griffith. 8vo. 5s.

Hall (E. H.) Lands of Plenty, for Health, Sport, and Profit. British North America. A Book for all Travellers and Settlers. By E. Hepple Hall, F.S.S. Crown 8vo., with Maps. 6s.

Hall's Trigonometry. The Elements of Plane and Spherical Trigonometry. With an Appendix, containing the solution of the Problems in Nautical Astronomy. For the use of Schools. By the Rev. T. G. Hall, M.A., Professor of Mathematics in King's College, London. 12mo. 2s.

Hancock (E. C.) The Amateur Pottery and Glass Painter. With Directions for Gilding, Chasing, Burnishing, Bronzing, and Groundlaying. By E. Campbell Hancock. Illustrated with Chromo-Lithographs and numerous Woodcuts. Fourth Edition. 8vo. 6s.

—— **Copies for China Painters.** By E. Campbell Hancock. With Fourteen Chromo-Lithographs and other Illustrations. 8vo. 10s.

Handbook of Reference to the Maps of India. Giving the Lat. and Long. of places of note. 18mo. 3s. 6d.

*** *This will be found a valuable Companion to Messrs. Allen & Cos.' Maps of India.*

Harcourt (Maj. A. F. P.) Down by the Drawle. By Major A. F. P. Harcourt, Bengal Staff Corps, author of "Kooloo, Lahoul, and Spiti," "The Shakespeare Argosy," &c. 2 Vols. in one, crown 8vo. 6s.

Hardwicke (Herbert Junius) Health Resorts and Spas; or, Climatic and Hygienic Treatment of Disease. By Herbert Junius Hardwicke, M.D., &c. Fcap. 2s. 6d.

Harting (J. E.) Sketches of Bird Life. By James Edmund Harting, Author of a "Handbook of British Birds." 8vo., with numerous Illustrations. 10s. 6d.

Heine (Heinrich) The Book of Songs. By Heinrich Heine. Translated from the German by Strathier. Cr. 8vo. 7s. 6d.

Helms (L. V.) Pioneering in the Far East, and Journeys to California in 1849, and to the White Sea in 1878. By Ludwig Verner Helms. With Illustrations from original Sketches and Photographs, and Maps. 8vo. 18s.

Hensman (Howard) The Afghan War, 1879–80. Being a complete Narrative of the Capture of Cabul, the Siege of Sherpur, the Battle of Ahmed Khel, the brilliant March to Candahar, and the Defeat of Ayub Khan, with the Operations on the Helmund, and the Settlement with Abdur Rahman Khan. By Howard Hensman, Special Correspondent of the "Pioneer" (Allahabad) and the "Daily News" (London). 8vo. With Maps. 21s.

General Sir Frederick Roberts writes in regard to the letters now re-published:—

"Allow me to congratulate you most cordially on the admirable manner in which you have placed before the public the account of our march from Cabul, and the operations of 31st August and 1st September around Candahar. *Nothing could be more accurate or graphic.* I thought your description of the fight at Charasai was one that any soldier might have been proud of writing; but your recent letters are, if possible, even better."

Holden (E. S.) Sir William Herschel. His Life and Works. By Edward S. Holden, United States Naval Observatory Washington. Cr. 8vo. 6s.

Holland.
By Edmondo de Amicis. Translated from the Italian by Caroline Tilton. Crown 8vo. 10s. 6d.

Holmes (T. R. E.) A History of the Indian Mutiny, and of the Disturbances which accompanied it among the Civil Population. By T. R. E. Holmes. 8vo., with Maps and Plans. 21s.

Hough (Lieut.-Col. W.) Precedents in Military Law.
8vo. cloth. 25s

Hughes (Rev. T. P.) Notes on Muhammadanism.
Second Edition, Revised and Enlarged. Fcap. 8vo. 6s.

Hunt and Kenny. On Duty under a Tropical Sun.
Being some Practical Suggestions for the Maintenance of Health and Bodily Comfort, and the Treatment of Simple Diseases; with Remarks on Clothing and Equipment for the Guidance of Travellers in Tropical Countries. By Major S. Leigh Hunt, Madras Army, and Alexander S. Kenny, M.R.C.S.E., A.K.C., Senior Demonstrator of Anatomy at King's College, London, Author of "The Tissues and their Structure." Second Edition. Crown 8vo. 4s.

—— **Tropical Trials.**
A Handbook for Women in the Tropics. By Major S. Leigh Hunt, and Alexander S. Kenny. Cr. 8vo. 7s. 6d.

Hutton (J.) Thugs and Dacoits of India.
A Popular Account of the Thugs and Dacoits, the Hereditary Garotters and Gang Robbers of India. By James Hutton. Post 8vo. 5s.

India Directory (The).
For the Guidance of Commanders of Steamers and Sailing Vessels. Founded upon the Work of the late Captain James Horsburgh, F.R.S.

Part I.—The East Indies, and Interjacent Ports of Africa and South America. Revised, Extended, and Illustrated with Charts of Winds, Currents, Passages, Variation, and Tides. By Commander Alfred Dundas Taylor, F.R.G.S., Superintendent of Marine Surveys to the Government of India. £1 18s.

Part II.—The China Sea, with the Ports of Java, Australia and Japan and the Indian Archipelago Harbours, as well as those of New Zealand. Illustrated with Charts of the Winds, Currents, Passages, &c. By the same. (*In preparation.*)

Indian and Military Law.

Mahommedan Law of Inheritance, &c. A Manual of the Mahommedan Law of Inheritance and Contract; comprising the Doctrine of the Soonee and Sheea Schools, and based upon the text of Sir H. W. Macnaghten's Principles and Precedents, together with the Decisions of the Privy Council and High Courts of the Presidencies in India. For the use of Schools and Students. By Standish Grove Grady, Barrister-at-Law, Reader of Hindoo, Mahommedan, and Indian Law to the Inns of Court. 8vo. 14s.

Hedaya, or Guide, a Commentary on the Mussulman Laws, translated by order of the Governor-General and Council of Bengal. By Charles Hamilton. Second Edition, with Preface and Index by Standish Grove Grady. 8vo. £1 15s.

Institutes of Menu in English. The Institutes of Hindu Law or the Ordinances of Menu, according to Gloss of Collucca. Comprising the Indian System of Duties, Religious and Civil, verbally translated from the Original, with a Preface by Sir William Jones, and collated with the Sanscrit Text by Graves Chamney Haughton, M.A., F.R.S., Professor of Hindu Literature in the East India College. New edition, with Preface and Index by Standish G. Grady, Barrister-at-Law, and Reader of Hindu, Mahommedan, aud Indian Law to the Inns of Court. 8vo., cloth. 12s.

Indian Code of Criminal Procedure. Being Act X. of 1872, Passed by the Governor-General of India in Council on the 25th of April, 1872. 8vo. 12s.

Indian Code of Civil Procedure. Being Act X. of 1877. 8vo 6s.

Indian Code of Civil Procedure. In the form of Questions and Answers, with Explanatory and Illustrative Notes. By Angelo J. Lewis. Barrister-at-law 12mo. 12s. 6d.

Indian Penal Code. In the Form of Questions and Answers. With Explanatory and Illustrative Notes. By Angelo J. Lewis, Barrister-at-Law. Post 8vo. 7s. 6d.

Hindu Law. Defence of the Daya Bhaga. Notice of the Case on Prosoono Coomar Tajore's Will. Judgment of the Judicial Committee of the Privy Council. Examination of such Judgment. By John Cochrane, Barrister-at-Law. Royal 8vo. 20s.

Law and Customs of Hindu Castes, within the Dekhan Provinces subject to the Presidency of Bombay, chiefly affecting Civil Suits. By Arthur Steele. Royal 8vo. £1 1s.

Moohummudan Law of Inheritance. (See page 35.)

Chart of Hindu Inheritance. With an Explanatory Treatise, By Almaric Rumsey. 8vo. 6s. 6d.

Manual of Military Law. For all ranks of the Army, Militia and Volunteer Services. By Colonel J. K. Pipon, Assist. Adjutant

General at Head Quarters, & J. F. Collier, Esq., of the Inner Temple, Barrister-at-Law. Third and Revised Edition. Pocket size. 5s.

Precedents in Military Law; including the Practice of Courts-Martial; the Mode of Conducting Trials; the Duties of Officers at Military Courts of Inquests, Courts of Inquiry, Courts of Requests, &c., &c. The following are a portion of the Contents:—

1. Military Law. 2. Martial Law. 3. Courts-Martial. 4. Courts of Inquiry. 5. Courts of Inquest. 6. Courts of Request. 7. Forms of Courts-Martial. 8. Precedents of Military Law. 9. Trials of Arson to Rape (Alphabetically arranged.) 10. Rebellions. 11. Riots. 12. Miscellaneous. By Lieut.-Col. W. Hough, late Deputy Judge-Advocate-General, Bengal Army, and Author of several Works on Courts-Martial. One thick 8vo. vol. 25s.

The Practice of Courts Martial. By Hough & Long. Thick 8vo. London, 1825. 26s.

Indian Criminal Law and Procedure,

Including the Procedure in the High Courts, as well as that in the Courts not established by Royal Charter; with Forms of Charges and Notes on Evidence, illustrated by a large number of English Cases, and Cases decided in the High Courts of India; and an Appendix of selected Acts passed by the Legislative Council relating to Criminal matters. By M. H. Starling, Esq., LL.B. & F. B. Constable, M.A. Third edition. 8vo. £2 2s.

In the Company's Service.

A Reminiscence. 8vo. 10s. 6d.

Irwin (H. C.) The Garden of India; or, Chapters on Oudh History and Affairs. By H. C. Irwin, B.A. Oxon., Bengal Civil Service. 8vo. 12s.

Jackson (Lt.-Col. B.) Military Surveying, &c. 8vo. 14s. (See page 28).

Jackson (Lowis D'A.) Canal and Culvert Tables.

Based on the Formula of Kutter, under a Modified Classification. with Explanatory Text and Examples. By Lowis D'A. Jackson, A.M.I.C.E., author of "Hydraulic Manual and Statistics," &c. Roy. 8vo. 28s.

—— **Pocket Logarithms and other Tables for Ordinary** Calculations of Quantity, Cost, Interest, Annuities, Assurance, and Angular Functions, obtaining Results correct in the Fourth figure. By Lowis D'A. Jackson. Cloth, 2s. 6d.; leather, 3s. 6d.

Jackson (Lowis D'A.) Accented Four-Figure Logarithms, and other Tables. For purposes both of Ordinary and of Trigonometrical Calculation, and for the Correction of Altitudes and Lunar Distances. Arranged and accented by LOWIS D'A. JACKSON, A.M.I.C.E., Author of "Canal and Culvert Tables," "Hydraulic Manual," &c. Crown 8vo. 9s.

—— Accented Five-Figure Logarithms of Numbers from 1 to 99999, without Differences. Arranged and accented by LOWIS D'A. JACKSON. Royal 8vo. 16s.

—— Units of Measurement for Scientific and Professional Men. By LOWIS D'A. JACKSON. Cr. 4to. 2s.

James (A. G. F. Eliot) Indian Industries.
By A. G. F. ELIOT JAMES, Author of "A Guide to Indian Household Management," &c. Crown 8vo. 9s.

CONTENTS:—Indian Agriculture; Beer; Cacao; Carpets; Cereals; Chemicals; Cinchona; Coffee; Cotton; Drugs; Dyeing and Colouring Materials; Fibrous Substances; Forestry; Hides; Skins and Horns; Gums and Resins; Irrigation; Ivory; Mining; Oils; Opium; Paper; Pottery; Ryots; Seeds; Silk; Spices; Sugar; Tea; Tobacco; Wood; Wool. Table of Exports. Index.

Jenkinson (Rev. T. B.) Amazulu.
The Zulu People: their Manners, Customs, and History, with Letters from Zululand descriptive of the Present Crisis. By THOMAS B. JENKINSON, B.A., sometime of Springvale, Natal, and Canon of Maritzburg. Crown 8vo. 6s.

Joyner (Mrs.) Cyprus: Historical and Descriptive.
Adapted from the German of Herr FRANZ VON LÖHER. With much additional matter. By Mrs. A. BATSON JOYNER. Crown 8vo. With 2 Maps. 10s. 6d.

Kaufman (R.) Our Young Folk's Plutarch.
Edited by ROSALIE KAUFMAN. With Maps and Illustrations. 8vo. 10s. 6d.

Kaye (Sir J. W.) The Sepoy War in India.
A History of the Sepoy War in India, 1857—1858. By Sir JOHN WILLIAM KAYE, Author of "The History of the War in Afghanistan." Vol. I., 8vo. 18s. Vol. II. £1. Vol. III. £1.

CONTENTS OF VOL. I.:—BOOK I.—INTRODUCTORY.—The Conquest of the Punjab and Pegu.—The "Right of Lapse."—The Annexation of Oude.—Progress of Englishism. BOOK II.—THE SEPOY ARMY: ITS RISE, PROGRESS, AND DECLINE.—Early History of the Native Army.—Deteriorating Influences.—The Sindh Mutinies.—The Punjaub Mutinies. Discipline of the

Bengal Army. BOOK III.—THE OUTBREAK OF THE MUTINY.—Lord Canning and his Council.—The Oude Administration and the Persian War.—The Rising of the Storm.—The First Mutiny.—Progress of Mutiny.—Excitement in Upper India.—Bursting of the Storm.—APPENDIX.

CONTENTS OF VOL. II.:—BOOK IV.—THE RISING IN THE NORTH-WEST.–The Delhi History.—The Outbreak at Meerut.—The Seizure of Delhi.—Calcutta in May.—Last Days of General Anson.—The March upon Delhi. BOOK V.—PROGRESS OF REBELLION IN UPPER INDIA.—Benares and Allahabad.—Cawnpore.—The March to Cawnpore.—Re-occupation of Cawnpore. BOOK VI.—THE PUNJAB AND DELHI.—First Conflicts in the Punjab.—Peshawur and Rawul Pinder.—Progress of Events in the Punjab.—Delhi.—First Weeks of the Siege.—Progress of the Siege.—The Last Succours from the Punjab.

CONTENTS OF VOL. III.:—BOOK VII.—BENGAL, BEHAR, AND THE NORTH-WEST PROVINCES.—At the Seat of Government.—The Insurrection in Behar.—The Siege of Arrah.—Behar and Bengal. BOOK VIII.—MUTINY AND REBELLION IN THE NORTH-WEST PROVINCES.—Agra in May.—Insurrection in the Districts.—Bearing of the Native Chiefs.—Agra in June, July, August and September. BOOK IX.—LUCKNOW AND DELHI.—Rebellion in Oude.—Revolt in the Districts.—Lucknow in June and July.—The siege and Capture of Delhi.

(For continuation, *see* "History of the Indian Mutiny," by Colonel G. B. MALLESON, p. 23.)

Kaye (Sir J. W.) History of the War in Afghanistan.
New edition. 3 Vols. Crown 8vo. £1. 6s.

—— Lives of Indian Officers.
By Sir JOHN WILLIAM KAYE. 3 vols. Cr. 8vo. 6s. each.

Keatinge (Mrs.) English Homes in India.
By MRS. KEATINGE. Part I.—The Three Loves. Part II.—The Wrong Turning. Two vols., Post 8vo. 16s.

Keene (H. G.) Mogul Empire.
From the death of Aurungzeb to the overthrow of the Mahratta Power, by HENRY GEORGE KEENE, B.C.S. Second edition. With Map. 8vo. 10s. 6d.

This Work fills up a blank between the ending of Elphinstone's and the commencement of Thornton's Histories.

—— Administration in India.
Post 8vo. 5s.

Keene (H. G.) Peepul Leaves.
Poems written in India. Post 8vo 5s.

—— **Fifty-Seven.**
Some account of the Administration of Indian Districts during the Revolt of the Bengal Army. By HENRY GEORGE KEENE, C.I.E., M.R.A.S., Author of "The Fall of the Mughal Empire." 8vo. 6s.

—— **The Turks in India.**
Historical Chapters on the Administration of Hindostan by the Chugtai Tartar, Babar, and his Descendants. 12s. 6d.

King (D. B.) The Irish Question. By DAVID BENNETT KING, Professor in Lafayette College, U.S.A. Cr. 8vo. 9s.

Lane-Poole (S.) Studies in a Mosque. By STANLEY LANE-POOLE, Laureat de l'Institut de France. 8vo.

Latham (Dr. R. G.) Russian and Turk,
From a Geographical, Ethnological, and Historical Point of View. 8vo 18s.

Laurie (Col. W. F. B.) Our Burmese Wars and Relations with Burma. With a Summary of Events from 1826 to 1879, including a Sketch of King Theebau's Progress. With various Local, Statistical, and Commercial Information. By Colonel W. F. B. LAURIE, Author of "Rangoon," "Narrative of the Second Burmese War," &c. 8vo. With Plans and Map. 16s.

—— **Ashé Pyee, the Superior Country**; or the great attractions of Burma to British Enterprise and Commerce. By Col. W. F. B. LAURIE, Author of "Our Burmese Wars and Relations with Burma." Crown 8vo. 5s.

Lee (F. G.) The Church under Queen Elizabeth.
An Historical Sketch. By the Rev. F. G. LEE, D.D. Two Vols., Crown 8vo. 21s.

—— **Reginald Barentyne**; or Liberty Without Limit. A Tale of the Times. By FREDERICK GEORGE LEE. With Portrait of the Author. Crown 8vo. Second Edition. 5s.

—— **The Words from the Cross**: Seven Sermons for Lent, Passion-Tide, and Holy Week. By the Rev. F. G. LEE, D.D. Third Edition revised. Fcap. 3s. 6d.

—— **Order Out of Chaos.** Two Sermons.
By the Rev. FREDERICK GEORGE LEE, D.D. Fcap. 2s. 6d.

Lee's (Dr. W. N.) Drain of Silver to the East.
Post 8vo. 8s.

Le Messurier (Maj. A.) Kandahar in 1879.
Being the Diary of Major A. LE MESSURIER, R.E., Brigade Major R.E. with the Quetta Column. Crown 8vo. 8s.

Lethbridge (R.) High Education in India. A Plea for the State Colleges. By ROPER LETHBRIDGE, C.I.E., M.A. Crown 8vo. 5s.

Lewin (T. H.) Wild Races of the South Eastern Frontier of India. Including an Account of the Loshai Country. By Capt. T. H. LEWIN, Dep. Comm. of Hill Tracts. Post 8vo. 10s. 6d.

Lewis (A. J.) Indian Penal Code
In the Form of Questions and Answers. With Explanatory and Illustrative Notes. By ANGELO J. LEWIS. Post 8vo. 7s. 6d.

—— **Indian Code of Civil Procedure.**
In the Form of Questions and Answers. With Explanatory and Illustrative Notes. By ANGELO J. LEWIS. Post 8vo. 12s. 6d.

Liancourt's and Pincott's Primitive and Universal Laws ot the Formation and Development of Language; a Rational and Inductive System founded on the Natural Basis of Onomatops. 8vo. 12*s*. 6*d*.

Lloyd (J. S.) Shadows of the Past.
Being the Autobiography of General Kenyon. Edited by J. S. LLOYD, Authoress of "Ruth Everingham," "The Silent Shadow," &c. Second Edition. Crown 8vo. 6s.

—— **Honesty Seeds, and How they Grew**; or, Tony Wigston's Firm Bank. Cr. 8vo. Illustrated. 2s. 6d.

Lockwood (Ed.) Natural History, Sport and Travel.
By EDWARD LOCKWOOD, Bengal Civil Service, late Magistrate of Monghyr. Crown 8vo. With numerous Illustrations. 9s.

Lovell (Vice-Adm.) Personal Narrative of Events from 1799 to 1815. With Anecdotes. By the late Vice-Adm. WM. STANHOPE LOVELL, R.N., K.H. Second edition. Crown 8vo. 4s.

Low (Charles Rathbone) Major-General Sir Frederick S. Roberts, Bart., V.C., G.C.B., C.I.E., R.A.: a Memoir. By CHARLES RATHBONE LOW, Author of "History of the Indian Navy," &c. 8vo., with Portrait. 18s.

Lupton (J. I.) The Horse, as he Was, as he Is, and as he Ought to Be. By JAMES IRVINE LUPTON, F.R.C.V.S., Author of "The External Anatomy of the Horse," &c. &c. Illustrated. 3s. 6d.

Macdonald (D. G. F.) Grouse Disease; its Causes and Remedies. By DUNCAN GEORGE FORBES MACDONALD, LL.D., C.E., J.P., F.R.G.S., Author of "What the Farmers may do with the Land," "Estate Management," "Cattle, Sheep, and Deer," &c. 8vo. Illustrated. Third Edition. 10s. 6d.

MacGregor (Col. C. M.) Narrative of a Journey through the Province of Khorassan and on the N. W. Frontier of Afghanistan in 1875. By Colonel C. M. MACGREGOR, C.S.I., C.I.E., Bengal Staff Corps. 2 vols. 8vo. With map and numerous illustrations. 30s.

—— **Wanderings in Balochistan.** By MAJOR-GENERAL SIR C. M. MACGREGOR, K.C.B., C.S.I., C.I.E., Bengal Staff Corps, and Quartermaster-General in India. 8vo. With Illustrations and Map. 18s.

Mackay (C.) Luck, and what came of it. A Tale of our Times. By CHARLES MACKAY, LL.D. Three vols. 31s. 6d.

Mackenzie (Capt. C. F.) The Romantic Land of Hind. By EL MUSANNIF (Capt. C. F. MACKENZIE). Crown 8vo. 6s.

Maggs (J.) Round Europe with the Crowd. Crown 8vo. 5s.

Magenis (Lady Louisa) The Challenge of Barletta. By Massimo D'Azeglio. Rendered into English by Lady LOUISA MAGENIS. 2 vols., crown 8vo. 21s.

Malabari (B. M.) Gujerat and the Gujeratis. Pictures of Men and Manners taken from Life. By BEHRAMJI M. MALABARI, Author of "The Indian Muse in English Garb," "Pleasures of Morality," &c. Crown 8vo. 6s.

Malleson (Col. G. B.) Final French Struggles in India and on the Indian Seas. Including an Account of the Capture of the Isles of France and Bourbon, and Sketches of the most eminent Foreign Adventurers in India up to the period of that Capture. With an Appendix containing an Account of the Expedition from India to Egypt in 1801. By Colonel G. B. MALLESON, C.S.I. Crown 8vo. 10s. 6d.

—— **History of the Indian Mutiny, 1857–1858,** commencing from the close of the Second Volume of Sir John Kaye's History of the Sepoy War. Vol. I. 8vo With Map. 20s.

Contents.—Calcutta in May and June.—William Tayler and Vincent Eyre.—How Bihar and Calcutta were saved.—Mr. Colvin and Agra.—Jhansi and Bandalkhand.—Colonel Durand and Holkar.—Sir George Lawrence and Rajputana.—Brigadier Polwhele's great battle and its results.—Bareli, Rohilkhand, and Farakhabad.—The relation of the annexation of Oudh to the Mutiny.—Sir Henry Lawrence and the Mutiny in Oudh.—The siege of Lakhnao.—The first relief of Lakhnao.

Vol. II.—The Storming of Delhi, the Relief of Lucknow, the Two Battles of Cawnpore, the Campaign in Rohilkhand, and the movements of the several Columns in the N.W. Provinces, the Azimgurh District, and on the Eastern and South-Eastern Frontiers. 8vo. With 4 Plans. 20s.

Vol. III.—Bombay in 1857. Lord Elphinstone. March of Woodburn's Column. Mr. Seton-Karr and the Southern Maratha Country. Mr. Forjett and Bombay. Asirgarh. Sir Henry Durand. March of Stuart's Column. Holkar and Durand. Malwa Campaign. Haidarabad. Major C. Davidson and Salar Jang Sagar and Narbadi Territory. Sir Robert Hamilton and Sir Hugh Rose. Central India Campaign. Whitlock and Kirwi. Sir Hugh Rose and Gwaliar. Le Grand Jacob and Western India. Lord Canning's Oudh policy. Last Campaign in, and pacification of, Oudh. Sir Robert Napier, Smith, Michell, and Tantia Topi. Civil Districts during the Mutiny. Minor Actions at Out-stations. Conclusion. 8vo. With Plans. 20s.

Malleson (Col. G. B.) History of Afghanistan, from the Earliest Period to the Outbreak of the War of 1878. 8vo. Second Edition. With Map. 18s.

—— **The Decisive Battles of India,** from 1746–1849. With a Portrait of the Author, a Map, and Three Plans. By Col. G. B. Malleson, C.S.I., Author of the "Life of Lord Clive," &c. 8vo. 18s.

—— **Herat: The Garden and Granary of Central Asia.** With Map and Index. 8vo. 8s.

—— **Founders of the Indian Empire.** Clive, Warren Hastings, and Wellesley. Vol. I.—LORD CLIVE. By Colonel G. B. Malleson, C.S.I., Author of "History of the French in India," &c. 8vo., with Portraits and 4 Plans. 20s.

Manning (Mrs.) Ancient and Mediæval India. Being the History, Religion, Laws, Caste, Manners and Customs, Language, Literature, Poetry, Philosophy, Astronomy, Algebra, Medicine, Architecture, Manufactures, Commerce, &c., of the Hindus, taken from their writings. Amongst the works consulted and gleaned from may be named the Rig Veda, Sama Veda, Yajur Veda, Sathapatha Brahmana, Bhagavat Gita, The Puranas, Code of Manu, Code of Yajnavalkya, Mitakshara, Daya Bhaga, Mahabharata, Atriya, Charaka, Susruta, Ramayana, Raghu Vansa, Bhattikavya, Sakuntala, Vikramorvasi, Malati and Madhava, Mudra Rakshasa, Ratnavali. Kumara Sambhava, Prabodha, Chandrodaya, Megha Duta, Gita Govinda. Panchatantra, Hitopadesa, Katha Sarit, Sagara, Ketala, Pancnavinsati, Dasa Kumara Charita, &c. By Mrs. Manning, with Illustrations. 2 vols., 8vo. 30s.

Marvin (Chas.) Merv, the Queen of the World and the Scourge of the Men-stealing Turcomans. By Charles Marvin, author of "The Disastrous Turcoman Campaign," and "Grodekoff's Ride to Herat." With Portraits and Maps. 8vo. 18s.

—— **Colonel Grodekoff's Ride from Samarcand to Herat,** through Balkh and the Uzbek States of Afghan Turkestan. With his own March-route from the Oxus to Herat. By Charles Marvin. Crown 8vo. With Portrait. 8s.

—— **The Eye-Witnesses' Account of the Disastrous Russian** Campaign against the Akhal Tekke Turcomans: Describing the March across the Burning Desert, the Storming of Dengeel Tepe, and the Disastrous Retreat to the Caspian. By Charles Marvin. With numerous Maps and Plans. 8vo. 18s.

—— **The Russians at Merv and Herat,** and their Power of Invading India. By Charles Marvin, Author of "Disastrous Russian Campaign against the Turcomans," "Merv, the Queen of the World," &c. 8vo., with Twenty-four Illustrations and Three Maps. 24s.

Mateer (Samuel) Native Life in Travancore. By the Rev. Samuel Mateer, of the London Missionary Society, Author of "The Land of Charity." With Numerous Illustrations and Map. 8vo. 18s.

Matson (Nellie) Hilda Desmond, or Riches and Poverty. Crown 8vo. 10s. 6d.

Mayhew (Edward) Illustrated Horse Doctor.

Being an Accurate and Detailed Account, accompanied by more than 400 Pictorial Representations, characteristic of the various Diseases to which the Equine Race are subjected; together with the latest Mode of Treatment, and all the requisite Prescriptions written in Plain English By EDWARD MAYHEW, M.R.C.V.S. 8vo. 18s. 6d.

CONTENTS.—The Brain and Nervous System.—The Eyes.—The Mouth.—The Nostrils.—The Throat.—The Chest and its contents.—The Stomach, Liver, &c.—The Abdomen.—The Urinary Organs.—The Skin.—Specific Diseases.—Limbs.—The Feet.—Injuries.—Operations.

"The book contains nearly 600 pages of valuable matter, which reflects great credit on its author, and, owing to its practical details, the result of deep scientific research, deserves a place in the library of medical, veterinary, and non-professional readers."—*Field.*

"The book furnishes at once the bane and the antidote, as the drawings show the horse not only suffering from every kind of disease, but in the different stages of it, while the alphabetical summary at the end gives the cause, symptoms and treatment of each."—*Illustrated London News.*

—— Illustrated Horse Management.

Containing descriptive remarks upon Anatomy, Medicine, Shoeing, Teeth, Food, Vices, Stables; likewise a plain account of the situation, nature, and value of the various points; together with comments on grooms, dealers, breeders, breakers, and trainers; Embellished with more than 400 engravings from original designs made expressly for this work. By E. MAYHEW. A new Edition, revised and improved by J. I. LUPTON. M.R.C.V.S. 8vo. 12s.

CONTENTS.—The body of the horse anatomically considered. PHYSIC.—The mode of administering it, and minor operations. SHOEING.—Its origin, its uses, and its varieties. THE TEETH.—Their natural growth, and the abuses to which they are liable.

FOOD.—The fittest time for feeding, and the kind of food which the horse naturally consumes. The evils which are occasioned by modern stables. The faults inseparable from stables. The so-called "incapacitating vices," which are the results of injury or of disease. Stables as they should be. GROOMS.—Their prejudices, their injuries, and their duties. POINTS.—Their relative importance and where to look for their development. BREEDING.—Its inconsistencies and its disappointments BREAKING AND TRAINING.—Their errors and their results

Mayhew (Henry) German Life and Manners.
As seen in Saxony. With an account of Town Life—Village Life—Fashionable Life—Married Life—School and University Life, &c. Illustrated with Songs and Pictures of the Student Customs at the University of Jena. By Henry Mayhew, 2 vols., 8vo., with numerous illustrations. 18s.

A Popular Edition of the above. With illustrations. Cr. 8vo. 7s

"Full of original thought and observation, and may be studied with profit by both German and English—especially by the German." ***Athenæum.***

Mayo (Earl of) De Rebus Africanus.
The Claims of Portugal to the Congo and Adjacent Littoral. With Remarks on the French Annexation. By the Earl of Mayo, F.R.G.S. 8vo., with Map. 3s. 6d.

McCarthy (T. A.) An Easy System of Calisthenics and Drilling. Including Light Dumb-Bell and Indian Club Exercises. By T. A. McCarthy, Chief Instructor at Mr. Moss's Gymnasium, Brighton. Fcap. 1s. 6d.

McCosh (J.) Advice to Officers in India.
By John McCosh, M.D. Post 8vo. 8s.

Meadow (T.) Notes on China.
Desultory Notes on the Government and People of China and on the Chinese Language. By T. T. Meadows. 8vo. 9s.

Menzies (S.) Turkey Old and New: Historical, Geographical, and Statistical. By Sutherland Menzies. With Map and numerous Illustrations. Second Edition. 2 vols., 8vo. 21s.

Military Works—chiefly issued by the Government.

Field Exercises and Evolutions of Infantry. Pocket edition, 1s.

Queen's Regulations and Orders for the Army. Corrected to **1881. 8vo. 3s. 6d. Interleaved, 5s. 6d. Pocket Edition, 1s. 6d.**

Musketry Regulations, as used at Hythe. 1s.

Dress Regulations for the Army. (Reprinting.)

Infantry Sword Exercise. 1875. 6d.

Infantry Bugle Sounds. 6d.

Red Book for Sergeants. By William Bright, Colour-**Sergeant, 19th Middlesex R.V. 1s.**

Cavalry Regulations. For the Instruction, Formations, and **Movements of Cavalry. Royal 8vo. 4s. 6d.**

Manual of Artillery Exercises, 1873. 8vo. 5s.

Manual of Field Artillery Exercises. 1877. 3s.

Principles and Practice of Modern Artillery. By Lt.-Col. C. H. OWEN, R.A. 8vo. Illustrated. 15s.

Volunteer Artillery Drill-Book. By Captain W. BROOKE HOGGAN, R.A., Adjutant 1st Shropshire and Staffordshire V.A. 2s.

Artillerist's Manual and British Soldiers' Compendium. By Major F. A. GRIFFITHS. 11th Edition. 5s.

Compendium of Artillery Exercises—Smooth Bore, Field, and Garrison Artillery for Reserve Forces. By Captain J. M. McKenzie. 3s. 6d.

Principles of Gunnery. By JOHN T. HYDE, M.A., late Professor of Fortification and Artillery, Royal Indian Military College, Addiscombe. Second edition, revised and enlarged. With many Plates and Cuts, and Photograph of Armstrong Gun. Royal 8vo. 14s.

Text Book of the Construction and Manufacture of Rifled Ordnance in the British Service. By STONEY & JONES. Second Edition. Paper, 3s. 6d., Cloth, 4s. 6d.

Treatise on Fortification and Artillery. By Major HECTOR STRAITH. Revised and re-arranged by THOMAS COOK, R.N., by JOHN T. HYDE, M.A. 7th Edition. Royal 8vo. Illustrated and Four Hundred Plans, Cuts, &c. £2 2s.

Elementary Principles of Fortification. A Text-Book for Military Examinations. By J. T. HYDE, M.A. Royal 8vo. With numerous Plans and Illustrations. 10s. 6d.

Military Surveying and Field Sketching. The Various Methods of Contouring, Levelling, Sketching without Instruments, Scale of Shade, Examples in Military Drawing, &c., &c., &c. As at present taught in the Military Colleges. By Major W. H. RICHARDS, 55th Regiment, Chief Garrison Instructor in India, Late Instructor in Military Surveying, Royal Military College, Sandhurst. Second Edition, Revised and Corrected. 12s.

Treatise on Military Surveying; including Sketching in the Field, Plan-Drawing, Levelling, Military Reconnaissance, &c. By Lieut.-Col. BASIL JACKSON, late of the Royal Staff Corps. The Fifth Edition. 8vo. Illustrated by Plans, &c. 14s.

Instruction in Military Engineering. Vol. 1., Part III. 4s.

Military Train Manual. 1s.

The Sappers' Manual. Compiled for the use of Engineer Volunteer Corps. By Col. W. A. FRANKLAND, R.E. With numerous Illustrations. 2s.

Ammunition. A descriptive treatise on the different Projectiles Charges, Fuzes, Rockets, &c., at present in use for Land and Sea Service, and on other war stores manufactured in the Royal Laboratory. 6s.

Hand-book on the Manufacture and Proof of Gunpowder. as carried on at the Royal Gunpowder Factory, Waltham Abbey. 5s.

Regulations for the Training of Troops for service in the Field and for the conduct of Peace Manœuvres. 2s.

Hand-book Dictionary for the Militia and Volunteer Services, Containing a variety of useful information, Alphabetically arranged. Pocket size, 3s. 6d.; by post, 3s. 8d.

Gymnastic Exercises, System of Fencing, and Exercises for the Regulation Clubs. In one volume. Crown 8vo. 1877. 2s.

Text-Book on the Theory and Motion of Projectiles; the History, Manufacture, and Explosive Force of Gunpowder; the History of Small Arms. For Officers sent to School of Musketry. 1s. 6d.

Notes on Ammunition. 4th Edition. 1877. 2s. 6d.

Regulations and Instructions for Encampments. 6d.

Rules for the Conduct of the War Game. 2s.

Medical Regulations for the Army, Instructions for the Army, Comprising duties of Officers, Attendants, and Nurses, &c. 1s. 6d.

Purveyors' Regulations and Instructions, for Guidance of Officers of Purveyors' Department of the Army. 3s.

Priced Vocabulary of Stores used in Her Majesty's Service. 4s.

Lectures on Tactics for Officers of the Army, Militia, and Volunteers. By Major F. H. DYKE, Garrison Instructor, E.D. 3s. 6d.

Transport of Sick and Wounded Troops. By DR. LONGMORE. 5s.

Precedents in Military Law. By LT-COL. W. HOUGH. 8vo. 25s.

The Practice of Courts-Martial, by HOUGH & LONG. 8vo. 26s.

Reserve Force; Guide to Examinations, for the use of Captains and Subalterns of Infantry, Militia, and Rifle Volunteers, and for Serjeants of Volunteers. By Capt. G. H. GREAVES. 2nd edit. 2s.

The Military Encyclopædia; referring exclusively to the Military Sciences, Memoirs of distinguished Soldiers, and the Narratives of Remarkable Battles. By J. H. STOCQUELER. 8vo. 12s.

The Operations of War Explained and Illustrated. By Col. HAMLEY. New Edition Revised, with Plates. Royal 8vo. 30s.

Lessons of War. As taught by the Great Masters and Others; Selected and Arranged from the various operations in War. By FRANCE JAMES SOADY, Lieut.-Col., R.A. Royal 8vo. 21s.

The Surgeon's Pocket Book, an Essay on the best Treatment of Wounded in War. By Surgeon Major J. H. PORTER. 7s. 6d.

A Precis of Modern Tactics. By COLONEL HOME. 8vo. 8s. 6d.

Armed Strength of Austria. By Capt. COOKE. 2 pts. £1 2s.

Armed Strength of Denmark. 3s.

Armed Strength of Russia. Translated from the German. 7s.

Armed Strength of Sweden and Norway. 3s. 6d.

Armed Strength of Italy. 5s. 6d.

Armed Strength of Germany. Part I. 8s. 6d.

The Franco-German War of 1870—71. By CAPT. C. H. CLARKE. Vol. I. £1 6s. Sixth Section. 5s. Seventh Section 6s. Eighth Section. 3s. Ninth Section. 4s. 6d. Tenth Section. 6s. Eleventh Section. 5s. 3d. Twelfth Section. 4s. 6d.

The Campaign of 1866 in Germany. Royal 8vo. With Atlas, 21s.

Celebrated Naval and Military Trials. By PETER BURKE. Post 8vo., cloth. 10s. 6d.

Military Sketches. By SIR LASCELLES WRAXALL. Post 8vo. 6s.

Military Life of the Duke of Wellington. By JACKSON and SCOTT. 2 Vols. 8vo. Maps, Plans, &c. 12s.

Single Stick Exercise of the Aldershot Gymnasium. 6*d.*

Treatise on Military Carriages, and other Manufactures of the Royal Carriage Department. 5s.

Steppe Campaign Lectures. 2s.

Manual of Instructions for Army Surgeons. 1s.

Regulations for Army Hospital Corps. 9d.

Manual of Instructions for Non-Commissioned Officers, Army Hospital Corps. 2s.

Handbook for Military Artificers. 3s.

Instructions for the use of Auxiliary Cavalry. 2s. 6d.

Equipment Regulations for the Army. 5s. 6d.

Statute Law relating to the Army. 1s. 3d.

Regulations for Commissariat and Ordnance Department 2s.

Regulations for the Commissariat Department. 1s. 6d.

Regulations for the Ordnance Department. 1s. 6d.

Artillerist's Handbook of Reference for the use of the Royal and Reserve Artillery, by WILL and DALTON. 5s.

An Essay on the Principles and Construction of Military Bridges. by SIR HOWARD DOUGLAS. 1853. 15s.

Mill's History of British India,

With Notes and Continuation. By H. H. WILSON. 9 vols. cr. 8vo. £2 10s.

Mitchinson (A. W.) The Expiring Continent; A Narrative of Travel in Senegambia, with Observations on Native Character; Present Condition and Future Prospects of Africa and Colonisation. By ALEX. WILL. MITCHINSON. With Sixteen full-page Illustrations and Map. 8vo. 18s.

Mitford (Maj. R. C. W.) To Caubul with the Cavalry Brigade. A Narrative of Personal Experiences with the Force under General Sir F. S. Roberts, G.C.B. With Map and Illustrations from Sketches by the Author. By Major R. C. W. MITFORD, 14th Beng. Lancers. 8vo. Second Edit. 9s.

Modern Parallels to the Ancient Evidences of Christianity. Being an Attempt to Illustrate the Force of those Evidences by the Light of Parallels supplied by Modern Affairs. 8vo. 10s. 6d.

Muller's (Max) Rig-Veda-Sanhita.
The Sacred Hymns of the Brahmins; together with the Commentary of Sayanacharya. Published under the Patronage of the Right Honourable the Secretary of State for India in Council. 6 vols., 4to. £2 10s. per volume.

Misterton, or, Through Shadow to Sunlight. By UNUS. Crown 8vo. 5s.

Mysteries of the Vatican;
Or Crimes of the Papacy. From the German of DR. THEODOR GRIESENGER. 2 Vols. post 8vo. 21s

Neville (Ralph) The Squire's Heir.
By RALPH NEVILLE, Author of "Lloyd Pennant." Two Vols. 21s.

Nicholson (Capt. H. W.) From Sword to Share; or, a Fortune in Five Years at Hawaii. By Capt. H. WHALLEY NICHOLSON. Crown 8vo. With Map and Photographs. 12s. 6d.

Nirgis and Bismillah.
NIRGIS; a Tale of the Indian Mutiny, from the Diary of a Slave Girl: and BISMILLAH; or, Happy Days in Cashmere. By HAFIZ ALLARD. Post 8vo. 10s. 6d.

Norris-Newman (C. L.) In Zululand with the British, throughout the War of 1879. By CHARLES L. NORRIS-NEWMAN, Special Correspondent of the London "Standard," Cape Town "Standard and Mail," and the "Times" of Natal. With Plans and Four Portraits. 8vo. 16s.

Norris-Newman (C. L.) With the Boers in the Transvaal and Orange Free State in 1880–81. By C. L. NORRIS-NEWMAN, Special War Correspondent, Author of "In Zululand with the British." 8vo. With Maps. 14s.

Notes on the North Western Provinces of India.
By a District Officer. 2nd Edition. Post 8vo., cloth. 5s.

CONTENTS.—Area and Population.—Soils.—Crops.—Irrigation.—Rent.—Rates.—Land Tenures.

O'Donoghue (Mrs. P.) Ladies on Horseback.
Learning, Park Riding, and Hunting. With Notes upon Costume, and numerous Anecdotes. By Mrs. POWER O'DONOGHUE, Authoress of "The Knave of Clubs," "Horses and Horsemen," "Grandfather's Hunter," "One in Ten Thousand," &c. &c. Cr. 8vo. With Portrait. Second Edition. 5s.

Oldfield (H. A.) Sketches from Nipal, Historical and Descriptive; with Anecdotes of the Court Life and Wild Sports of the Country in the time of Maharaja Jang Bahadur, G.C.B.; to which is added an Essay on Nipalese Buddhism, and Illustrations of Religious Monuments, Architecture, and Scenery, from the Author's own Drawings. By the late HENRY AMBROSE OLDFIELD, M.D., of H. M.'s Indian Army, many years Resident at Khatmandu. Two vols. 8vo. 36s.

Oliver (Capt. S. P.) On and Off Duty.
Being Leaves from an Officer's Note Book. Part I.—Turania; Part II.—Lemuria; Part III.—Columbia. By Captain S. P. OLIVER. Crown 4to. With 38 Illustrations. 14s.

—— On Board a Union Steamer.
A compilation. By Captain S. P. OLIVER. To which is added "A Sketch Abroad," by MISS DOVETON. 8vo. With Frontispiece. 8s.

Osborne (Mrs. W.) Pilgrimage to Mecca (A).
By the Nawab Sikandar Begum of Bhopal. Translated from the Original Urdu. By MRS. WILLOUGHBY OSBORNE. Followed by a Sketch of the History of Bhopal. By COL. WILLOUGHBY OSBORNE, C.B. With Photographs, and dedicated, by permission, to HER MAJESTY, QUEEN VICTORIA. Post 8vo. £1. 1s.

This is a highly important book, not only for its literary merit, and the information it contains, but also from the fact of its being the first work written by an Indian lady, and that lady a Queen.

Oswald (Felix S.) Zoological Sketches: a Contribution to the Out-door Study of Natural History. By Felix S. Oswald, Author of "Summer-land Sketches of Mexico and Central America." 8vo., with 36 Illustrations by Hermann Faber. 7s. 6d.

Owen (Sidney) India on the Eve of the British Conquest. A Historical Sketch. By Sidney Owen, M.A. Reader in Indian Law and History in the University of Oxford. Formerly Professor of History in the Elphinstone College, Bombay. Post 8vo. 8s.

Oxenham (Rev. H. N.) Catholic Eschatology and Universalism. An Essay on the Doctrine of Future Retribution. Second Edition, revised and enlarged. Crown 8vo. 7s. 6d.

—— **Catholic Doctrine of the Atonement.** An Historical Inquiry into its Development in the Church, with an Introduction on the Principle of Theological Development. By H. Nutcombe Oxenham, M.A. 3rd Edition and Enlarged. 8vo. 14s.

"It is one of the ablest and probably one of the most charmingly written treatises on the subject which exists in our language."—*Times.*

—— **The First Age of Christianity and the Church.** By John Ignatius Döllinger, D.D., Professor of Ecclesiastical History in the University of Munich, &c., &c. Translated from the German by Henry Nutcombe Oxenham, M.A., late Scholar of Baliol College, Oxford. Third Edition. 2 vols. Crown 8vo. 18s.

Ozanam's (A. F.) History of Civilisation in the Fifth Century. From the French. By The Hon. A. C. Glyn. 2 Vols., post 8vo. 21s.

Pebody (Charles) Authors at Work. Francis Jeffrey—Sir Walter Scott—Robert Burns—Charles Lamb—R. B. Sheridan—Sydney Smith—Macaulay—Byron Wordsworth—Tom Moore—Sir James Mackintosh. Post 8vo. 10s. 6d.

Pelly (Sir Lewis). The Miracle Play of Hasan and Husain. Collected from Oral Tradition by Colonel Sir Lewis Pelly, K.C.B., K.C.S.I., formerly serving in Persia as Secretary of Legation, and Political Resident in the Persian Gulf.

Revised, with Explanatory Notes, by ARTHUR N. WOLLASTON, H.M. Indian (Home) Service, Translator of Anwar-i-Suhaili, &c. 2 Vols. royal 8vo. 32s.

Pen and Ink Sketches of Military Subjects. By "IGNOTUS." Reprinted by permission from the "Saturday Review." Crown 8vo. 5s.

Pincott (F.) Analytical Index to Sir JOHN KAYE'S History of the Sepoy War, and Col. G. B. MALLESON'S History of the Indian Mutiny. (Combined in one volume.) By FREDERIC PINCOTT, M.R.A.S. 8vo. 10s. 6d.

Pinkerton (Thomas A.) Agnes Moran.
A Story of Innocence and Experience. By THOMAS A. PINKERTON. 3 vols. 31s. 6d.

Pittenger (Rev. W.) Capturing a Locomotive.
A History of Secret Service in the late American War. By Rev. W. PITTENGER. Crown 8vo. With 13 Illustrations. 6s.

Pollock (Field Marshal Sir George) Life & Correspondence.
By C. R. Low. 8vo. With portrait. 18s.

Pope (G. U.) Text-book of Indian History; with Geographical Notes, Genealogical Tables, Examination Questions, and Chronological, Biographical, Geographical, and General Indexes. For the use of Schools, Colleges, and Private Students. By the Rev. G. U. POPE, D.D., Principal of Bishop Cotton's Grammar School and College, Bangalore; Fellow of the Madras University. Third Edition, thoroughly revised. Fcap. 4to. 12s.

Practice of Courts Martial.
By HOUGH & LONG. 8vo. London. 1825. 26s.

Prichard's Chronicles of Budgepore, &c.
Or Sketches of Life in Upper India. 2 Vols., Foolscap 8vo. 12s.

Prinsep (H. T.) Historical Results.
Deducible from Recent Discoveries in Affghanistàn. By H. T. PRINSEP. 8vo. Lond. 1844. 15s.

—— Tibet, Tartary, and Mongolia.
By HENRY T. PRINSEP, Esq. Second edition. Post 8vo. 5s.

Prinsep (H. T.) Political and Military Transactions in India. 2 Vols. 8vo. London, 1825. 18s.

Private Theatricals.
Being a Practical Guide to the Home Stage, both before and behind the Curtain. By AN OLD STAGER. Illustrated with Suggestions for Scenes after designs by Shirley Hodson. Crown 8vo. 3s. 6d.

Ramann (L.) Franz Liszt, Artist and Man, 1811–1840. By L. RAMANN. Translated from the German by Miss E. Cowdery. 2 vols. 21s.

Richards (Major W. H.) Military Surveying, &c.
12s. (See page 28.)

Rowe (R.) Picked up in the Streets; or, Struggles for Life among the London Poor. By RICHARD ROWE, "Good Words" Commissioner, Author of "Jack Afloat and Ashore," &c Crown 8vo. Illustrated. 6s.

Rumsey (Almaric) Moohummudan Law of Inheritance, and Rights and Relations affecting it. Sunni Doctrine. Comprising, together with much collateral information, the substance, greatly expanded, of the author's "Chart of Family Inheritance." By ALMARIC RUMSEY, of Lincoln's Inn, Barrister-at-Law, Professor of Indian Jurisprudence at King's College, London. Author of "A Chart of Hindu Family Inheritance." 8vo. 12s.

—— A Chart of Hindu Family Inheritance.
Second Edition, much enlarged. 8vo. 6s. 6d.

Sachau (Dr. C. Ed.) The Chronology of Ancient Nations. An English Version of the Arabic Text of the Athar-ut Bâkiya of Albîrûnî, or "Vestiges of the Past." Collected and reduced to writing by the Author in A.H. 390–1, A.D. 1,000. Translated and Edited, with Notes and Index, by Dr. C. EDWARD SACHAU, Professor in the Royal University of Berlin. Published for the Oriental Translation Fund of Great Britain and Ireland. Royal 8vo. 42s.

Sanderson (G. P.) Thirteen Years among the Wild Beasts of India; their Haunts and Habits, from Personal Observation; with an account of the Modes of Capturing and Taming Wild Elephants. By G. P. SANDERSON, Officer in

Charge of the Government Elephant Keddahs at Mysore. With 21 full page Illustrations and three Maps. Second Edition. Fcp. 4to. £1 5s.

Scudamore (F. I.) France in the East.
A Contribution towards the consideration of the Eastern Question. By Frank Ives Scudamore, C.B. Crown 8vo. 6s.

Sewell (R.) Analytical History of India.
From the earliest times to the Abolition of the East India Company in 1858. By Robert Sewell, Madras Civil Service. Post 8vo. 8s.

*** The object of this work is to supply the want which has been felt by students for a condensed outline of Indian History which would serve at once to recall the memory and guide the eye, while at the same time it has been attempted to render it interesting to the general reader by preserving a medium between a bare analysis and a complete history.

Shadow of a Life (The) A Girl's Story.
By Beryl Hope. 3 vols., post 8vo. 31s. 6d.

Sherer (J. W.) The Conjuror's Daughter.
A Tale. By J. W. Sherer, C.S.I. With Illustrations by Alf. T. Elwes and J. Jellicoe. Cr. 8vo. 6s.

—— **Who is Mary?**
A Cabinet Novel, in one volume. By J. W. Sherer, Esq., C.S.I. 10s. 6d.

—— **At Home and in India.**
A Volume of Miscellanies. By J. W. Sherer, C.S.I. Crown 8vo., with Frontispiece. 5s.

Signor Monaldini's Niece.
A Novel of Italian Life. Crown 8vo. 6s.

Simpson (H. T.) Archæologia Adelensis; or, a History of the Parish of Adel, in the West Riding of Yorkshire. Being an attempt to delineate its Past and Present Associations, Archæological, Topographical, and Scriptural. By Henry Traill Simpson, M.A., late Rector of Adel. With numerous etchings by W. Lloyd Ferguson. Roy. 8vo. 21s.

Small (Rev. G.) A Dictionary of Naval Terms, English and Hindustani. For the use of Nautical Men trading to India, &c. By Rev. G. Small, Interpreter to the Strangers' Home for Asiatics. Fcap. 2s. 6d.

Solymos (B.) Desert Life. Recollections of an Expedition in the Soudan. By B. SOLYMOS (B. E. FALKONBERG), Civil Engineer. 8vo. 15s.

Songs of a Lost World.
By a NEW HAND. Crown 8vo. 6s.

Starling (M. H.) Indian Criminal Law and Procedure.
Third edition. 8vo. £2 2s. See page 18.

Steele (A.) Law and Customs of Hindu Castes.
BY ARTHUR STEELE. Royal 8vo. £1. 1s. (See page 18.)

Stent (G. C.) Entombed Alive,
And other Songs and Ballads. (From the Chinese.) By GEORGE CARTER STENT, M.R.A.S., of the Chinese Imperial Maritime Customs Service. Crown 8vo. With four Illustrations. 9s.

—— **Scraps from my Sabretasche.** Being Personal Adventures while in the 14th (King's Light) Dragoons. By GEORGE CARTER STENT, M.R.A.S. Crown 8vo. 6s.

—— **The Jade Chaplet,** in Twenty-four Beads.
A Collection of Songs, Ballads, &c. from the Chinese. By GEORGE CARTER STENT, M.R.A.S. Second Edition. Crown 8vo. 5s.

Stothard (R. T.) The A B C of Art.
Being a system of delineating forms and objects in nature necessary for the attainments of a draughtsman. By ROBERT T STOTHARD, F.S.A., late H.D.S.A. Fcap. 1s.

Swinnerton (Rev. C.) The Afghan War. Gough's Action at Futtehabad. By the Rev. C. SWINNERTON, Chaplain in the Field with the First Division, Peshawur Valley Field Force. With Frontispiece and Two Plans. Crown 8vo. 5s.

Taunton (A. G.) The Family Register. A Key to such Official Entries of Births, Marriages, and Deaths at the Registrar-General's Office as may refer to any particular family. Edited by ALFRED GEORGE TAUNTON. Folio Cloth. 21s.

Tayler (W.) Thirty-eight Years in India, from Juganath to the Himalaya Mountains. By WILLIAM TAYLER, Esq., Retired B.C.S., late Commissioner of Patna. In 2 vols. 25s. each.

Contains a memoir of the life of Mr. William Tayler, from 1829 to 1867—during the Government of eight Governors General—from Lord William Bentinck to Lord Lawrence, comprising numerous incidents and adventures, official, personal, tragic, and comic, "from grave to gay, from lively to severe" throughout that period. These volumes contain upwards of two hundred illustrations, reproduced by Mr. Tayler himself, from original sketches taken by him on the spot, in Bengal, Behar, N.W. Provinces, Darjeeling, Nipal, and Simla.

Tayler (Wm.) The Patna Crisis; or Three Months at Patna during the Insurrection of 1857. By WILLIAM TAYLER, late Commissioner of Patna. Third Edition. Fcap. 2s.

Thoms (J. A.) A Complete Concordance to the Revised Version of the New Testament, embracing the Marginal Readings of the English Revisers as well as those of the American Committee. By JOHN ALEXANDER THOMS. 6s.

Thomson's Lunar and Horary Tables.

For New and Concise Methods of Performing the Calculations necessary for ascertaining the Longitude by Lunar Observations, or Chronometers; with directions for acquiring a knowledge of the Principal Fixed Stars and finding the Latitude of them. By DAVID THOMSON. Sixty-fifth edit. Royal 8vo. 10s.

Thornton (P. M.) Foreign Secretaries of the Nineteenth Century. By PERCY M. THORNTON.

Contains—Memoirs of Lord Grenville, Lord Hawkesbury, Lord Harrowby, Lord Mulgrave, C. J. Fox, Lord Howick, George Canning, Lord Bathurst, Lord Wellesley (together with estimate of his Indian Rule by Col. G. B. Malleson, C.S.I.), Lord Castlereagh, Lord Dudley, Lord Aberdeen, and Lord Palmerston. Also, Extracts from Lord Bexley's Papers, including lithographed letters of Lords Castlereagh and Canning, which, bearing on important points of public policy, have never yet been published; together with other important information culled from private and other sources. With Ten Portraits, and a View shewing Interior of the old House of Lords. (Second Edition.) 2 vols. 8vo. 32s. 6d.

Vol. III. 8vo. With Portraits. 18s

Thornton's History of India.

The History of the British Empire in India, by Edward Thornton, Esq. Containing a Copious Glossary of Indian Terms, and a Complete Chronological Index of Events, to aid the Aspirant for Public Examinations. Third edition. 1 vol. 8vo. With Map. 12s.

**** The Library Edition of the above in 6 volumes, 8vo., may be had, price £2 8s.*

Thornton's Gazetteer of India.

Compiled chiefly from the records at the India Office. By Edward Thornton. 1 vol., 8vo., pp. 1015. With Map. 21s.

*** *The chief objects in view in compiling this Gazetteer are:—*

1st. To fix the relative position of the various cities, towns, and villages with as much precision as possible, and to exhibit with the greatest practicable brevity all that is known respecting them; and

2ndly. To note the various countries, provinces, or territorial divisions, and to describe the physical characteristics of each, together with their statistical, social, and political circumstances.

To these are added minute descriptions of the principal rivers and chains of mountains; thus presenting to the reader, within a brief compass, a mass of information which cannot otherwise be obtained, except from a multiplicity of volumes and manuscript records.

The Library Edition.

4 vols., 8vo. Notes, Marginal References, and Map. £2 16s.

—— **Gazetteer of the Punjaub, Affghanistan, &c.**

Gazetteer of the Countries adjacent to India, on the north-west, including Scinde, Affghanistan, Beloochistan, the Punjaub, and the neighbouring States. By Edward Thornton, Esq. 2 vols. 8vo. £1 5s.

Thornton (T.) East India Calculator.

By T. Thornton. 8vo. London, 1823. 10s.

—— **History of the Punjaub,**

And of the Rise, Progress, and Present Condition of the Sikhs. By T. Thornton. 2 Vols. Post 8vo. 8s.

Tilley (H. A.) Japan, the Amoor and the Pacific.

With notices of other Places, comprised in a Voyage of Circumnavigation in the Imperial Russian Corvette *Rynda*, in 1858–1860. By Henry A. Tilley. Eight Illustrations. 8vo. 16s.

Tincker (Mary Agnes) The Jewel in the Lotos.

A Novel. By the Author of "Signor Monaldini's Niece," &c. Crown 8vo., with 5 Illustrations. 7s. 6d.

Tod (Col. Jas.) Travels in Western India.

Embracing a visit to the Sacred Mounts of the Jains, and the most Celebrated Shrines of Hindu Faith between Rajpootana and the Indus, with an account of the Ancient City of Nehrwalla. By the late Lieut.-Col. James Tod, Illustrations. Royal 4to. £3 3s.

*** *This is a companion volume to Colonel Tod's Rajasthan.*

Torrens (W. T. McC.) Reform of Procedure in Parliament to Clear the Block of Public Business. By W. T. McCullagh Torrens, M.P. Second Edition. Crown 8vo. 5s.

Trimen (Capt. R.) Regiments of the British Army, Chronologically arranged. Showing their History, Services, Uniform, &c By Captain R. Trimen, late 35th Regiment. 8vo. 10s. 6d.

Trotter (L. J.) History of India. The History of the British Empire in India, from the Appointment of Lord Hardinge to the Death of Lord Canning (1844 to 1862). By Captain Lionel James Trotter, late Bengal Fusiliers. 2 vols. 8vo. 16s. each.

—— Lord Lawrence. A Sketch of his Career. Fcap. 1s. 6d.

—— Warren Hastings, a Biography. By Captain Lionel James Trotter, Bengal H. P., author of a "History of India," "Studies in Biography," &c. Crown 8vo. 9s.

Tupper (M. F.) Three Five-Act Plays and Twelve Dramatic Scenes. Suitable for Private Theatricals or Drawing-room Recitation. By Martin F. Tupper, Author of "Proverbial Philosophy," &c. Crown 8vo. Gilt. 5s.

Under Orders: a Novel. By the Author of "Invasions of India from Central Asia." Third Edition. 3 vols. 31s. 6d.

Underwood (A. S.) Surgery for Dental Students. By Arthur S. Underwood, M.R.C.S., L.D.S.E., Assistant Surgeon to the Dental Hospital of London. 5s.

Valbezen (E. De) The English and India. New Sketches. By E. De Valbezen, late Consul-General at Calcutta, Minister Plenipotentiary. Translated from the French (with the Author's permission) by a Diplomate. 8vo. 18s.

Vambery (A.) Sketches of Central Asia. Additional Chapters on My Travels and Adventures, and of the Ethnology of Central Asia. By Armenius Vambery. 8vo. 16s.

"A valuable guide on almost untrodden ground."—*Athenæum.*

Vibart (Major H. M.) The Military History of the Madras Engineers and Pioneers. By Major H. M. VIBART, Royal (late Madras) Engineers. In 2 vols., with numerous Maps and Plans. 2 vols. 8vo. 32s. each.

Victoria Cross (The) An Official Chronicle of Deeds of Personal Valour achieved in the presence of the Enemy during the Crimean and Baltic Campaigns and the Indian, Chinese, New Zealand, and African Wars. From the Institution of the Order in 1856 to 1880. Edited by ROBERT W. O'BYRNE. Crown 8vo. With Plate. 5s.

Vyse (G. W.) Egypt: Political, Financial, and Strategical. Together with an Account of its Engineering Capabilities and Agricultural Resources. By GRIFFIN W. VYSE, late on special duty in Egypt and Afghanistan for H.M.'s Government. Crown 8vo. With Maps. 9s.

Wall (A. J.) Indian Snake Poisons, their Nature and Effects. By A. J: WALL, M.D., F.R.C.S. England, of the Medical Staff H.M.'s Indian Army. Crown 8vo. 6s.

Waring (E. J.) Pharmacopœia of India.
By EDWARD JOHN WARING, M.D., &c. 8vo. 6s. (See page 2.)

Watson (M.) Money.
By JULES TARDIEU. Translated from the French by MARGARET WATSON. Crown 8vo. 7s. 6d.

Watson (Dr. J. F.) and J. W. Kaye, Races and Tribes of Hindostan. The People of India. A series of Photographic Illustrations of the Races and Tribes of Hindustan. Prepared under the Authority of the Government of India, by J. FORBES WATSON, and JOHN WILLIAM KAYE. The Work contains about 450 Photographs on mounts, in Eight Volumes, super royal 4to. £2. 5s. per volume.

Webb (Dr. A.) Pathologia Indica.
Based upon Morbid Specimens from all parts of the Indian Empire. By ALLAN WEBB, B.M.S. Second Edit. 8vo. 14s.

Wellesley's Despatches.
The Despatches, Minutes, and Correspondence of the Marquis Wellesley, K.G., during his Administration in India. 5 vols. 8vo. With Portrait, Map, &c. £6. 10s.

This work should be perused by all who proceed to India in the Civil Services.

Wellington in India.
Military History of the Duke of Wellington in India

White (S. D.) Indian Reminiscences.
By Colonel S. Dewe' White, late Bengal Staff Corps. 8vo. With 10 Photographs. 14s.

Wilberforce (E.) Franz Schubert.
A Musical Biography, from the German of Dr. Heinrich Kreisle von Hellborn. By Edward Wilberforce, Esq., Author of "Social Life in Munich." Post 8vo. 6s.

Wilk's South of India.
3 vols. 4to. £5. 5s.

Wilkin (Mrs.) The Shackles of an Old Love.
By Mārā (Mrs. Wilkin). Crown 8vo. 7s. 6d.

Wilkins (W. N.) Visual Art; or Nature through the Healthy Eye. With some remarks on Originality and Free Trade, Artistic Copyright, and Durability. By Wm. Noy Wilkins, Author of "Art Impressions of Dresden," &c. 8vo. 6s.

Williams (F.) Lives of the English Cardinals.
The Lives of the English Cardinals, from Nicholas Breakspeare (Pope Adrien IV.) to Thomas Wolsey, Cardinal Legate. With Historical Notices of the Papal Court. By Folkestone Williams. 2 vols., 8vo. 14s.

—— Life, &c., of Bishop Atterbury.
The Memoir and Correspondence of Francis Atterbury, Bishop of Rochester, with his distinguished contemporaries. Compiled chiefly from the Atterbury and Stuart Papers. By Folkestone Williams, Author of "Lives of the English Cardinals," &c., 2 vols. 8vo. 14s.

Williams (S. Wells) The Middle Kingdom.
A Survey of the Geography, Government, Literature, Social Life, Arts, and History of the Chinese Empire and Its Inhabitants. By S. Wells Willams, LL D., Professor of the Chinese Language and Literature at Yale College, Author of Tonic and Syllabic Dictionaries of the Chinese Language. Revised Edition, with 74 Illustrations and a New Map of the Empire. 2 vols. Demy 8vo. 42s.

Wilson (H. H.) Glossary of Judicial and Revenue Terms, and of useful Words occurring in Official Documents relating to the Administration of the Government of British India. From the Arabic, Persian, Hindustani, Sanskrit, Hindi, Bengali, Uriya, Marathi, Guzarathi, Telugu, Karnata, Tamil, Malayalam, and other Languages. Compiled and published under the authority of the Hon. the Court of Directors of the E. I. Company. 4to., cloth. £1 10s.

Wollaston (Arthur N.) Anwari Suhaili, or Lights of Canopus. Commonly known as Kalilah and Damnah, being an adaptation of the Fables of Bidpai. Translated from the Persian. Royal 8vo., 42s.; also in royal 4to., with illuminated borders, designed specially for the work, cloth, extra gilt. £3 13s. 6d.

—— Elementary Indian Reader.
Designed for the use of Students in the Anglo-Vernacular Schools in India. Fcap. 1s.

Woolrych (Serjeant W. H.)
Lives of Eminent Serjeants-at-Law of the English Bar. By Humphry W. Woolrych, Serjeant-at-Law. 2 vols. 8vo. 30s.

Wraxall (Sir L., Bart.) Caroline Matilda.
Queen of Denmark, Sister of George 3rd. From Family and State Papers. By Sir Lascelles Wraxall, Bart. 3 vols., 8vo. 18s.

Young (J. R.) Course of Mathematics.
A Course of Elementary Mathematics for the use of candidates for admission into either of the Military Colleges; of applicants for appointments in the Home or Indian Civil Services; and of mathematical students generally. By Professor J. R. Young. In one closely-printed volume 8vo., pp. 648. 12s.

"In the work before us he has digested a complete Elementary Course, by aid of his long experience as a teacher and writer; and he has produced a very useful book. Mr. Young has not allowed his own taste to rule the distribution, but has adjusted his parts with the skill of a veteran."—*Athenæum.*

Young (M.) and Trent (R.) A Home Ruler.
A Story for Girls. By Minnie Young and Rachel Trent, Illustrated by C. P. Colnaghi. Crown 8vo. 3s. 6d.

Works in the Press.

Malleson's Capt Musafir's Rambles in Alpine Lands.
By Colonel G. B. Malleson, C.S.I. 4to. 10s. 6d.

Life of Gustave Doré.
By Blanchard Jerrold.

Personal Reminiscences of General Skobeleff.
By Nemirovitch-Dantchenko. Translated by E. A. Brayley Hodgetts. With 3 Portraits.

A Land March from England to Ceylon Forty Years Ago.
By Edward Mitford. With Map and Numerous Illustrations.

At Home in Paris.
By Blanchard Jerrold. 2 Vols., Crown 8vo. 21s.

My Musical Life.
By the Rev. H. R. Haweis, Author of "Music and Morals." With Portraits.

Coruña to Sevastopal.
By Colonel F. A. Whinyates.

Thoughts on Reading Shakespeare.
By The Hon. A. S. G. Canning.

Games of Cards for Three Players.
By "Aquarius." Author of "Écarté."

Piquet and Cribbage.
By the same Author.